The Great Adventure

100 Years at The Arts & Letters Club

To Don Sutherland
– warm regards
Margaret McBurney

The Great Adventure

100 Years at The Arts & Letters Club

Margaret McBurney

Library and Archives Canada Cataloguing in Publication

McBurney, Margaret, 1931–
The great adventure : 100 years of the Arts & Letters Club / Margaret McBurney.

Includes bibliographical references and index.
ISBN 978-0-9694588-2-1

1. Arts and Letters Club of Toronto--History.
I. Arts and Letters Club of Toronto II. Title.

HS2735.T6A782 2007 706'.0713541 C2007-904166-3

Produced for the Arts and Letters Club of Toronto by Malcolm Lester & Associates
Editor: Ann Schabas
Copy Editor: Andrea Knight
Book Design: Jack Steiner Design

Printed and bound in Canada by Friesens.

07 08 09 3 2 1

Above the fireplace let us set the emblem of the Club

—the Viking ship with the sails full spread before the rising sun,

to remind us of the open sea and the great adventure.

—C. W. Jefferys, November 1911

TABLE OF CONTENTS

Preface

One of our charter members, historian Jesse Middleton, wrote in a 1912 prefatory note to Newton McConnell's *A Portfolio of Caricatures* that "a preface is an annoying interruption between the title-page and the text." He was undoubtedly correct, but sometimes that interruption seems necessary when a subject such as the Arts and Letters Club is involved. Its history has been complex, challenging, and, to me, utterly fascinating.

This book was started in the early days of 1997 when eight committed members gathered in the club library to discuss producing a club history. We called ourselves the history committee. We first addressed the question of structure—how to pull together a story spanning one hundred years of the club's existence, years ranging from heady success to terrifying near failure. We soon decided to divide the story into six chapters, the first covering the club's beginnings up to the end of World War I; the next taking us through the Roaring Twenties and the Great Depression; the third covering the years of World War II and the approach to our fiftieth birthday in 1958; the fourth culminating in the admission of women members in 1985; the fifth bringing us into the first years of this century; and the last a brief overview of the four years leading up to our centenary celebrations.

Our publishing adviser, Ian Montagnes, reinforced this decision. "Tell the story chronologically," he said. I have, and I think it has worked. Another bit of Ian's always valuable counsel was "Stick to what happened within the walls of the club." It was simple but good advice, and, by and large, that is what I have done. I found that I was able to include countless bits and pieces of historical lore that kept cropping up—what journalist George Bain calls "lint from the pant cuffs of history"—and to bring alive the disparate, quirky, and charming nature of this remarkable institution. Our committee also decided to include six brief essays by other club members, five to outline each of our LAMPS disciplines and the sixth to cover our spring revues, a tradition since 1930.

So how to begin? During the course of the century, making it happen, were our loyal and (God knows) individualistic members, several thousand of them. How could I contain the accounts of so many diverse people within one readable story? Reflecting on this diversity and exploring reasons for the club's continuing success always brought me back to the individuals involved. Their stories are the short and long strands that weave together to form a colourful and intricate fabric. Some of them achieved lasting renown—Sir Frederick Banting, Robertson Davies, and Marshall McLuhan immediately spring to mind—but they were not necessarily the people who helped make the club the success that it is today. Others, such as Augustus Bridle, Vincent Massey, Healey Willan, and various members of the Group of Seven weave in and out through much of the narrative. And still others appear only briefly, either because their involvement with the club was short-lived or, like many of us, they served mainly as spectators rather than as front-and-centre participants. Sprinkled throughout the story are the names of the six members who were honoured with knighthoods, two recipients of Nobel Prizes, some of the twenty-two who have been named persons of national historic significance, and some of the more than 150 who have received the Order of Canada.

My main source of information has been the club archives, with its numerous files—alphabetical for people and subjects, chronological for years. They contain a rich collection of newspaper clippings, programs, letters, diaries, photographs, and drawings. There are also club publications, executive minutes, scrapbooks, audio tapes, video tapes, and artifacts. Without a doubt, the most unusual artifact was an unopened bottle of Chateauneuf du Pape 1928.

Some of the club's archives are now on long-term loan to the Thomas Fisher Rare Book Library, including our massive leather-bound scrapbooks and other valuable and fragile items. The scrapbooks include humorous sketches (originals!) by members of the Group of Seven and others, programs for early plays staged at the club, numerous photographs—including one of the first Boar's Head—and many letters and cards, some from our members fighting in Europe during World War I. They contain, in fact, more about that war and our members' involvement in it than do our brief executive minutes and other historical records of that time. I have also drawn on material from a number of books—the most useful to me are listed in the bibliography. The Ontario Archives is another goldmine: it holds the photographs and personal journals of our early member M. O. Hammond.

There have been surprises. Until beginning research for this book, for instance, I had always assumed that Vincent Massey had no sense of humour; I was wrong. This became evident while perusing the records of his time as club president from 1920 to 1922. Happy insights such as this occurred frequently as my colleagues and I pored over the material. We discovered that members we had previously known of simply as Canadian cultural icons were indeed complex, fascinating, and fully human. Something in the atmosphere at the club allowed them to unwind and be themselves.

During the research for the book I came to feel that I knew many of the members. Leading the parade was the club's founder, Augustus Bridle. His 1945 book, *The Story of the Club*, is rich with lore. Another remarkable member was the aforementioned Hammond, a great observer whose personal journals—full of anecdotes about the club—are an invaluable record of the club's first twenty-five years. An avid photographer, he also left dozens of photographic portraits of early club members.

Many of the audio tapes are interviews of club members by our first archivist, Hunter Bishop. They provide glimpses of the club's day-to-day life, little sidelights that could not have been discovered without their help. Particularly helpful to me were those with violinist Horace Corner, a member from 1914 until 1977, and architect Walter Moorhouse, a member from 1912 until 1977.

Names—how to refer to people—have been an ongoing challenge. I have chosen to be as informal as the records and context permit. For some, I have chosen to use the full name at first mention, but a shortened version after that. Franklin Arbuckle, for instance, was known at the club, as Archie. For style and to ensure consistency, I have generally been guided by *The Globe and Mail Style Book*, co-authored by our own Warren Clements. Who could argue? In regard to quotes, I admit to taking occasional and very minor liberties to improve readability without distorting the sense. Also for readability, not all quotes are attributed. As much as possible, error checking has been a priority. Nonetheless, if some factual errors have slipped through, I take full responsibility and apologize for them. And if I have annoyed some of you—the readers—from time to time, I do *not* apologize. As Kingsley Amis has written, "If you can't annoy somebody some of the time, there's no point in writing."

The fact that this book is readable is due, in large part, to my editor, Ann Schabas. She brought to this daunting project an extensive knowledge of the Arts and Letters Club—her father, Barker Fairley, was a distinguished member for nearly seventy years, so she grew up hearing about the club and its members. Her long academic career as professor of library and information science at the University of Toronto honed her editorial skills—skills that are manifest on nearly every page. There are several important passages, for which she deserves credit as co-author. I could not have asked for a finer collaborator. As George F. Kaufman once wrote, "Collaboration is marriage without sex, and subject to many vexations. But pay no attention to them, because in one respect at least it is wonderful. The total result is frequently far more than the combined abilities of two people...and if I don't know about collaboration, who the hell does!"

I am profoundly grateful as well to the club's archivist, Scott James, who chaired our history committee. His unfailing good humour and his ready assistance as I worked my way through our extensive archives has made the research for this project much more enjoyable. Scott was also responsible for choosing the visual material for the book—a task requiring extensive knowledge of the club's holdings—and writing the captions. My good friend Raymond Peringer, our "archivist emeritus," was also a great help. He read the manuscript as it evolved, adding thoughtful and unerringly good advice throughout, as did Jim Hubbard, a life member who as a boy helped his father backstage at the spring revues. Jim's insights and stories of the club's middle years have been invaluable. Special thanks are due as well to the others on our history committee who served loyally and well for ten long years—Pat Wardrop with her extensive knowledge of music in Canada; Ann Robson, an author and academic with a fine mind and a ready wit; and Eve Yates who, with great determination, tackled the transcription of several years of early handwritten minutes. And everyone helped me plough through the plentitude of rich resources.

This brings me to the six essays. All required extensive research. Their authors, by cutting across the timelines, have been able to synthesize their subjects and provide important additions to the text. Their tasks were not easy and I am most grateful to them for pulling it off. And not to be forgotten are my many colleagues with whom, during my more than twenty years as a club member, I have had numerous conversations. From them, I have been able to store up the events and insights that found their way into the text. You may recognize your subtle input. I am very grateful for your willingness to talk with me and share your memories. Many thanks also to Ray Cattell and Tom McNeely for their designs of the initials for each of the essays.

All the images in this book had to be digitized. Those from our own collections were prepared at the club. For those at the Fisher Library, I thank Anne Dondertman. I am grateful, too, to the Archives of Ontario for the Hammond photographs. The City of Toronto Archives also provided photos, as did various members. The photo of playwright Herman Voaden was from his niece, Jane Ricketts. Compiling the lists of honours was the work of Pat Wardrop and Ann Schabas—not an easy task. If there are any errors or omissions, please accept their apologies.

Permission to include artwork has been received from Janet Cauffiel and the Arthur Lismer Estate; the Office of the Governor General; St. Anne's Anglican Church; and club members Andy Donato, Carole Vaughan, Lesley Fairfield, Warren Clements, Tom McNeely, and our many artists, past and present, who produced our presidential portraits and executive lists. George Lobb enthusiastically photographed many of the contemporary subjects.

My thanks to the club's Publication Committee—co-chairs Peter Large and Julian Mulock, along with Wally Coulthard, Chester Gryski, Scott James, and Lorna Kelly—all of whom provided ongoing encouragement and dedication to this project. And to the Centenary Committee too, with chair John Lawson and vice chair Mary Jane Large, who never got discouraged as they addressed countless challenges with our hundredth birthday approaching.

As Sandra Gwyn once wrote, the challenge in writing social history is "not to get the facts straight—the records are there for the looking—but to get the context right. Being truthful is much more difficult than being accurate." Those of us who have searched with pleasure and determination through the club's rich store of historical material have tried to get the context right and to follow the dictum given me by past-president Jack Yocom. He looked me in the eye as we discussed his many devoted years with the club and said firmly—Jack said *everything* firmly—"It was *never* always wonderful in 'the old days.' Make sure that you tell it like it was!" And that is what I have tried to do.

Why Another Club?

At the dawn of the twentieth century, Toronto was a town of innate conservatism, stiff with Victorian intolerance and prudery, and dominated by a prosperous merchant class. The city's Protestant churches held sway, with many a charismatic fire-breathing preacher attracting huge crowds to Sunday services.

Private men's clubs played a major role in Toronto's social and business life. They were where the prominent and successful business elite met to conduct their affairs discreetly and effectively, and, to quote a British aphorism, "to escape their wives, their mistresses, and their creditors."

There were also professional clubs and associations. In 1908, the year the Arts and Letters Club of Toronto was established, the *Canadian Magazine* listed a number in the arts, including the Graphic Arts Club, the Canadian Art Club, the Ontario Society of Artists, the Authors' Club, the Ontario Association of Architects, the Clef Club, and the Toronto Press Club. Most of these also limited their memberships to men. It is not surprising that the founders of the Arts and Letters Club, while never specifically *excluding* women from membership, never gave any thought to including them either. It probably never entered their minds. There were, after all, several clubs for women interested in the arts—the Women's Musical Club, the Women's Art Association, the Toronto Ladies' Club, and the University Women's Club.

Unlike many clubs of that time, the Arts and Letters Club never officially discriminated on the basis of race or religion—and this at a time when such prejudices were endemic. People of colour were overtly ignored and anti-Semitism was a fact of life. Even Catholics had difficulty being accepted in Toronto society, and, all too often, anyone who spoke with a foreign accent was viewed with great suspicion. Toronto was an outpost of the empire, and deference to all things British was reflected within our club. Most of the first members were, if not born in Britain, of British stock—and proud of it. Even in the thirties, Arthur Irwin, the editor of *Maclean's* magazine, was, according to his biographer David MacKenzie, put off by the "Englishness of the place and the people in it."

What really set the club apart, however, was how it brought together the professional and the amateur, the artist and the patron, the traditional and the modern. The club sought out and promoted artistic differences—all in an effort to create a culture for English Canada. Which indeed it did. From its very beginning, non-professionals enjoyed sharing lunchtime chats with musicians, writers, artists, architects, dramatists, and critics. Visiting celebrities often joined the members to share in the spirited conversations and cultural diversions offered at the club, a tradition that has continued for the better part of a century. Names such as Rupert Brooke, Wilfrid Laurier, Paul Robeson, and Peter Ustinov appear on a lengthy list of distinguished visitors—a veritable who's who in the arts, politics, and science. Even, on occasion, women were admitted as guests—Margaret Laurence, Nellie McClung, Mazo de la Roche, and Emily Pankhurst, to name a few.

Today, the club enjoys the largest membership in its history. As George Locke decreed, it never became an "upholstered" club, which is one reason for its success, the other being that we still adhere to Augustus Bridle's dictum of a "shirtsleeve democracy."

CHAPTER 1

Getting Started 1908–1919

Finding a home
Founding fathers
Financial woes
Our soldiers return

It was a diverse group of men who met in the spring of 1908 to toss around a few ideas about forming a new club. Some were prosperous and well-known, some were young and ambitious, and some were struggling to establish themselves as artists in a city where commerce held sway. Among them were several painters, musicians, and architects, an actor, a sculptor, a few journalists, some academics, and even a few businessmen. They seemed, at first glance, to have little in common, other than a longing to enrich their lives in some as yet untried way. Certainly none of them could have imagined that, within a few years, the club that they were about to found would not only become successful as a club, but would also boast a list of members envied simply because they belonged.

One man, Augustus Bridle, was chiefly responsible for the founding of the Arts and Letters Club of Toronto. A determined and energetic journalist brimming with enthusiasm, he managed to entice some of Toronto's brightest and most creative young men (and a few who were middle-aged or older) to meet, on March 23, 1908, at the St. Charles Hotel on Yonge Street between King and Melinda to discuss the arts. The thirty-nine-year-old Bridle—known as Gus to his friends—believed that the arts in the city had been neglected too long. His zeal must have been contagious because seventy men turned up that evening to see what the excitement was all about. Toronto was then a pale Protestant town in the grip of a depression, but nothing deterred them. After the meeting, *Saturday Night*'s editor, Joe Clark, wrote, "It seemed to me that I had been fraternizing with a group of men this evening whose main object in life is not to make money." The startling thing about that meeting was its immediate success. It was

An informal gathering prior to the founding of the club, possibly at Mossop's Hotel, 1907. From left to right: Sid Howard, A. H. Robson, R. F. Gagen, F. Halliday, Fergus Kyle, unknown, Ivor Lewis, W. W. Alexander, Fred Brigden, Tom Mitchell, unknown, J. D. Kelly, C. W. Jefferys, Robert Holmes, unknown. (*A. A. Gleason*)

(Above) Gus Bridle, "Fellow Member Number One," 1913. (*M. O. Hammond*)

(Above right) St. Charles Hotel, Yonge and Melinda streets, 1908. (*William James*)

quite obvious that Bridle, Clark, and the others were on to something—and a simple lack of money wasn't going to stop them.

Bridle's way with words was likely of considerable help when it came to rounding up prospective members for this new and imaginative venture. Many were soon caught up by his enthusiasm and, by the end of April, they headed happily to a second meeting, this one held at a gallery used by the Ontario Society of Artists (OSA) above the Princess Theatre on King Street West. A few days later, Bridle, in his inimitable style, wrote in the *Canadian Magazine* of this "gathering of gentlemen who met to weigh the advantages that might result from frequent association of ideas, motives, temperaments, and aspirations, all, of course, tracing their sources to at least one of the higher arts—painting, literature, architecture, sculpture, music."

The third meeting, held in May 1908, was at the same gallery. Agar Adamson wrote in his journal the next day, "Mabel and I went to the meeting of the Arts and Letters Club and the ceremony of christening it by the above name." There were several other women on hand as well—somewhat surprising since it would be seventy-seven years before women were admitted as members.

William A. Langton, President, 1908–1909. (*Wyly Grier*)

McConkey's Restaurant, 27 King Street West, early 1900s.

On an evening in late October 1908, the club's first official meeting took place, this time in the popular Palms Room at McConkey's restaurant on King Street West. A dignified fifty-four-year-old architect, William A. Langton, was named the first president. His reserved but impressive demeanor struck just the right note for the fledgling organization. His hope for the new club, he stated, was that it would become "an art society where the jingle of the coin would not be part of the music." The club, he felt, should live in a garret. Langton himself, however, had little acquaintance with garret life.

Cover design by J. E. H. MacDonald for *A Gathering of the Arts*, 1908. The club's first publication introduced the LAMPS disciplines.

(Above right) Horatio Walker in his studio, c.1927. (*M. O. Hammond*)

The son of Canada's first auditor general, he was a founder of the Ontario Association of Architects (OAA) and was instrumental in the establishment of the School of Architecture at the University of Toronto (U of T). It was no wonder that, years later, the architectural historian Eric Arthur described Langton as "a great gentleman, and a great architect in the widest sense of the word."

In January 1909, the club met for dinner in the spacious studio of artist Wyly Grier at the Imperial Bank Chambers on Leader Lane, two blocks east of Yonge, between Front and King. The invitation promised that "several expert gentlemen" would carve for the company and there would be "plenty of smoking, light refreshments, and sociability." On the agenda was the club's recently completed statement of purpose: "A society for the promotion of intercourse among those who work in and those who encourage the arts of literature, architecture, music, painting, and sculpture." The initials of these five disciplines became the club's acronym—LAMPS. Some years later, "sculpture" would be changed to "stage" and "painting" would include "sculpture and the other visual arts."

In the club's formative years, actors were not considered professional enough for membership—in Samuel Johnson's words, "not clubable." In any case, most actors at that time were transients. After dinner, members leaned back, lit up their cigarettes, pipes, and cigars, and launched into a serious discussion about "Ideals in Art."

The opportunity to meet visiting celebrities—one of the greatest pleasures of club membership—dates back to those very first years. Within one week in April 1909, for instance, there were two notable visitors. The first was dinner guest Dr. Wilfred Grenfell of Newfoundland and Labrador. A medical missionary, Grenfell had built the first hospital at Battle Harbour on the southern coast of Labrador and raised funds from around the world for hospitals, nursing stations, and orphanages. The next day's lunch guest was the internationally recognized Quebec painter Horatio Walker, described by one member as "about fifty or fifty-five and turning gray, with a mustache and a large Pierpont Morgan sort of nose." He joined the club four years later.

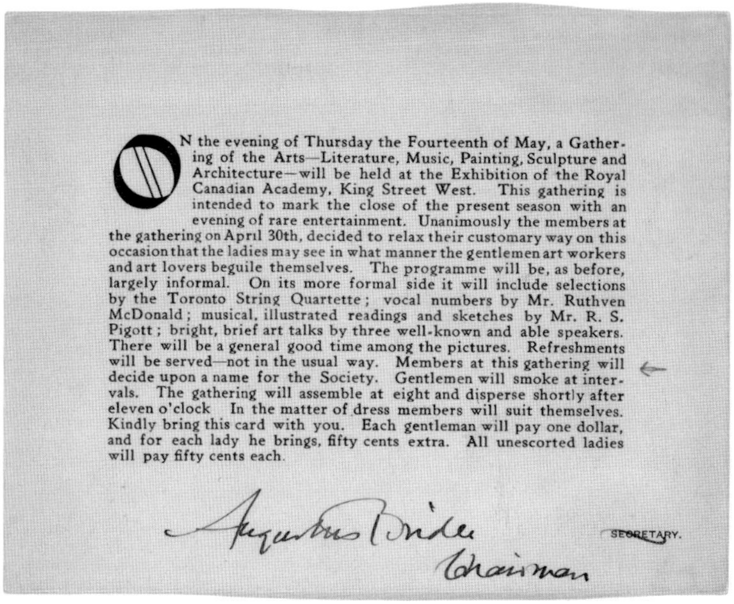
ON the evening of Thursday the Fourteenth of May, a Gathering of the Arts—Literature, Music, Painting, Sculpture and Architecture—will be held at the Exhibition of the Royal Canadian Academy, King Street West. This gathering is intended to mark the close of the present season with an evening of rare entertainment. Unanimously the members at the gathering on April 30th, decided to relax their customary way on this occasion that the ladies may see in what manner the gentlemen art workers and art lovers beguile themselves. The programme will be, as before, largely informal. On its more formal side it will include selections by the Toronto String Quartette; vocal numbers by Mr. Ruthven McDonald; musical, illustrated readings and sketches by Mr. R. S. Pigott; bright, brief art talks by three well-known and able speakers. There will be a general good time among the pictures. Refreshments will be served—not in the usual way. Members at this gathering will decide upon a name for the Society. Gentlemen will smoke at intervals. The gathering will assemble at eight and disperse shortly after eleven o'clock In the matter of dress members will suit themselves. Kindly bring this card with you. Each gentleman will pay one dollar, and for each lady he brings, fifty cents extra. All unescorted ladies will pay fifty cents each.

Augustus Bridle SECRETARY.
Chairman

Notice of the first "ladies'" event, May 14, 1908.

On May 20, with the club a little more than one year old, members embarked on their first organized "meeting with the ladies"—these ladies being members of the newly formed women-only Heliconian Club. According to Bridle, the Arts and Letters Club was, by its very existence, the Heliconian Club's unwitting progenitor. With regard to women, our club was much like its London counterpart, the Arts Club, where "women were seen as the enemy to be repelled whenever necessary from this male citadel." Bridle, in particular, was rarely in favour of women at club functions no matter what the occasion. Nevertheless, the following year, so as "not to exclude the feminine," our club decided to inaugurate a monthly series of Saturday vesper musicales featuring "plain teas and simple, good programs of uncommon merit."

Dinners continued to be held once a month at various locations. Early in October, it was time for the first annual meeting, held at the St. Charles Hotel. The evening was highlighted by the election of Wyly Grier as the club's second president. Grier was at the same time serving as president of the OSA. An artist renowned for his portraits (Sir John A. Macdonald once sat for him), he was a man who knew what he liked—and what he didn't like. Years later, when his presidential portrait was done by André Lapine, Grier was not impressed. He replaced it with a self-portrait, and the Lapine effort was relegated

Wyly Grier, President, 1909–1910. (*Wyly Grier*)

(Above right) Wyly Grier. (*Andre Lapine*)

to a storage cupboard. Grier went on to become president of the Royal Canadian Academy of Arts (RCA) from 1930 to 1939. He was knighted in 1935.

Three weeks after Grier became president, members moved with great rejoicing into their first permanent quarters—two spacious albeit unpretentious rooms above the Brown Betty Luncheon & Tea Rooms at 42 King Street East, across from the King Edward Hotel. It was at this time that J. E. H. (Jim) MacDonald, although not yet a member, designed the club's logo for its first letterhead—"a Viking ship with sails full spread before the rising sun," to remind members of "the open sea and the great adventure." The heraldic representation of a Viking longboat originated with Norse and Swedish kings of the seventh century and can also be seen in Scottish family crests, including that of the MacDonald clan.

By the end of the year, 117 men had joined and came to be known as the charter members. All were determined that the Arts and Letters Club would become something more than simply a run-of-the-mill social organization. Members were urged to develop a sense of community and outreach. Bridle asked, "What is the A&LC doing to help civic art? The field is wide, opinions many, and the A&LC is the only place where a common ground for opinions can be determined."

The first newsletter was published in January 1910. It was a modest four-page pamphlet entitled *The Lamps* and featured a brief "Story of the A.L.C." outlining the club's not quite two-year history. Also included were the first two staves of J. D. A. Tripp's "Woodland Love Song"; a photograph of Walter Allward's recently unveiled statue of Ontario's first premier, John Sandfield Macdonald; and a sensitive article entitled "The Art of Appreciation" by musician Robert Stuart Pigott. "Many people think that fault-finding is the highest criticism," he wrote, "but anyone can find fault, whereas it takes wide knowledge and true culture to praise judiciously." A column entitled "Turn of the Wick"—a play on the LAMPS acronym—gave brief mention of several members. A sketch by Fergus Kyle showed members enjoying their new clubrooms.

Masthead of *The Lamps*, featuring the Viking ship logo designed by J. E. H. MacDonald, 1910.

The club's stay above the Brown Betty was short-lived. Less than a year after moving in, Bridle was discovered punching a hole through a wall—apparently in order to install a dumb waiter to bring meals up from the restaurant. "The landlord," he wrote, "kicked us casually into the street." But the move was not really unwelcome, since membership continued to grow and more space was needed.

And so it was that, on the first day of September 1910, members enthusiastically took possession of spacious new quarters on the second floor of the County of York Court House, a massive Greek Revival structure still standing at 57 Adelaide Street East. When it opened its doors in 1853, it housed not only courts but also basement cells for prisoners; Toronto's last public hanging took place in its courtyard to the south. After 1900, when the courts moved to the new city hall on Queen Street at Bay, the building became the County of York Municipal Building, although it continued to house prisoners and to be called the courthouse. Here the Arts and Letters men felt that they had found their true home. They loved it. As was the case with most such organizations, privacy was the order of the day—there was no doorplate to identify the club's presence. This desire for anonymity would continue for years and even the club's phone number was kept private for a long time. To enter the building, members walked along a dingy lane between a

York County Court House, south door, 1910. (*Stanley Turner*)

Said a well-known worker in the Club at luncheon not long ago, "Art is surely going to the dogs. Do these men ever work?"—(Quick-fire sketch by F. K.)

"Do these men ever work?" *The Lamps*, 1910. (*Fergus Kyle*)

Hector Charlesworth. (*M. O. Hammond*)

manure pile and a stack of firewood, went in through the back door on Court Lane—now Court Street—and, once inside, passed by a lockup where they would often hear prisoners yelling or singing. From there they happily climbed up a graceful spiral staircase to the old assize courtroom, a magnificent and inviting space with soaring windows and a thirty-foot ceiling—in Bridle's words, "a gaunt, glorious room." It was, he said with satisfaction, "the most impressive and inaccessible room in Toronto."

The club's initial success could not have been achieved without the enthusiasm and energy of its first members and a brief look at some of them is in order. Literature (the L of LAMPS) was particularly well represented, mainly by journalists, several from the weekly *Saturday Night*. One of the latter was Hector Charlesworth, who wrote negative—often vituperative—opinions about current trends in painting. His antipathy toward the work of some of the club's innovative painters would become legend. *The Globe*'s literary editor, M. O. Hammond, was in almost daily attendance since his office was within easy walking distance of the club's first meeting rooms. Mild-mannered and popular, he was a man of simple tastes and few pretensions and his daily journals are full of club lore. Another notable writer was Peter McArthur, who may have joined the club because, as he wrote, "a club is a place where a gentleman can get drunk respectably."

There were also an impressive number of architects (the A of LAMPS). Most were relatively young, with careers stretching invitingly before them. Some, including Alfred Chapman, John Pearson, and John C. B. Horwood, were busy rebuilding Toronto's downtown core after the disastrous fire of 1904. Eden Smith was creating a popular new style in house design—according to historian Donald Jones, "everyone with money wanted to live in a house designed by Eden Smith." He became so prominent in his field that when he died in 1949, the Royal Architectural Institute of Canada referred to him as "the last of that great group of architects who contributed so much to the architecture of Toronto prior to the First World War." And Ford Howland had recently completed the design for St. Anne's Anglican Church on Gladstone Avenue, one of the few Byzantine structures in Canada and now a national historic site. St. Anne's would feature in several club-related affairs over the next century.

Augustus Vogt. (*Charles Aylett*)

The music side (the M of LAMPS) included pianist Frank Welsman, conductor of the first Toronto Symphony Orchestra (TSO), organist Augustus Vogt, founder and conductor of the Toronto Mendelssohn Choir, and cellists Paul Hahn and Leo Smith. These and other musician members often performed for their fellow members, sometimes with visiting musician friends.

Among the visual artists (the P and S of LAMPS), one of the first on the scene was twenty-three-year-old Lawren Harris. Born to a wealthy family that owned part of the giant Massey Harris farm machinery company, he studied art in Berlin, returning to Toronto in 1908. Fellow charter member and illustrator C. W. Jefferys described him as "inclined to be headstrong but...not spoiled when you consider his being brought up in luxury." Others included the obstreperous Curtis Williamson, an artist of great virtuosity; George Reid, principal of the Ontario College of Art (OCA), who brought with him a number of his teachers; and architect-sculptor Walter Allward, who later produced the magnificent memorial to Canada's war dead at Vimy Ridge. Sculptor Emanuel Hahn and painter Gustav Hahn were brothers of Paul Hahn—not the only trio of brothers to join the club, but the first.

This brings us to the stage (later to be the S of LAMPS). The club's early activities in this area were dominated by one man: Roy Mitchell, a writer and director, but, above all, a passionate lover of theatre—one of the avant-garde who fervently denounced its commercial aspects, claiming that they betrayed its artistic integrity.

George Reid at home, 1907. (*M. O. Hammond*)

Although the club was formed for the professional arts and letters community, the members recognized from the start that while membership should be weighted to professionals, there was also a need to include nonprofessionals. And so, even in those early years, there were a number of members who had no claim to professional status, but possessed a keen interest in the arts and letters. Among them were lawyers Robert (Bob) Defries and Sir William Mulock, who, at this time, was chief justice of the Exchequer Division of the Supreme Court of Ontario. Another was banker and philanthropist Sir Edmund Walker. All three would be members of the club for many years.

Roy Mitchell conducting a "fireside chat," 1915. (*M. O. Hammond*)

In September 1910, just a week after moving into the courthouse, the tired but cheerful members were ready to celebrate. They did so with great fanfare at a splendid inaugural dinner, during which a number of "masterpieces" were staged. As reported in the December 1910 issue of *The Lamps*,

> Sir William Mulock was humorous; Sir Edmund Walker illuminative and historical; Mr. Jan Hambourg played "The Devil's Trill" almost divinely to the accompaniment of Mr. Frank Welsman; Mr. Leo Smith delicately empurpled the air with a cello piece by Brahms; Mr. McLean Borthwick, baritone, sang delightfully—and it was discovered that the old courthouse has almost ideal acoustics.

George Locke, President, 1910–1912. (*Andre Lapine*)

A few days after this memorable event, an excited Gus Bridle wrote to Sir William Glenholme Falconbridge, chief justice of the Queen's Bench division of Ontario's High Court of Justice, inviting him to come to the club to hear the legendary English actor J. Forbes Robertson, "the greatest Hamlet of the times." The invitation noted that there would be a "Smoker" at 9:30 p.m., supper at 11:20 p.m., followed by music by the Toronto String Quartet, and finally Robertson's talk—so late, no doubt, because of an earlier stage appearance. According to President Grier, when the big night arrived the walls of the formal chamber were "warmed and enlivened by pictures and its severe architectural features softened by the blue haze of ascending tobacco smoke." Robertson, the guest of Walker and Mulock, was "the embodiment of grace." He reminded his audience of their high calling as "assembled Bohemians."

A month later, it was time for the next annual meeting and the inauguration of the third president, George Locke, a tall, impressive, genial figure who was then head of the Toronto Public Library. The evening's dinner was introduced with great panache and silliness. "Eight pie bearers in vestments of improvised cheesecloth and garlands of olive...each with two pies...entered the hall to the unprepared march of 'O Canada'." After dinner, Locke outlined the virtues of the club, reminding members that, "the highest pleasure is not in getting, but in giving.... There must exist an atmosphere of social service that will promote individual pleasure as well as social well-being. The parasite and the chameleon will not be comfortable amid such surroundings, and the social climber will prefer the shaded lights that accompany marshmallows and afternoon bridges, or the padded cushions, menus, and conversation of more luxurious surroundings." Not for Locke an "upholstered" club.

With or without upholstered surroundings, members were determined to have fun in their spacious new quarters—and wasted no time in doing so. Our first Boar's Head ceremony was held that December, with colourful pageantry that originated in Tudor times. It all began with a dignified procession or, as Bridle put it, "a trail-in from the kitchen." It was led by a jester, who was followed by wardens, a sergeant-at-arms, and the marshal. Once the president and other dignitaries were seated, several candle-bearers entered, followed by the chef carrying aloft a boar's head. Others carrying platters with turkey and beef joined the parade—all to the accompaniment of a boys' choir singing "Caput Apri Defero Reddens Laudes Domino," a carol first printed in 1521. As Hammond, greatly impressed, recorded later that evening,

> Best of all was the Xmas tree with Mr. [Frederick] Bell-Smith as Santa Claus. There was a present for just about everyone and the fun this brought was simply sidesplitting.

George Locke with the club executive "at his feet," 1910. Clockwise from Locke are W. W. Alexander, Fergus Kyle, Roy Mitchell, R. S. Pigott, Jan Hambourg, Gustav Hahn, Eden Smith, C. W. Jefferys, Gus Bridle, Wyly Grier, and R. L. Defries. (*M. O. Hammond*)

> Sir William Mulock got a supposed bottle of wine, a "gift of the government," but it was hollow and filled with candies. Michael Hambourg got a toy piano, Jan Hambourg a toy violin, Ed Morris a set of paints, another artist some dolls as models, others mechanical toys & so on. I laughed till I was sore.

The second issue of *The Lamps*—now grown to twelve pages—also appeared that month. It featured a dramatic cover illustration by Lawren Harris depicting the clock tower of St. James Cathedral as seen from a south window of the courthouse clubrooms, a view that can still be enjoyed from that same window today.

Paintings and painters were always hot topics at the club. Even when the club was little more than a bright idea in the mind of Gus Bridle, he had written of the challenge facing the city's visual artists. "Unfortunately for art in Ontario, particularly the art of painting, there has been a good deal of indulgence in quibblings and petty animosities amongst painters, with a result that has caused a marked division of interest." A new club, he had continued hopefully, "would have a tendency to set aside even long-standing grievances." Hammond remembered one heated discussion when the artist Carl Ahrens was his guest. They were joined by the *Canadian Magazine*'s Newton MacTavish, a central figure in the literary world and influential in art circles, the dogmatic Henry Franklin

View of St. James Cathedral from the Court House south window. Sketch for cover of *The Lamps*, 1910. (*Lawren Harris*)

Newton McTavish (left) and M. O. Hammond. (*M. O. Hammond*)

Gadsby of the *Toronto Daily Star*, and artist, John Russell. Before long, Hammond made a remark praising the work of Horatio Walker, a fine but traditional painter, described years later by the critic Paul Duval as one of the best watercolour painters flourishing at the turn of the century. MacTavish and Gadsby disagreed with Hammond. "It drew a hornet's nest about my ears," Hammond recalled, "and the two artists were soon pitching into Walker fiercely." Ahrens claimed that Walker was an assimilative artist, while Russell insisted that his work would not live. This led to a dispute about whether laymen could discuss art intelligently. In the end, MacTavish got them to admit that "artists could not write about art and that some laymen knew more about art than some artists."

Hammond was back at the club in January for the first members' dinner of 1911. That evening's entertainment featured a talk on Egypt and its politics by Charles Currelly, curator of the Royal Ontario Museum (ROM). Under his leadership the museum acquired one of the outstanding archaeological collections on the continent. His talk was followed by five Egyptian friezes, each representing a LAMPS discipline with performers wearing little but a towel around their nether regions—in a drafty hall in January—and appropriate headgear. All this was thanks to the fertile imagination of the club's "prankmeister" Roy Mitchell.

"Death to the Chairman of the First Hanging Committee," 1911. One of five friezes mounted by Roy Mitchell at a dinner addressed by C. T. Currelly. Arthur Lismer is the figure in the centre. (*M. O. Hammond*)

In February, members at the monthly dinner were treated to a performance of Haydn's *Toy Symphony* by the club orchestra, with Paul Hahn conducting. Several of the toy musical instruments that had adorned the Christmas tree two months earlier were included. It was all in good fun, according to a bit of doggerel in an early scrapbook:

Saturday we heard it played;
On the platform were arrayed
Thirty men, and not a dub
At the Arts and Letters Club.
Big musicians kept it going,
Played the stuff so smooth and flowing,
While some bright and clever boys
Were performing on the toys.

Ottawa poet Duncan Campbell Scott was a visitor at the club for lunch one day in March. He was a friend of many of the members and loved chatting with them. Scott said that in Ottawa he lacked "stimulation from contact with other writers" such as he found at the club. Two years later he became a member.

Roy Mitchell and his fellow enthusiasts took to the stage in late April. Mitchell's unflagging devotion to theatre had led them to form the Arts and Letters Players the previous year, one of several little theatre groups that were cropping up at about this time in various Ontario centres. The Players' first venture was Maurice Maeterlinck's *Interior*, directed by Mitchell and performed on a platform made up of movable boxes. Unfortunately, the only place where this improvised stage could be set up was directly in front of the wall where club painters displayed their pictures. Whenever pictures were taken down for a play or covered by scenery, the painters were, to say the least and to no one's surprise, not amused. As journalist Poynter Bell noted in *The Lamps*, the resulting conflicts were "unfortunate." It seems amazing that these theatrical efforts were as successful as they were, but somehow it all came together—thanks to Mitchell and the club's writers, critics, and amateur theatre enthusiasts. They made it happen. As Merrill Denison later wrote, "The Arts and Letters Players...had an absolute freedom in their choice of plays. They could do anything they felt was interesting or worth doing.... Their one adamant rule was never to produce anything that had been done in Canada before."

After what Bridle described as "one winter in that cold-storage chamber," the executive decided that what was really needed in the new clubrooms was a fireplace. Eden Smith was put in charge—and he accomplished the task so well that he became revered

Eden Smith, architect and designer of the fireplace. (*Ivor Lewis*)

Characters from *Then Came Fire*, the fireplace dedication ceremony, October 1911: Caveman (Francis Coombs), Zoroastrian (Roy Mitchell), Roman Sentry (Eugene Beaupré), and Scandinavian (Harry Smith). (*M. O. Hammond*)

within the club. When the fireplace was ready to be installed in October, it was carried up on steel-reinforced beams, built onto the south wall, and immediately became the focal point of every club function. Horace Corner, a new member at the time, recalled that "the fireplace was really necessary—it was often pretty cold up there. Members would toast their rolls by the fire on long toasting forks." He also described how, on arrival, each member would carry up a stick of firewood for the fireplace. Later in the month, the "greatest fireplace in Canada" was officially dedicated. Members packed the club-rooms to enjoy the theatrical extravaganza *Then Came Fire*! The text had been written by Alan Sullivan, with music by Leo Smith and costumes by Mitchell. When it finally came to an end, a flaming torch was thrown into the firewood and the club's *saengerbund* burst into song:

Oh, a song by the fire!
Fill the pipes, pass the bowl
Oh, a song by the fire!
With a skoal, with a skoal!

Following all the entertainment, President Locke formally dedicated the fireplace to "the domestic uses of the club."

At this time, there were three members of the Hambourg family in the club—Michael and two of his sons, Boris and Jan—all gifted musicians who had recently emigrated from England. As a present-day member has commented, had these assimilated Jews been born in Toronto, they might not have been so well received. A third son, pianist Mark, had stayed in England, but visited from time to time as he went on to an international career. A fourth much younger son, Clement, was not yet old enough to join. One evening in late October, Mark obligingly sat down at the club's less-than-wonderful piano to perform for the members. The always enthusiastic Hammond came to hear him, and recorded in his diary that Hambourg, who was then about thirty-two, "pounded out one of Liszt's rhapsodies.... When he quit there was a perfect hurricane of applause." Hambourg then sank back into a chair but was promptly escorted to the kitchen, where he autographed a cushion top for a church and donated ten cents. "My Lord," he said later, "I am usually paid half a crown for my autograph, and for a church too—and me an atheist!"

The Hambourg Trio: Jan, Boris, and Professor Michael Hambourg, 1912. (*M. O. Hammond*)

The third issue of *The Lamps* landed on members' desks that month. Its focus was, of course, the magnificent fireplace and its dedication—included was a painting of the fireplace by Jim MacDonald, a lengthy article by Langton, a shorter tribute by Homer Watson, photos by Hammond, every deathless word of the long stage production, and sketches of its players. It also carried an ecstatic review of a concert given by the Hambourg family. "Boris did not bore us," claimed the reviewer, who concluded that the Hambourgs were "a mutually responsive ensemble such as one has seldom heard equaled." The same issue mentioned that membership "had reached the limit of 175, with 50 on a waiting list," and George Reid reported on a suggested redecoration of the main hall. "A meeting of architects and artists enthusiastically discussed the scheme. Opinions differed." *Plus ça change....* Women, on occasion, managed to find their place in the scheme of things, as noted in a brief item on the back page: "Here's to the kitchen—which never a day since October last has failed to give every man his due.... Twenty kind ladies—mainly the wives of members—have been diligently preserving fruit for the club pantry; for the management of which much thanks is due to Messrs. Mitchell and Henry Button."

"Academicians are sometimes actors when pictures become a play," *The Lamps,* December 1911. (*Arthur Lismer*)

Lawren Harris, April 1926.
(*M. O. Hammond*)

No doubt buoyed by the enthusiastic reception of the October 1911 issue, a fourth issue of *The Lamps* appeared just two months later. In it, Lawren Harris wrote of a recent RCA show at the club, offering his outspoken opinions as to why, on occasion, voices were raised and buns hurled across the clubroom when views about art differed. He spared no one. "If from one quarter to one half the pictures and all the sketches in the exhibition had been rejected by the hanging committee, the exhibition would have been one of very high standard." Harris had a few words of praise for two fellow club members: "Homer Watson's *The Stronghold* is...powerful, great and strong of line," he wrote, and "Mr. Jefferys' pictures are notable for a refinement of line and design." Other members fared less well. "Mr. Harry Britton's *Cornish Fishing Boats* invites criticism, as does the work of Mr. W. St. Thomas-Smith, Mr. Gagen, Mr. Manly, Mr. F. M. Bell-Smith, Mr. G. A. Reid, and many others.... Mr. Beatty's *Wood Interior* is a big thing...an admirable bit of work. The frame, however, injured the tone of the picture."

A fifth issue of *The Lamps*, mostly essays, appeared in June 1912, the last one to be published until December 1919. It was not a shining venture—self-indulgent and full of meaningless prose, trivial poetry, and second-rate art. The club continued to welcome guests on a regular basis and one guest who visited in September 1912 was the Yukon poet Robert W. Service. He was hesitant about receiving praise for his work and seemed astonished that he was so well-known and appreciated.

The annual meeting that fall saw J. W. (Bill) Beatty elected the club's fourth president. Beatty was one of a kind. Dignified? Well, no. Genial? No, not really. Virtually everyone who knew him described him as a fine painter, but volatile and something of a rough diamond. "He had that Irish sentimentality," wrote Bridle. It made him "a glorious truculent bigot, ready for action with either fists or vocabulary." But he was fiercely loyal to his friends and to the club. "He talked like an anarchist," recalled another member, "but painted like a grand old Tory with imagination." Beatty had enlisted as a bugle boy during the Riel Rebellion when he was sixteen, served for eleven years as a fireman with the Toronto Fire Department until he was thirty, then studied painting in Paris, London, and the Low Countries. He was forty-three when he became president. That same year he joined the staff at the OCA, where he was an inspiring and highly regarded teacher.

J. W. Beatty, President, 1912–1913.
(*J. E. Sampson*)

One of Beatty's first duties as president was to introduce club members to one of the world's leading violinists. Visiting musicians were always welcome at the club, and many of international stature performed for those fortunate enough to be on hand. Such was the case one December day when young Mischa Elman, the guest of Frank Welsman, agreed to play. Elman, a Russian child prodigy, was then twenty-one and had been touring the United States and Europe for several years. He was coaxed to play by Michael Hambourg but, as he had not brought his violin with him and refused to play Robert Flaherty's "old pick-up violin," he had his own instrument fetched from his hotel. He performed a Handel sonata. Hammond described Elman as "a short, temperamental Russian Jew who had the crowd at his feet." Another member, revealing the pervasive anti-Semitism that was never far from the surface in Toronto society, described him as "a queer-looking little fellow.... I was told he is loose in his morals. He is obviously coarse in his tastes...but, with his instrument in his hands he can produce wonderful harmonies. He seemed to mesmerize everybody."

"Boy wonder" Mischa Elman.

The New Year's Eve celebration that year was a rowdy, men-only event. Hammond cheerfully described the evening that began with a hot punch—"an invidious alluring concoction." Before long, half or more of the crowd was drunk or close to it. Songs were sung, short speeches made, poems recited, dances danced, the piano played. "It was all a happy, merry, good-natured crowd."

In January 1913, the Norwegian explorer, Roald Amundsen, was at the club to recount his adventures through the Northwest Passage in 1905 and his trip to reach the South Pole in 1911. At the conclusion of his talk, the club choir, led by Percy Hollinshead, launched into a rousing version of the Norwegian national anthem.

Percy Hollinshead, 1912.
(*M. O. Hammond*)

That spring, the club welcomed back Augustus Vogt with a fine dinner in his honour. He was just home from a year-long stay in Europe. The purpose of his trip had been to arrange a tour for his choir, but the plans were abandoned due to concerns about the coming war. A more important outcome for the country and the club was that while abroad he met with organist Healey Willan and encouraged him to move to Canada—which he soon did.

At about this time, Percy Hollinshead, the club's enthusiastic tenor, left for Milan to further his musical studies. The portly and popular Hollinshead was an exuberant participant in club functions and his fellow members hated to see him leave. As a farewell gift he was presented with a small and exquisite book containing on each page either a painting, an engraving, a poem, or a few bars of music created lovingly by a fellow member. On his death in 1937, Hollinshead's widow kindly returned this volume to the club. It now is safely stored in the Thomas Fisher Rare Book Library, but a copy is available at the club for all to enjoy. Reproductions of some of its pages have been framed and are now presented as gifts to guest speakers and musicians.

Rupert Brooke, *The Lamps*, 1919. (*Franz Johnston*)

Then as now, conversation at the luncheon table was spirited, but only a few of the exchanges have been retained for posterity in the diaries of early members. In May, Arnot Craick wrote that one discussion had turned to the new Pellatt mansion, Casa Loma. Construction of the castle had begun in 1911 and would be completed in 1914. "It seems to be conceded that the whole scheme is vulgar."

In July, the English poet Rupert Brooke appeared at the club one day and settled down by the fireplace. In Bridle's words, he was, "a pink-cheeked sprawler in tweeds with a big, floppy hat." Handsome, talented, and upper class, Brooke was then about twenty-six and one of the brightest stars in the literary firmament. In a somewhat condescending, world-weary, here-I-am-in-the-colonies tone, he wrote to his friend Edward Marsh,

> I've found here an Arts & Letters Club of poets, painters, journalists, etc., where they'd heard of me and read *Georgian Poetry*, and, oh Eddie, one fellow actually possessed my "Poems." Awful Triumph. Every now & then, one comes up & presses my hand & says "Wal, Sir, you cannot know how memorable a Day in my life this is." Then I do my pet boyish modesty stunt & go pink all over, and everyone thinks it too delightful.... But they're really quite an up-to-date lot and very cheery and pleasant.

Rufus Hathaway, the club's librarian, recalled that Brooke was like a young Greek god, "pleasant and agreeable, rather reserved, if not indeed shy." Brooke had agreed to sign a copy of his *Georgian Poetry* for Hathaway, and while doing so altered the title of the sonnet "Libido" to "Lust," explaining that the latter was his original title, but his publishers would not have it, and consequently he sought to get even with them by restoring it whenever opportunity offered. Perry Meisel wrote that "Brooke is remembered less for his poems than for his good looks and less for his good looks than for the way he abused his friends." Brooke had been a guest that day of painter Edmund Morris, who drowned tragically in Quebec a few weeks after their lunch at the age of forty-two. His métier was sensitive portraits of Canada's native Indians and he had amassed a fine collection of Indian artifacts. Morris's work received little public notice during his lifetime, but today many of his portraits and artifacts can be seen in major galleries and museums across the country.

In September, while Arnot Craick was having lunch with Lindsay Crawford of *The Globe*, Vincent Massey came by and was very friendly. With something less than enthusiasm, Craick wrote in his journal that Massey "seems a nice fellow and will doubtless improve on acquaintance." Massey, who had joined the club two years earlier, was at the time a junior lecturer in modern history at U of T. He had recently returned from Balliol College, Oxford, and, along with his teaching duties, was deeply involved with the construction of Hart House. He and Lawren Harris would often joke at the club about their families' Massey Harris company: "Blessed be the binder that twines!"

Painter A. Y. (Alec) Jackson, recently arrived from Montreal, joined the club that year. He soon fell in with a number of like-minded young radical artists—Lawren Harris, Jim MacDonald, Arthur Lismer, Fred Varley, Frank Johnston, and others—and this, at times, made him a target for abuse from the more traditional artists. Jackson later wrote that Curtis Williamson, who had studied art for years in Europe, "had no sympathy for what we were doing, and not much respect for anything done in Canada." The lack of respect was mutual. Jackson went on, "Heming only made pencil portraits of pretty women, and Beatty could never free himself from traditional ways of painting. About all that Williamson, Heming, and Beatty had in common was a hearty dislike of one another."

These three and several other club artists were, however, soon to be neighbours in a new and remarkable structure then rising on Severn Street in the Rosedale Ravine near Yonge and Bloor streets. Called the Studio Building, it was another of Eden Smith's memorable designs, and the first building in Canada constructed specifically for artists' studios in the hope that favourable surroundings would promote good art and good discussion—which it did. No sooner had its doors opened than artists moved in to enjoy the camaraderie, comfort, and reasonable rent of its bright, spacious studios. Among the first tenants were Williamson, Heming, Beatty, Harris, and MacDonald. The building was financed by Harris with the help of ophthalmologist James MacCallum, who had joined the club the previous year. It was MacCallum who had urged Alec Jackson to move to Toronto, and he had generously promised to provide him with living expenses and a studio for a year. The Studio Building is now a national historic site.

In spite of occasional disagreements—or perhaps because of them—the club was thriving. At the annual meeting in October, it was announced that only seven out of sixty applicants had been accepted as members. They had been carefully selected after a long wait, owing to the ever-growing list of men who were anxious to join. So it seemed that the time had arrived for Gus Bridle to become president—not a surprising turn of events given his complete devotion to the club. To this day he is still referred to as "Fellow Member Number One."

Bridle's early life had been incredibly difficult. Born fatherless in England to an orphaned teenager, he was only two years old when his mother died. Young Gus was placed in an orphanage for a few years, then shipped off to Canada in 1878 when he was ten. It was another eight years before he received any schooling, when a kindly schoolteacher in Chatham, Ontario took him under her wing. Remarkably, this determined and hardworking young man eventually graduated from U of T in 1900 with a gold medal

Studio Building, Severn Street, 2006. (*John Blumenson*)

Augustus Bridle, President, 1913–1914. (*Wyly Grier*)

in classics. By the time the idea of a club devoted to the arts came into his fertile mind, Bridle was an established journalist. Although admired by most who knew him, Bridle was not—to put it kindly—a man of few words. His pen flowed with abundant and idiosyncratic grace, often leaving his readers wondering just what in the world he was trying to say. For most of his working life, he was the book review editor, drama editor, and music critic for the *Toronto Daily Star*. As such he was, in the words of William Kilbourn, "a kind of communal shamanic memory."

In those first heady days, club elections could be heated and, at times, divisive. Such was the case when Bridle was nominated for president. His opponent was Alan Sullivan, whose election had seemed a sure thing until a move favouring Bridle quietly gathered momentum, partly because of all that Bridle had done for the club, partly "to get him out of the perpetual secretaryship," and partly because Bridle, then forty-five, was soon to be married. "The romance of the old bachelor...fired the emotions." There was also a hint of enmity towards Sullivan. Tempers rose but, at the last moment, Sullivan graciously withdrew and was promptly nominated vice president. He confided to Hammond the following day that he was aware of all the club meant to Bridle. In Sullivan's words, Bridle had had, after all, "no very clear birth, no start in life, nothing but what he had earned and made for himself, and I resolved to step aside."

At lunch on the day of the election Bridle was presented with a cheque in recognition of his upcoming marriage. A ceremony of some sort was staged—Arnot Craick recalled "a musical program of some length, a short and most effective pantomime, and then the presentation. I cannot say that I was much impressed by the last item. It was too stagy in effect—nothing spontaneous about it, and Bridle piled up words in a most unconcerned way." Which, of course, was not surprising. Even on an ordinary day, Bridle piled up words. On this occasion, with his wedding ahead of him, he may have understandably been more than a little nervous. Two weeks later, when he returned from his honeymoon, the new bridegroom presided at a members' dinner—his first as president. He made "a long-winded and tiresome speech," wrote Hammond, "and his conduct of the meeting was anything but brisk and businesslike." Perhaps he was tired.

In December, former Prime Minister Sir Wilfrid Laurier came for lunch and chatted with a clutch of club bigwigs including Sir Edmund Walker, Sir William Mulock, Wyly Grier, and some of the leading academics of the day. Also on hand was *Toronto Daily Star* news editor H. C. Hindmarsh. Bridle wrote:

> In the old Assize Court, Laurier discovered a type of bohemian democracy that he had never met. The great hall was full of members at lunch—all dining when the eminent

O, WEDNESDAY, DECEMBER 17, 1913.—TWENTY PAGES. Last Edition.

SIR WILFRID LAURIER, AND OTHER WELL-KNOWN MEN, SKETCHED DURING A CHEERFUL AND INFORMAL HALF-HOUR AROUND THE CLUB FIRESIDE

ONE OF THE MOST PLEASANT DAYS EVER SPENT IN TORONTO BY FORMER PRIME MINISTER.

The artist was successful yesterday in securing a sketch that is not without historic value. Among the gentlemen around the lounging room may be seen some who hold a high place in the public and professional life of the country. The names of many of these men are often associated with the formality of office, but here they are seen in the happier moments of relaxation.

Sir Wilfrid Laurier lunches at the club, *Toronto Daily Star*, December 17, 1913.

> personage came in.... The moment he stepped into the hall of the great fireplace, all the members rose to cheer in a flutter of napkins. Such an ovation had never been tendered to him by both Grits and Tories. Supremely at home, chatting in his impeccable English, he was a figure that instantly ten club artists yearned to paint; the focus of a great occasion in the most unconventional club premises he had ever seen. Even Paris could scarcely have surpassed that spontaneous *vie de la Bohème.*

Laurier was presented with a copy of *The Yearbook of Canadian Art 1913*, which had been published by the club a few months earlier. It was the first major survey of the arts in this country and members were justly proud of this well-illustrated publication. Instigated by Bridle, it comprised "a record of the progress made by a young nation in literature, architecture, music, painting, and sculpture, during the years 1912–13." The book features brief essays outlining accomplishments in all the arts in all parts of Canada. It had been put together by a determined and hardworking committee of Peter Donovan, Jesse Middleton, M. O. Hammond, Alan Sullivan, Albert H. Robson, and Jim MacDonald who, although remembered today primarily as a painter, was also a fine writer. The book was a major undertaking, produced with the encouragement of its ebullient publisher, charter

Sir William Mulock and Sir Wilfrid Laurier, 1913. (*William James*)

Lunch at the club, c.1916.
(*Pringle & Booth*)

member Henry Button. "Pop" Button, as he was affectionately called, was then managing director of the firm J. M. Dent and Sons.

At some point during the year, Roy Mitchell and his theatre contingent had assembled a platform of sorts and staged *The Glittering Gate* by the Anglo-Irish aristocrat Lord Dunsany. It was Dunsany's first play, written in 1909 at the urging of William Butler Yeats and already a success in Ireland. Yeats described Dunsany as "a man of genius."

As 1914 began, the club's treasurer, Bob Defries, faced the ongoing problem of unpaid membership fees—many by then several months overdue—and normal practice required that he pursue the delinquents. At a meeting in April, Hammond, who was on the membership committee, was clearly exasperated: "We had a list of forty or fifty members who had not paid fees.... I heard various excuses made on behalf of some, while others were allowed to be dropped."

But the issue of unpaid fees faded into insignificance when, on August 4, Britain declared war on Germany. Canada, as a fiercely loyal member of the British Empire, automatically became a participant. Within weeks, many Arts and Letters men flocked to the colours. The city's prevailing mood changed dramatically, no longer reflecting the optimism that had been current when Joe Clark wrote in 1908 that "aeroplanes and the possibility of aerial bombardment meant an end to war. " No one, he felt, would be "silly enough to drop bombs on cities." But how could anyone have prophesied the horrors that lay ahead?

In its earliest days the war fostered a somewhat chivalrous and upbeat attitude in the young since it was generally assumed that this particular conflict would be dealt with promptly and would, in all likelihood, be over by Christmas. Consequently, there was an almost frantic eagerness to enlist. One of the first from the club was Thomas H. Plummer, who was on the ocean for England within a week and survived the war with a Distinguished Service Order. But it wasn't just the young men who were eager to serve. Agar Adamson, a man of great courage and legendary charm, was pushing forty-nine when he joined the army and left home on August 10, having been offered a captaincy in the Princess Patricia's Canadian Light Infantry. He had served with distinction in the Boer War, but, after developing typhoid fever, had been invalided home. The outbreak of World War I offered him another chance at soldiering, which he considered his true calling. He leaped at the opportunity.

Henry Campbell Osborne, also in his forties, enlisted on August 20. Others who joined up that year included architects Robert B. McGiffin and Ford Howland. McGiffin was put in charge of setting up hospitals and barracks. Howland served overseas and, in early 1919, was sent to Vladivostok as a staff officer with the 16th Infantry Brigade. Lawyer Norman Scarth Macdonnell (years later a justice of the Supreme Court of Ontario) was on the front lines in a matter of weeks, as was Saint-Elme de Champ, a colourful and much-loved professor of French at U of T. William Langton, at the age of sixty, gave up his architectural practice to devote all his time to the Serbian Relief Committee.

Despite the events of the war, life at the club continued much as before. At the 1914 annual meeting, the executive addressed a complaint regarding the presence of ladies. Similar complaints had been surfacing with almost monotonous regularity. But that seems to have been the only contentious issue in the proceedings, during which Alan Sullivan was finally sworn in as president.

Sullivan was born in Montreal in 1868, studied industrial engineering at U of T, and then headed for northern Ontario and a career in surveying and gold mining. He returned to Toronto in 1904 and became a writer of fiction and poetry. At some point he moved to the upper-class enclave known as Wychwood Park, where he lived in a house that would, nearly half a century later, become the home of Marshall and Corinne McLuhan. Sullivan impressed his fellow members by usually walking the three miles from his home

Saint-Elme de Champ in 1934. (*Arthur Lismer*)

Allan Sullivan, President, 1914–1915. (*J. E. Sampson*)

Robert Flaherty.

to the club's Adelaide Street quarters. He published his first novel, *Blantyre Alien*, the year he became president. After a brief stint with the Royal Flying Corps during the war, he wrote *Aviation in Canada 1917–18*, and then went on to write a total of forty-three works of fiction. In his heyday he was widely read and reviewed. One novel, *Three Came to Ville Marie*, won the 1941 Governor General's Award for Fiction.

Hammond's daily journal offers innumerable insights into what was going on at the club. In December, when he dropped in for lunch with Gus Bridle, Peter Donovan, and Robert Flaherty, Hammond recalled that Flaherty, who had been making a name for himself with his Arctic adventures, entertained his luncheon colleagues with "racy side-lights on Eskimo life, he having just returned from fifteen months in the Arctic.... He says white men wintering up there always take an Eskimo girl each for the time, who esteems it an honour, never thinks of any stigma. It seems to him a biological necessity, and when they left there was much weeping on both sides." (A recent visitor from the Arctic tells us that there are still quite a few Flahertys there, who cherish their heritage.) It's not much wonder that members were anxious to attend the screening of his documentary about the Arctic. To accompany the film, Flaherty brought "reliques, costumes, tools, hunting gear. For weeks the club was a small Eskimo museum." He went on to a stellar career as a documentary filmmaker. When he died in 1951, e. e. cummings called Flaherty "a god among men," and Orson Welles described him as "one of the two or three greatest people who ever worked in the medium." He stayed a club member for only four years.

The club's fifth Boar's Head, held at the end of the month, was, according to the impressionable Hammond, the best they ever had.

> Huge crowd of 150 or more and many had trouble getting seats. I sat between Rowe, the architect, and Varley, the painter.... Beaupré put on a good little Xmas stunt at the start, dressed with head of jackass. It was an astonishing lineup of musical talent that evening as the Adanac Quartet sang three or four songs, after which Mark Hambourg played two Bach selections. A string octet, including Mark's brothers, Boris and Jan, followed. The evening concluded with a chorus led by Vogt, the whole numbering thirty people or more of the best orchestra players and professional singers in the city.

In January 1915, Bridle announced an upcoming "symposium," a playlet intriguingly titled *Love and the Arts*, written by Alan Sullivan, and dealing with "different phases of the marriage question and women in general." Ah, to have been there. Unfortunately, women were not invited. We'll never know just what it entailed, since no one thought—

Scene from *The Post Office* by Rabindranath Tagore, 1915. The club's performance in December 1914 was the first in North America. (*M. O. Hammond*)

(Above left) Augustus Vogt, founder of the Mendelssohn Choir, conducts. (*Newton McConnell*)

or dared—to keep a copy of the script. A more ambitious production, *The Post Office*, written by the celebrated Indian writer Rabindranath Tagore and directed by Roy Mitchell, was also staged that month—its first performance in North America. (Tagore had won the Nobel Prize for literature a year before and would soon be knighted.) The cast included Arthur Lismer, Henry Button, James Kitchener, and the Misses Ferris and Chrichton (of whom nothing is known). Then, at the monthly dinner in March, Mitchell and "his cohorts"—as Hammond put it—produced J. M. Synge's *The Shadow of the Glen*, a performance repeated twice in the following weeks.

The first of the club painters to head for Europe was Alec Jackson, who left in late April. Stunned by the devastating Canadian casualties sustained during the first battle of Ypres, he enlisted immediately. Lawren Harris had suggested that Jackson apply for a commission and offered to pay all expenses, but Jackson, because he "knew nothing about soldiering," decided to start at the bottom as a private in the infantry. On the home front, the club's architects and engineers formed the Arts and Science Rifle Association, "a program of self-improvement based on patriotism." We don't know who took part in this venture or what it entailed, nor do we know how long it lasted. That same spring, fees of members who were serving in the war were waived.

Alfred DeLury, President, 1915–1916. (*F. S. Challener*)

One day in July, Alan Sullivan, C. W. Jefferys, Peter Donovan, Francis (Frank) Moore, Rufus Hathaway, and a few others met in the club library to hear Pelham Edgar, a much loved and highly regarded professor of English at Victoria College, read a new poem by Duncan Campbell Scott, written in memory of Edmund Morris, who had drowned so tragically two years earlier. The poem was, claimed Edgar, "the best thing in Canadian poetry so far." The library was a fitting spot for all of them to meet, as Morris had left his extensive collection of books to the club.

Sullivan's presidency was not without its conflicts. At the annual meeting in October, he had a run-in with the usually mild-mannered Hammond, who questioned the absence of a financial statement. The problem appeared to be about the funds spent by the theatre committee during the year. Not everyone, it seemed, was as supportive of stage activities as were Roy Mitchell and his friends. The actual sum was finally revealed when the treasurer, Bob Defries, joined Hammond in insisting on full disclosure—which showed that the theatre committee's expenses had reached a steep $532. After this confrontation, Sullivan may have been pleased that his presidency was for only one year.

Alfred Tennyson DeLury, an Irishman of great personal charm, was elected the next president. He was a popular professor of mathematics at U of T who shared his enthusiasm for Irish poetry and plays with fellow club members. He encouraged Roy Mitchell to direct the first North American productions of plays by J. M. Synge and William Butler Yeats, the latter being DeLury's guest at the club on several occasions.

Ernest Seitz playing at lunch, April 17, 1924. (*Arthur Lismer*)

The executive decided in November that it was time for the club to acquire its own piano rather than continuing to use Gus Bridle's. Ernest Seitz, a brilliant twenty-three-year-old pianist who had joined the club in 1911, was asked to choose the best that the Nordheimer Piano & Music Co. had on hand, which he did—a seven-foot Steinway concert grand built in New York two years previously that cost the club $1,000. Seitz had been studying in Berlin, but by great good fortune, or perhaps because he sensed what lay ahead, he had returned to Toronto a matter of weeks before the outbreak of war. He went on to forge an international career as a concert pianist, teacher, and composer. Seitz's most famous composition was a ballad, "The World is Waiting for the Sunrise," written in 1918 to lyrics by Gene Lockhart.

A show of Tom Thomson's sketches went up on the club walls in December—paintings that, to no one's surprise, elicited plenty of controversy. Although he was never a member, Thomson was a close friend of several of the club artists. On the day before the show opened, Hammond had met him for the first time at the Studio Building, where the painter shared a small shack at the rear with Arthur Lismer. He described the scene as follows:

> Thomson is a well-built chap with a clean face and the hard hands of the woodsman. But the place was awfully bare. He and Lismer work together and both are about bankrupt. There was no fire in the stove, and he explained it did not draw well for lack of enough pipe. But I perceive the real reason is no money for fuel. He showed me bunches of sketches by Jackson & Lismer, & praised them highly, but said nothing of himself save in answer to questions.

Ever gung-ho, the club's theatrical members produced yet another show. This time it was Thomas Hardy's epic poem *The Dynasts*, a lengthy drama in verse set in the Napoleonic period. Although staged at the Royal Alexandra Theatre, it was basically an Arts and Letters Club production, with the program designed by Fred Varley.

In February 1916, the club mounted Fred Varley's first one-man show. His fellow club member, Hector Charlesworth, would undoubtedly have seen the show—and would have disliked it intensely, but it was MacDonald's works in an OSA exhibition that became the target of a vicious diatribe by Charlesworth in *Saturday Night* the following month. Did he soften his words because MacDonald was a popular fellow member of the club? He did not. "If nature should come to imitate some of the paintings in that show," he declared, "we shall all have to wear smoked glasses." Charlesworth acknowledged grudgingly that MacDonald was gifted and that "his *Tangled Garden*...is a masterpiece as compared with *The Elements*, or *Rock and Maple* which, for all they can convey, might just as well have been called *Hungarian Goulash* and *Drunkard's Stomach*." A. J. Casson was a visitor at the club one day shortly after the *Saturday Night* article appeared and recalled that "Charlesworth came into the club with his high squeaky voice and Jim was at the table and said to me, 'Listen to that damned old rooster'."

Hector Charlesworth. (*Jack McLaren*)

Charlesworth, however, was not alone in his disapproval. He echoed the views of many of the club's more conservative members. Hammond, who was usually more upbeat in his approach to new ideas, described MacDonald's paintings as "so unusual as to be indecipherable and revolting. It is difficult to write of them with any restraint." Gadsby and Donovan had unleashed torrents of abuse in their respective journals. "Hot Mush," Gadsby had roared in a lengthy article in the *Toronto Daily Star*, describing the club's controversial young artists as "the advanced atomizers who spray a tube of paint at a canvas and call it 'Sunshine on the Cowshed'." This opinion had been echoed with equal scorn by Donovan in *Saturday Night*, who described one sketch as looking like "a Dutch head cheese having a quarrel with a chunk of French nougat." One can't help but wonder what on earth these men had to say to the young artists when they met at the club for lunch. It was no surprise that they usually sat at different tables.

Macdonald's *Tangled Garden* became the most contentious work of art ever painted in Canada. Controversy over it raged at the club and in the press, and provoked a gentle but beautifully pointed letter by MacDonald, published in *The Globe* on March 27, 1916:

> One would almost think that the critics are unaware of the fact that if the function of the artist is to see, the first duty of the critic is to understand what the artist saw. Yet they condemn apparently without understanding and without making an effort to understand, forgetful of Goethe's caution for doubtful cases, that "a genuine work of art usually displeases at first sight, as it suggests a deficiency in the spectator."

The OSA show was still a hot topic when, later that month, the club held another symposium on "Purpose in Art." The gloves came off. Frederick Bell-Smith, one of the club's more conservative painters, took a savage swipe at MacDonald and other "moderns," claiming that their influence was disturbing to art students. The OCA's George Reid agreed. "Students have to learn the basics," he said sternly. Lismer was almost alone in defending the moderns, saying that finding fresh forms of expression was always difficult, but that "all art depended on evolution, change, and new ideas, and this should not be condemned in its formative stages." Walter Allward quietly defended them as well, stating firmly that "the world would be better if more art students dropped out."

Membership had now reached 220, two-thirds of whom were professionals. Many members were, of course, serving in the armed forces and therefore not active in club activities. Captain Edward Kylie, a young professor of history at U of T, was the first to die on active service. He had been a close friend of Vincent Massey, who remembered him as "a great teacher, both in relation to the students who fell under his spell and in his influence on the people he met in a wider field." Massey joined the army in 1915 as a lieutenant-colonel. He had used Hart House as a venue for training newly recruited officers early in the war, having them fire at targets painted by his friend Lieutenant

Lawren Harris. He later served at Camp Borden in charge of musketry training, and went on to be a staff officer working for the War Committee of the Cabinet.

Fergus Kyle, a fine cartoonist with *The Globe*, also enlisted that year at the age of forty. While serving at the front, he was crippled for life when a horse stepped on his foot. Lacey Amy left for England in 1916 to work in a convalescent home established by the Massey Harris company, accompanied by his wife. For a long time they had wanted to help the war effort, and so jumped at the chance to "do something." Amy went on to serve as a war correspondent with the Canadian Army. He had joined the club in 1912 and remained a member until his death in 1962. He was a frequent contributor to *Saturday Night* and also the author of many detective novels. The first, *The Blue Wolf*, was written under his own name before the war. Following the war he wrote under the pseudonym Luke Allan—possibly thinking that his real name was not appropriate for a writer of crime fiction.

The club's eighth president was James MacCallum, an eccentric and sometimes difficult man, but one with a wide range of interests and a friend and benefactor of many club artists. In the summer of 1911, he invited Jim MacDonald and his family to stay on a houseboat moored by his Georgian Bay cottage on Go Home Bay. During the following two summers, Arthur and Esther Lismer spent time there as well.

Although the war in Europe had now been raging for two years, life within the club changed very little. The Ontario Temperance Act was passed that year, bringing prohibition to the province, but it did not seem to interfere with fun at club gatherings. Liquor could not be sold as a beverage and it was illegal to keep, give, or possess liquor, except in a private dwelling, but it was never forbidden to make alcoholic beverages—for export only, of course. While nothing is mentioned in the club records, it seems likely that creative ways were found around the situation. Mark Hambourg noted that at club social gatherings, "officially every entertainment was bone dry, just as unofficially one was almost drowned in the inevitable reaction."

There are other anecdotes about how club revelries carried on through this period. Curtis Williamson told Hammond about how he and Tom Thomson and another artist had enjoyed an all-night session (presumably at the Studio Building), got plastered, and mashed up Arthur Heming's hat, to show their contempt for him. He said he liked Arthur all right, but his old-maid habits of objecting to noise and going about with a broom for cigarette ashes made him tired. Heming, a man with firm conservative ideas, was described by one woman as a most desirable bachelor who never married because, in his words, he "had never met a lady who knew how to handle a book properly." He resigned from the club two months after the studio revel, possibly because of it. He rejoined five years later, resigned again, joined again, and then resigned for the last time in 1936.

Dr. James MacCallum, President, 1916–1918. (*Curtis Williamson*)

Arthur Heming, 1912. (*M. O. Hammond*)

Another hijinks story from about that time concerned James Mavor. According to his grandson Mavor Moore, he and five others won a draw, one stormy night, to stay overnight at the club in the six available beds. When it came time to retire, Mavor was missing. He reappeared two hours later, soaked to the skin. "I went home to get my pyjamas," he said.

At the members' dinner in January 1917, a dozen or so painters entered a speed contest—a race to paint pictures in twenty minutes from set subjects. Each artist was disguised with a long cloak, a hood, and a mask. Frank Johnston "was a sort of comedian and made funny drawings to divert the crowd," while George Reid, C. W. Jefferys, Wyly Grier, Jim MacDonald, J. E. (Sammy) Sampson, and other artists displayed their talents. Later that year, Frank Carmichael joined the club. He was then twenty-six, and a friend of the six other club painters who would, with him, form the Group of Seven three years later. Another new member was Barker Fairley, a professor of German at U of T and an articulate spokesman for the Group's ideals.

Charles Currelly spoke at the February members' dinner. His talk on "Life in the Orient" was illustrated with photographs by architect Jules Wegman. A month later, Sir Edmund Walker was the speaker. His collection of rare Japanese prints was on display at the club. "He gave quite an informing talk.... He seems to have a good knowledge of the art and spoke in a popular way of them." A renowned philanthropist, Sir Edmund later gave his prints to the ROM. As one of the founders of both the museum and Toronto's art gallery, he once remarked, "I can think of no privilege so great as to have founded any good or enduring thing in this country. I know the value of money, but I should rather have created one of the institutions of my country than to possess millions."

That same month, poet Joyce Kilmer—of "I think that I shall never see a poem lovely as a tree" fame—visited the club, where he was described by one member as a "youngish, bright, fresh-looking chap." Soon after Kilmer's visit, the renowned Belgian violinist Eugène Ysaÿe was the guest of Boris Hambourg. M. O. Hammond described Ysaÿe, known as the gentle giant of the violin, as a huge, tall, oily-haired, firm-faced man. "Bridle toasted him," one member recalled, "and Ysaÿe, probably not understanding, got up and drank too. They sat down and an awkward pause ensued. Presently Ysaÿe arose and replied in French and roused the enthusiasm of those who understood. Then they tried all possible wiles to get him to play, but he went to the lavatory and disappointed all."

As a gesture of war support, the club extended membership privileges to officers of the Royal Flying Corps who were training on Toronto Island courtesy of the American

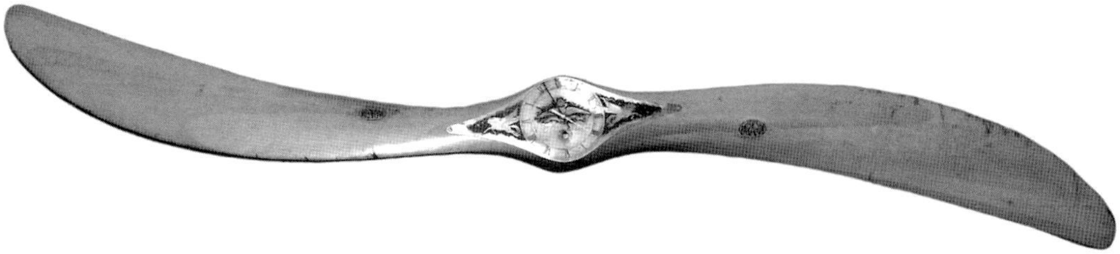

Curtiss Jenny propeller donated by members of the Royal Air Force, December 1918.

Curtiss Aeroplane Manufactory. At war's end, the Corps presented the club with a propeller from one of the Curtiss planes. It now hangs in the club library.

April 1917 saw two significant world events: The Americans entered the war and the Canadians, under the leadership of lieutenant colonel Agar Adamson, won a magnificent victory at the battle of Vimy Ridge—although with casualties numbering more than 10,000, over 3,500 of them fatal. It was a terrible price to pay for Canada's coming of age. Adamson remained in command until February 1918, and visitors to Vimy can still see his battered desk in a tiny underground office, part of an intricate system of tunnels that lie beneath the battlefield.

Torontonians were by now becoming increasingly aware of the horrendous events unfolding in Europe, as the daily papers continued to list the dead and missing and more and more wounded servicemen appeared on city streets. The club, as always, offered a

Members hard at work on the club farm, Hogg's Hollow, 1917. (*M. O. Hammond*)

refuge for its members. So did the club farm, a novel experiment that had been launched in the spring of 1915 to supplement wartime shortages of fresh fruit and vegetables. Jim MacDonald had first offered the use of his Thornhill grounds, but the executive chose an acreage a little closer to the city on Yonge Street just south of York Mills Road. The property was also just south of C. W. Jefferys' home—which, by the way, still stands today. And so, every Saturday during the summer, members cheerfully donned overalls and old shirts and clambered onto streetcars for the jaunt up to Hogg's Hollow where they planted, weeded, and harvested an acre or so of vegetables—and enjoyed themselves enormously. Their stay-at-home wives had the pleasure of pickling and preserving the resulting produce for use in the club kitchen.

Sammy Sampson had been working on a historic painting of twenty-eight club members enjoying lunch in our courthouse clubrooms for more than a year. Completed in 1917, it is a magnificent work. More than half of those included were charter members, four had served as president, another four would do so in coming years. "The figures were painted in at half hour sittings," wrote Charles (Chuck) Matthews many years later, "usually at lunch time in the Old Court Lane building. The likenesses are remarkable, each being a small-scale portrait, true to figure and stance, as well as facial features. It is regrettable that the artist did not include himself in this historical record." The strikingly handsome Peter Donovan is seen standing head and shoulders above the others. Matthews, who had known Donovan in the twenties, described him as "a suave and witty Irishman, tall and handsome with a mane of silvery white hair. How he managed to remain a bachelor was a mystery." This painting, certainly one of our most treasured possessions, hangs prominently in the club.

R. L. Defries. (*Charles Aylett*)

Tragedy that was closer than the fields of France struck on July 8 when Tom Thomson, a cherished colleague of many club members, went missing in Algonquin Park. His body was recovered from Canoe Lake more than a week later and several of his grieving friends designed a memorial cairn that was later erected at the site. The irascible but fierce-hearted Bill Beatty did much of the work. Dean of Canadian engravers W. W. Alexander—"Billy Alec" to his fellow members—etched a moving tribute, written by Jim MacDonald, onto the cairn's brass plaque. It said in part that Thomson "lived humbly but passionately with the wild. It made him brother to all untamed things of nature. It drew him apart and revealed itself wonderfully to him." The cairn still stands high atop a steep cliff overlooking Canoe Lake. Later that year, the club mounted a show of Thomson's larger paintings, followed by a show of his smaller oil sketches.

At the annual meeting in October, the more mundane but pressing question of unpaid fees came up again. To everyone's dismay, the worn-out and frustrated treasurer

Bob Defries announced his resignation. The executive, undoubtedly concerned about the potential loss of its loyal and hardworking officer, promptly appointed an assistant to help him. This did the trick. Defries agreed to stay on, and continued in this position until 1937. But his challenges didn't go away. By November the following year, he was facing similar, seemingly intractable problems. Members in arrears were to be notified on a pay-up-or-else basis—anyone who failed to do so by the end of December was to have his membership cancelled.

In November, the club sent a Christmas message to members serving overseas—a card featuring a painting of the beloved fireplace, along with some lighthearted doggerel, which read in part:

Still do all Toronto roads
Lead to old Court Lane
Still do veterans come and go
And come and go again
Bridle tamed and married
Jefferys from York Mills
Tattersall with music
Bob Defries with bills
Still MacCallum meekly bears
The presidential part
Still there's shepherd's pie for lunch
Still the boys talk art.

But it's much the same old club
That you knew before
Save for those good fellows gone
Like yourself to war
Now that Christmas brings again
Thoughts of ancient cheer
We all join together in
Wishing you were here
But the Kaiser still is kaising
And the Boches prance
So we have to send our greeting
Six weeks in advance
Filling up with two percent
All the law allows
We look t'wards you in Flanders
And we rises—likewise bows.

The war was never far from the minds of members, particularly of the visual artists. The Canadian War Memorials Fund had been set up by Lord Beaverbrook, an ambitious Canadian who in 1910 had left for England, where he became involved in politics and the newspaper business. The purpose of the Fund was to provide "suitable memorials in the form of tablets, oil paintings, etc." While recognizing the importance of films and photographs for use in propaganda, Beaverbrook believed that they couldn't capture the full truth about the war. "Only paintings," he wrote, "could provide the most permanent and vital form in which the great deeds of the Canadian nation in the war could

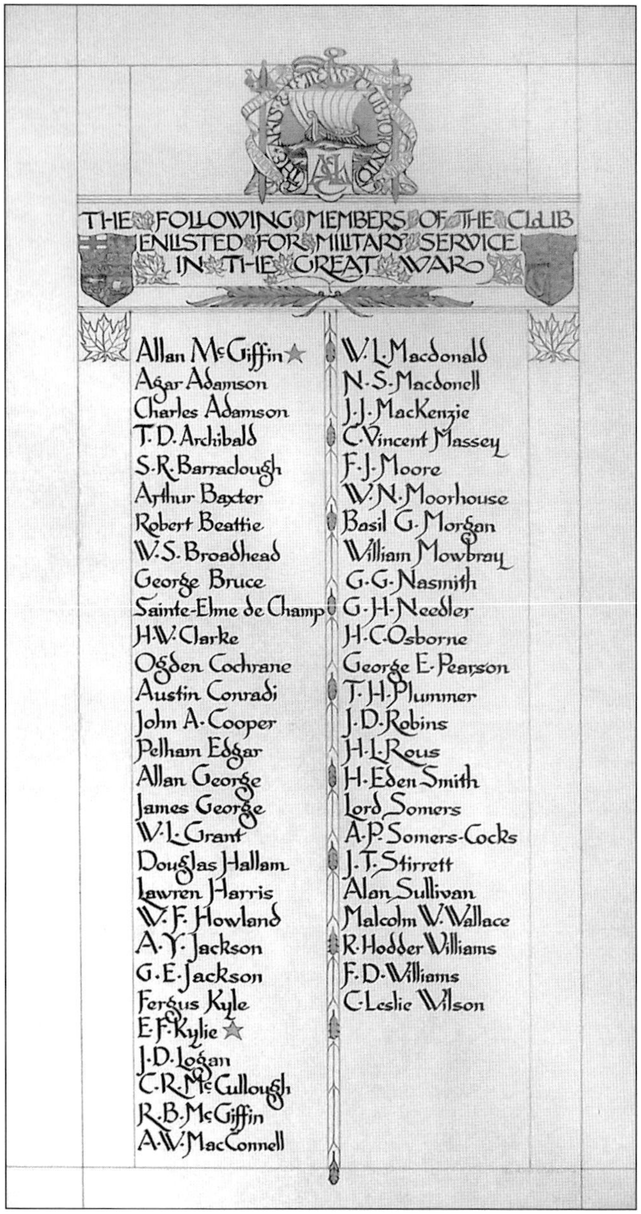

Members who served in the Great War, 1918. (*J. E. H. MacDonald*)

be enshrined for posterity." The first artist assigned to the project was Englishman Richard Jack. Alec Jackson, by then a lieutenant, was added in September 1917, but most of the other artists were British. Two months later, Sir Edmund Walker and Eric Brown (the director of the National Gallery of Canada) were put in charge of finding more Canadian painters, and another five were added, including C. W. Jefferys, one of Canada's finest historical artists, and Bill Beatty. Grier and the ever-feisty Beatty met with Sir Edmund to protest the continuing shortage of Canadian artists in this Canadian project. Sir Edmund vacillated, explaining to Beaverbrook that, "owing to the rather irritable minds of most artists," he was unwilling to suggest suitable names. Grier and Beatty were incensed. By the following May they had provided Walker with a sizable list of painters he could recommend, and within weeks Beatty and Varley were off to Europe to join Jackson at the front. Frank Johnston was also an official war artist by then, working with flying personnel training for overseas duty, and Lismer was painting warships in Halifax. Yet of the approximately 120 artists appointed to depict Canada's involvement in the war, only forty-three were Canadian. Fifteen were club members. The project had a profound effect on the artists who participated in it and both Jackson and Varley, in particular, were transformed by their war experiences.

Against this background of world events, there were ongoing day-to-day challenges at the club—some of them remarkably petty. The executive's December meeting, for instance, ended on a note of controversy when George Locke moved that guests be charged fifteen cents for tea at an upcoming ladies' day. Ivor Lewis and Donovan disagreed. They moved an amendment insisting that "tea be cut out altogether." In a further amendment, Bridle and Edwin Bell moved that "tea be served free, but cards be required for admission." The amendment to the amendment to the motion was carried, and it was duly decided that each member would be issued tickets for two friends.

The club produced a minstrel show in February 1918—its first and last—without Roy Mitchell's involvement. Minstrel shows were wildly popular with amateur groups at the time, but they were not up to Mitchell's theatrical or philosophical standards. In any event, the Old Court Minstrels happily reached into a vat of oily black burnt cork and produced a blackface show—"a great medley of wit and humour, starring Sambo, Rastus, Moses, and Rufus, along with the irrepressible Henrietta Buttonia in an original and entrancing Hawaiian hula dance." The show was so well received that it was staged again two weeks later. But that was the last time a blackface show appeared on our stage and the club was well ahead of many organizations in ceasing to produce such shows. Britain's Royal Opera House didn't do so until 2005, their spokesman saying belatedly, "It doesn't work. It is racially insensitive." Oddly enough, interested members could also have come to the club that afternoon to see George Bernard Shaw's *The Man of Destiny*, performed by professional actors from the Canadian Officers Training Corps. How the club managed to stage two such diverse productions within hours of each other remains a mystery.

Herbert Austin Fricker joined that year. One of Britain's ablest choirmasters, he had come to Toronto to replace Vogt as conductor of the Mendelssohn Choir. Fricker appeared for the first time with the choir at Massey Hall in February, performing with the Philadelphia Orchestra under the baton of his friend Leopold Stokowski. Not surprisingly, Fricker brought Stokowski to the club as a guest.

The Ontario Temperance Act was still in effect and would remain in force for nine more years. M. O. Hammond went to dinner at the club one night in May of that year and became embroiled in "a lively tilt with Carter, Kihl, Sampson, and others about the Lord's Day Alliance and prohibition. I was a minority of one in saying anything good of either, so was surrounded and jumped on. But they said I held up my end well. They are narrow and prejudiced, so easily upset by facts."

Robert Gagen, President, 1918–1920. (*Wyly Grier*)

All of this was trivial in the extreme as the relentless barrage of bad news from France continued. Robert McGiffen's brother Allan, a charter member who had been a literary reporter for the *Toronto Daily Star*, became the second club member to die on active service. He was killed during an attack on Upton Wood on August 27, 1918, at the age of thirty-six, only weeks before the war ended. He had been seriously wounded at Courcelette in 1916 and was sent back to Canada to recover, but insisted on returning to the battlefields. His grave is in Sun Quarry Cemetery, Pas de Calais, France. Fortunately, his brother, also a charter member, survived the war.

With the daily lists of casualties appearing in Canadian papers, it is difficult to understand why, to some, the war seemed remote and not of their concern. Robert Gagen, for instance, who became the club's ninth president in November 1918, was noted for his fine marine paintings and had done some work as a war artist, painting mostly

"A Club Time-Table," *The Lamps*, 1919. (*Fergus Kyle*)

shipbuilding scenes. Not to his credit, Gagen demanded a higher price for his paintings than the Memorials Fund offered. Herbert Palmer did likewise. By contrast, Marie Tippett mentions how many other war artists gave their paintings to the Fund. And Vogt had insisted that the Mendelssohn Choir's fees be turned over to patriotic causes.

Of the club's first nine presidents, three were painters. A fourth, James MacCallum, was a great supporter of those artists who were, in spite of the inevitable naysayers, fast becoming the latest arbiters of taste. Lismer would mutter on occasion that Canada was still "a new country with old men," but, undeterred, he and his young friends continued to offer a panorama of startling and exciting new works. Meanwhile, the club's conservative constituency—Grier, Reid, and others—fiercely defended the traditionalists' approach. It made for heated exchanges, at the club and beyond.

World War I finally came to an end on November 11, 1918, after the loss of more than 66,000 Canadian lives. For those still overseas, there was little celebration. As Sandra Gwyn has written, "The atmosphere was curiously muted.... Everyone was too tired." But, in Toronto, Eaton's big "wild-cat" siren sounded at three in the morning and, before long, joyful crowds were surging up Yonge Street, beating pans and blowing whistles. Hammond and his wife were asleep when their phone rang. "We were told by *The Globe* of the news.... We lay quietly for a half hour. Then a news boy with extras came along and his voice wakened many on the street. Soon there were other boys...tooting motors, whistles, and the din did not end till midnight or more."

Five days later, it was time for the club's annual meeting. Not surprisingly, members were in an upbeat mood and happily climbed the spiral staircase to the spacious room above and settled in to enjoy the evening. After the business details had been dealt with, the entertainment began, this time taking its cue from the recent harvesting activities at the club's farm. One member wrote,

> The entertainment was most amusing. Bridle was its author and director. The curtain divided on a scene representing the interior of a barn. Messrs. Button and Lismer held the floor and, after considerable chatter, those members of the club who had figured in farming operations during the summer put in an appearance. Singing was interlarded among a good deal of burlesque goings-on and there were numerous vaudeville stunts of a more or less amusing character. Altogether it was quite a good show, all things considered.

George G. Nasmith, 1912. (*Arthur S. Goss*)

With the war at an end, the club gradually welcomed back into the fold its returning servicemen and war artists. They were wiser and more mature, few, if any, of them untouched by their experiences. Some, like Agar Adamson, after almost three years in the trenches, were lifelong emotional casualties. According to Sandra Gwyn, Adamson failed to establish another career and, thanks to the financial support of his wife's family, "whiled away the time drinking too much champagne in gentlemen's clubs with companions of whom she disapproved." Others, such as Fergus Kyle, dealt with continuing physical handicaps. The heroic four-foot-six George G. Nasmith had become one of the country's most celebrated soldiers. When war broke out, he had been serving as Toronto's first deputy health officer. His small stature would have made him unacceptable to the army, except for his brilliant mind. He went first to England where he oversaw the inoculation of 9,000 soldiers against typhoid, and then to France where he deliberately exposed himself to German chlorine gas in order to analyze its effects. He went on to design the first gas mask used in the war. On his return to Canada he wrote a military history, *Canada's Sons and Great Britain in the World War*, and an account of his personal war experiences, *On the Fringe of the Great Fight*. He lived to become a life member of the club.

As for the club's war artists, the hundreds of works they produced were initially shipped to the National Gallery, then later to Vimy House, the Canadian War Museum's storage facility in Ottawa. The vast majority of them (more than 150 painted by artists who later became the Group of Seven) remained there on sliding racks, unseen for decades. Now, with the opening of the new War Museum in 2005—"just a cannon shot west of Parliament Hill," more are on exhibit. Varley's magnificent painting titled *For What?* depicts a wagon load of corpses about to be dumped into an open pit on a barren battlefield. It is considered by many to be the finest Canadian work produced during World War I. It is so powerful that the museum didn't put it on display until the eighties, fearing that viewers might find it too upsetting.

"Men and Mary," *The Lamps*, 1919. (*J. E. H. MacDonald*)

THE LAMPS *December*

Men and Mary

(Court Street)

BY J. E. H. MACDONALD

Poor Mary rides in state,
I hear her laugh and talk;
Before the station gate
Her car draws to the walk.

I pause to see her light
And solemn men step out,
Who grip her by the arms,
Implacable and stout.

Her stringy hair is grey,
Her shaken head is bare;
The streets are sleety-wet
And chill the midnight air.

The sullen doors are swung
And Mary forced within,
Where burly men in blue
Sit to record her sin.

When Mary's withered cheek
Was round in morning light
Men came to her as friends
And stole her young delight.

She mounts the bitter steps,
And my heart follows too,
Praying that God may sit
Among those men in blue.

60

In August 1919, the club held "Blighty Night," a dinner to honour our men home from the war. In December, members turned their energies to producing another newsletter—the first since 1912. When it was finished, this edition of *The Lamps* was more like a small book, with ninety-two pages, fine artwork, and very readable essays. Fergus Kyle produced two pieces, "Chamber Music at the Club" and "A Club Time Table—Read Up." Grier, Johnston, Lismer, Beatty, and others supplied many illustrations. Jim MacDonald submitted a sensitive poem about a prostitute dragged unceremoniously into the police station on the ground floor below the clubrooms. Beverley Baxter's contribution was particularly notable—affectionate brief biographies of the "Members Who Served." He himself had served in France as a lieutenant with the Engineers.

M. O. Hammond's essay, "Down on the Farm," was a revealing piece about the club's 1915–1917 foray into patriotic agriculture. Some members, he said, would remember "gargantuan feasts of fruits and vegetables," some a romantic "return to the plow," and others the "natural beauty of the scene." More realistically, he suggested that what they really treasured was the memory of the cider press––its popularity due, no doubt, to the Ontario Temperance Act. Despite the law, it was decided that "the revels must continue through the winter, and the glorious work of filling the kegs went on for hours. Cocktail chemists proffered recipes to preserve the precious fluid, but something went wrong. There were furtive visits to the kegs for days to come, but soon what had been but a pleasant 'kick' became a battering ram...and the best of all farm produce—because it was at once so diverting and so legal—became only a memory."

By the end the year, the club had almost returned to its prewar pace—except for the presence of yet another devastating scourge. The year 1918 had seen the arrival of the Spanish flu epidemic, and it was still rampant at the end of the decade. Hammond and others became ill, and, while we know of no members who died from the flu, it sent one in six Canadians to their sick beds, and more than 60,000 died––this out of a population of only 8 million—almost as many as were lost in the war. It is little wonder that Arts and Letters men welcomed the opportunity to escape, even briefly, behind the sheltering walls of their beloved club. It remained, as Jesse Middleton once said, "a lighthouse in a tossing sea...where life is gentle, blithe and free."

Literature

On December 10, 1908, the club held its first formal discussion, "The Relation of Literature to Journalism in Canada." Someone must have made the point that it was at least in part a relation of dependency as nearly all the charter members who had published or would publish literary works—Augustus Bridle, Hector Charlesworth, Peter Donovan, M. O. Hammond, Jesse Middleton, J. H. Smith—were also journalists, it being almost impossible at that time for a writer in Canada to live by his or her books alone. Over the next few years the entry of several academics—Pelham Edgar, Barker Fairley, Malcolm Wallace—introduced a second traditional source of support for authors, and the admission of the major poet Duncan Campbell Scott a less frequent source, the civil service. A few early members did live by their literary work alone: the prolific novelist Alan Sullivan (by moving to England) and the equally prolific versifier Wilson MacDonald (by relentless barnstorming).

The making of literature, unlike that of some arts, is not a group enterprise, but the club did undertake some group activities related to literature. From the outset, it held discussions, readings, and debates, and entertained visiting authors, some of whom gave papers or readings. In January 1910 it produced the first issue of *The Lamps*, a magazine often including poems, stories, and essays that appeared at irregular intervals until 1939, when it succumbed to the pressures of World War II. In 1913, aware of its uniqueness as a centre for the arts in contemporary Canada, the club published *The Yearbook of Canadian Art*. Bertram Brooker, with other members, published a second yearbook in 1928 and a final one in 1936. In 1920, the *Canadian Bookman* was founded. Its editor, B. K. Sandwell, and five of its editorial committee were members of the club. When the *Canadian Forum* was founded in 1927, thirteen of its editorial committee were members.

After World War I, poets Ned Pratt and Robert Finch strengthened the university representation. Finch's poetry was as contained and economical as Pratt's was energetic and expansive. W. A. Deacon, Thomas B. Costain, and Beverley Baxter reinforced the literary journalists.

In mid-century, three literary and cultural academic critics—Northrop Frye, Marshall McLuhan, and Claude Bissell—joined the club, as did journalistic essayist and playwright Robertson Davies, just then becoming a novelist and academic. Playwrights John Coulter, Mavor Moore, Lister Sinclair, and Herman Voaden, and journalist-authors Ralph Allen, Kildare Dobbs, Blair Fraser, and Ron Hambleton also became members. In 1942 *The Monthly Letter* (which wasn't monthly) replaced the extinguished *Lamps* and in 1991, it became the current *LAMPSletter*.

In the final quarter of the twentieth century, novelist Hugh Hood, playwright Dan Needles, drama critic Herbert Whittaker, social historian Rod Austin, and major poet Richard Outram became members. The university contingent was strengthened by literary scholars William Blissett, Harry Girling, Alexander Leggatt, Michael Millgate, Brian Parker, William Rogers, Ernest Sirluck, Michael Tait, Milton Wilson, Michael Bliss, and Ezra Schabas. After an unconscionable delay, women were finally admitted in 1985, and the club gained poets Susan Ioannou, Evelyn Yates, and Polly Fleck, novelist Rosemary Aubert, playwright Samantha Swan, social historians Margaret McBurney, Mary Byers, and Lois Darroch, children's authors Kati Rekai and Madeline Freeman, journalist Kay

Kritzweiser, and literary scholars Zoë Girling and Dorothy Parker.

After a protracted effort, in 1982 memoirist and publisher Lovat Dickson succeeded in establishing the literary tables, weekly lunches to hear and discuss papers or readings. They were initially held in the LAMPS Room, whose intimate proportions encouraged genuine discussion and debate of quite recondite literary matters, but their success swelled the numbers until they had to be moved to a larger room, where discussion tends to be of the question-answer or single-observation kind. The literary tables have helped the club recruit literature-loving members and have also led to the formation of more specialized groups for writers and poets.

Ernest Sirluck

The growth of the literary tables is the most notable development on the club's literature side. They now occupy, and often fill, the Great Hall. For ten months each year, September through June, the meetings are held each Tuesday from noon to 2 p.m.—for lunch, a lecture or reading, and a brief period of questions and discussion. In the early days, all speakers were selected by the chairman, but this onerous task is now shared among members of the steering committee, who take turns—month by month—finding speakers. Special "star" speakers are selected for LAMPS weeks in mid-February—in 2005 it was Lieutenant Governor the Honourable James Bartleman, at the invitation of Carol McGirr.

Speakers are evenly divided between members and visitors. Over the last five years, our definition of literature has broadened in keeping with the changing times and the growth of multiculturalism in Toronto. Carol McGirr and Rod Carruthers have introduced us to oral literature, particularly the great Norse sagas. Margaret MacMillan's historical lectures on the "Treaty of Versailles" and "Women of the Raj" drew capacity audiences. There have been talks on dictionaries, libraries, letters and diaries, children's stories, fantasy, mysteries, science fiction, the electronic media, and opera libretti. We have enjoyed presentations about Broadway musicals illustrated by excerpts from performances that our sophisticated new equipment now makes possible. Multiculturalism has been reflected in talks about Indian, Caribbean, and African writers. In the May-June period there is always an attempt to devote two or three lectures to plays that will be performed by the Shakespeare and Shaw festivals or by downtown Toronto's Soulpepper Theatre. Around Armistice Day a topic of memorial significance is chosen. A member usually does a special reading before Christmas —John Rammell impersonating Dylan Thomas or Clifford Holland presenting Dickens' *Christmas Carol*. The literary table lunches end in June with a splendid *Fête Champêtre* —in recent years hosted by Lela Wilson, one of our charter women, who is herself an author.

Another major contributor has been the much lamented Richard Outram, who generously compiled an anthology of his own poetry, beautifully designed by his wife, Barbara Howard, and hand-printed on their press. Copies of it are now given to visiting speakers as a thank-you gift.

Popularity has its drawbacks, of course. The numbers now make extended discussion and argument impractical; but all in all, the club's interest in literature seems to be thriving.

Brian Parker

CHAPTER 2

From the Roaring Twenties to the Deepening Depression

1920–1939

Hail the new club house
Spring revues begin
Financial woes

The happy years in the courthouse came to an end in 1920 when the club was notified that its lease would not be renewed. Before long, negotiations were underway with the venerable St. George's Society about leasing a significant portion of St. George's Hall at 14 Elm Street. The society had been founded in 1834 to promote British traditions in Canada and had built the hall in 1891. It was now looking for a major tenant to help carry the financial load. The Arts and Letters Club appeared to be the answer to its prayers—at least at first blush.

St. George's Hall, 14 Elm Street, 1919 (*Arthur S. Goss*)

Our lawyer, Bob Defries, who was then also still serving as our long-suffering treasurer, began discussing terms with St. George's president Sir Frederick Stupart. Letters flew back and forth, with the club refusing to pay the suggested rental of $2,400 per annum and demanding substantial renovations. In the end, the sum of $2,000 per annum was agreed upon, with the club also responsible for taxes, heating, upkeep, and alterations. Animated discussions ensued.

The building was not in itself architecturally significant. Patricia McHugh, in her guide to Toronto architecture, describes it as a "late Victorian smorgasbord." But what it lacked in elegance it gained in dignity, with its somewhat stolid Romanesque Revival façade. Within a matter of weeks, architect Henry Sproatt and his partner, engineer Ernest Rolph, were ready with their imaginative redesign of the main hall that, until then, had been little more than a barn-like all-purpose space used by the society for its philanthropic activities. Conveniently, Sproatt and Rolph were also members of the St. George's Society, and their credentials were impeccable. They could count Hart House and additions to Vincent Massey's boyhood home on Jarvis Street among their past achievements. At Elm Street, their plans included a spectacular Tudor Great Hall featuring a baronial fireplace, a minstrels' gallery, six soaring gothic windows, and, tucked into the ceiling high above, several small dormer windows.

At the Club, 1921, showing the fireplace and windows installed by the club, and punning banners designed by J. E. H. MacDonald (*W. W. Alexander*)

Membership was growing. Soldiers home from the war were settling into what promised to be a bright new future. Most were young adults, returning from what Robert MacNeil called "the army of the disillusioned." Forty-three of the fifty-three members whose names are on Jim MacDonald's commemorative list returned to the club, as did all fifteen of our official war artists. Two members had died in service, while others resigned for various reasons shortly after the war. The club continued to be an inviting haven for writers, architects, musicians, painters, engravers, sculptors, and the occasional actor.

Sadly, some of our talented writers left for greener fields. Beverley Baxter and Peter Donovan sailed off to England and new careers with Lord Beaverbrook's *Daily Express*. Thomas B. Costain, who had joined in 1916, headed for the United States. All three maintained club membership for some time. Baxter is probably best remembered by Canadians for his "London Letter" that ran for many years in *Maclean's*. He was knighted in 1954, after which he would sometimes be referred to as "Sir Bax with the Axe" for his less than enthusiastic reviews. But the egotistical Hector Charlesworth remained in Toronto and continued to hold court at the club. He was by this time the assistant editor of *Saturday Night* and his *Cyclopedia of Canadian Biography* had just been published with almost five hundred entries—all male. His own entry was one of the longest!

Although Baxter, Donovan, and Costain were no longer at the club, other ambitious young writers were lining up to join, including the witty and shrewd B. K. Sandwell, as well as several young publishers. Hugh Eayrs, a new bright light, was only twenty-

Ernest MacMillan. (*Arthur Lismer*)

B. K. Sandwell, 1925. (*Arthur Lismer*)

(*Right*) *A Back Number of* Saturday Night, 1922. Charlesworth used his position as editor of *Saturday Night* magazine to criticize the Group of Seven. (*Arthur Lismer*)

Healey Willan. (*Arthur Lismer*)

six when he joined. Within the year he was president of the Macmillan Company of Canada. Two other publishers who joined were John McClelland and George Stewart of McClelland and Stewart Limited.

Three highly accomplished artists joined that year: A. J. Casson, another one of the avant-garde—so much so that he was sometimes referred to as the eighth member of the Group of Seven; Charles Comfort, famous for his murals and landscapes; and André Lapine, best known as Canada's most accomplished painter of animals. It was Lapine who painted the presidential portrait of Wyly Grier that was rejected by Grier.

As for musicians, the most important addition at this time was the jovial and gifted musician Ernest MacMillan. He joined soon after returning home from a German internment camp where he had spent four years as an enemy alien. He remained a member, and a very active one, until his death in 1973. Healey Willan had joined in 1917, and soon there were other new musician members, including violinists Harry Adaskin, Géza de Kresz, and Elie Spivak.

Another newcomer was playwright Merrill Denison. Although he had trained as an architect, his real love was the stage. Soon after he joined, Mitchell invited him to Hart House Theatre and he never looked back. His first play, *Brothers in Arms*, was staged there that year and became his most popular work.

Early in February, Yeats was back in town to speak at the University of Toronto about a "Theatre for the People." It was his third visit, and he was once again the guest of DeLury. A month later, the English novelist and poet Siegfried Sassoon was entertained at a lavish dinner hosted by Vincent Massey, and the next day a special luncheon was held in his honour. The following evening, the club co-sponsored with the Players Club at U of T a talk by Sassoon at Convocation Hall, a benefit for the renowned Canadian poet Bliss Carman, who was penniless and ill with tuberculosis. Sassoon was staying with Pelham Edgar and described his host as "a charmingly friendly but rather fatiguingly talkative man who was in a flutter of excitement about my performance." Hammond described Sassoon as "tall and rather spare and somewhat nervous in temperament. He has a lively open bare, boyish looking face and a quick manner of speech. His smile is contagious and helps for free intercourse, if he would only stay still long enough." Later that year, the club sent a cheque for $1,000 to Bliss Carman, who by that time was recovering.

The next bit of excitement took place in May at the Art Gallery of Toronto (AGT), where seven club artists launched their very first show. Members received invitations to the "Exhibition of the Group...to see the pictures and heckle the painters." This was the birth of the Group of Seven. The exhibit featured more than one hundred paintings by Frank Carmichael, Frank Johnston, Alec Jackson, Jim MacDonald, Arthur Lismer, Fred Varley, and Lawren Harris. They were, as the National Gallery's Charles Hill writes, "likc-minded artists who had joined together to articulate their ideas for the advancement of Canadian art." Reviews were mixed. The *Mail and Empire* and *The Globe* both published laudatory ones, but Fred Jacob, literary editor of the *Mail and Empire*, took umbrage, wondering if the artists were losing their individual identities. *Saturday Night*'s Hector Charlesworth responded with a deafening silence. The most positive reviewer was, to no one's surprise, Gus Bridle in the *Toronto News.*

A few months later, still in the courthouse, Lord Beaverbrook appeared at a dinner given for him by Beverley Baxter. More than two hundred men were invited. One admirer described him as "a strange attractive gnome with an odour of genius about him.... He spoke in a conversational way, often dropped his voice to a whisper. He has an expressive face with large eyes, and a smile flickers, coming and going quickly as he speaks."

That fall, thirty-three-year-old Vincent Massey, a "patrician by affinity" and a man of considerable culture, was named club president. Thanks to his degree in history from

Beaverbrook, 1928, *Canadian Forum,* August 1928. (*Jack McLaren*)

Members of the Group of Seven lunching at the Court House, 1920. From left to right: Fred Varley, Alec Jackson, Lawren Harris, friend and supporter Barker Fairley, Franz Johnston, Arthur Lismer, and Jim MacDonald. The absent Frank Carmichael was inserted into a later version of this image. (*Arthur S. Goss*)

Vincent Massey, President, 1920–1922. (*Fred Varley*)

Balliol College and his Oxonian style, he fitted right in with the club's deference for all things British. He was a popular president, often officiating at events with grace and dignity. He also had a wicked sense of humour that surfaced frequently, particularly in his quite brilliant club-related doggerel.

By this time, renovations to the Great Hall had been completed. Members said good-bye to the courthouse on November 20 and moved in to St. George's Hall on November 27, an event marked that evening with a celebratory dinner. The *Toronto World* described the approximately two hundred members marching in procession into the Great Hall, where President Massey, clad in scarlet robes and supported by costumed officials and beefeaters, received the keys of the building from Sir Frederick. For the first time, our large heraldic banners representing past presidents and members of that year's executive were on view. They had been painted by Jim MacDonald, whose gentle tongue-in-cheek humour was very evident and the members loved them. They still do. Another banner honouring Boris Hambourg was added later, for reasons now lost in time. After introductions were made, Sproatt, the architect responsible for the room's transformation, was "cheered and chaired," the fire lit, and dinner served. After dinner, scores of candles were lit and the lights turned out. A chorus of twenty launched into the "Pilgrim's Chorus," from *Tannhauser*, after which Boris Hambourg played the cello, and guest Campbell

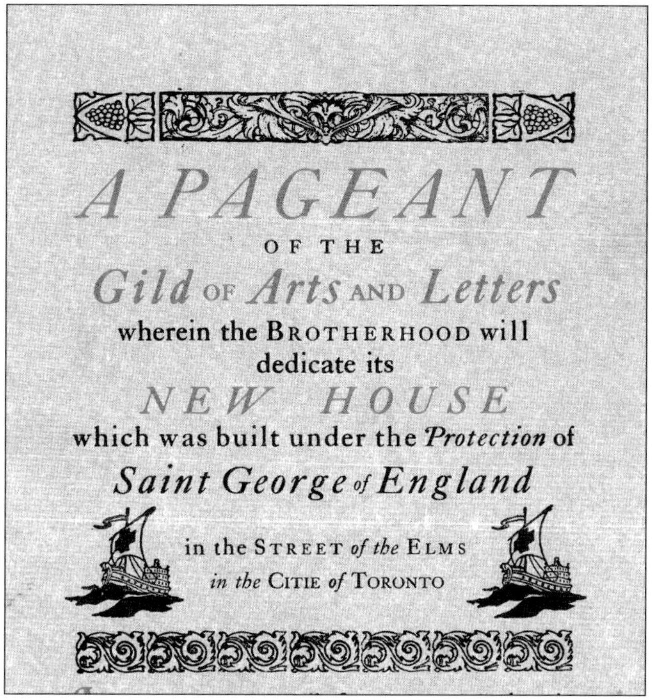
A PAGEANT
OF THE
Gild OF Arts AND Letters
wherein the BROTHERHOOD will
dedicate its
NEW HOUSE
which was built under the *Protection* of
Saint George of England
in the STREET *of the* ELMS
in the CITIE *of* TORONTO

Program for the dedication of the club's new quarters (extract), 1920.

(Right) The stage as it appeared in December 1920. Program illustration for the Second Candle-Light Chamber Music concert, February 14, 1921. (*Fergus Kyle*)

Second Candle-Light Chamber Music
at the Arts and Letters Club
Monday, February the Fourteenth, 1921
Ferdinand Fillion, *Violinist*
Carlos Buhler, *Pianist*

The soft glow of candles flickering lambently under lofty mediaeval beams suggests the stately days of Mozart and Haydn

McInnes—a fine baritone—sang a few songs. Everyone went home happy. To this day, the hall elicits gasps of admiration from all who step inside.

In December, the club held an auction of members' paintings, with proceeds to go to the building fund. Varley offered to paint a woman for $455, and Grier offered to paint a man for $280. A number of members chipped in five or ten dollars each to have Wyly Grier paint Bridle's portrait. That portrait now hangs in the club library—recently nicknamed "The Bridle Suite." The auction realized a handsome

Bliss Carman. (*M. O. Hammond*)

$3,200. One week later, club musicians climbed on the bandwagon to aid the building fund by embarking on a series of musical evenings.

January 1921 began quietly, except for the treasurer's ongoing lament about nonpayment of fees, but things picked up in early February when Bliss Carman, now restored to health and vigour, was welcomed as guest and speaker. A scant four months after receiving the club's generous financial help, he was embarking on a reading and lecture tour of Canada and the United States. British novelist G. K. Chesterton arrived at the club in February. When asked if he thought England would ever have prohibition, he replied, "The idea that the English governing class would ever do without its glass of champagne was drastic and so absurd that no sane man in England would ever entertain it." Over the next three weeks there were two more distinguished guests, Walter Damrosch, conductor of the New York Symphony Orchestra and English poet and playwright John Drinkwater.

In March, J. M. Synge's *The Shadow of the Glen* was staged by the ever-enthusiastic drama committee and was warmly received. This success helped persuade the executive to provide funds for the building of a stage in the Great Hall. By October, membership was at near capacity, with professionals numbering 213 and laymen 103. One of the new professionals was Campbell McInnes, whose previous application had been turned down because of his "periodical sprees" that had led to a very public and painful divorce. By the time of his second application for membership, he was said to have "reformed." It is unlikely, however, that Ernest MacMillan welcomed his membership. MacMillan's sister Dorothy had recently attempted to elope with McInnes, but when MacMillan found out, he raced to Montreal, found the couple on a ship bound for Europe, and persuaded her to return home. Perhaps not surprisingly, MacInnes resigned from the club in 1924. He went on to make a significant contribution to the musical life of Toronto.

The Great Hall, 1922, looking north showing the fireplace, MacDonald's banners, and the recently unveiled George Reid murals. (*Arthur S. Goss*)

On a brisk evening in mid-November, a special dinner was held to celebrate Canadian Book Week. Guests included Canadian novelists Nellie McClung and Lucy Maude Montgomery, and the famous British suffragette, Emily Pankhurst, "who just happened to be in town." Mrs. McClung, a confirmed teetotaler, made a particularly fine impression. She was "happy, breezy, and bright." But the

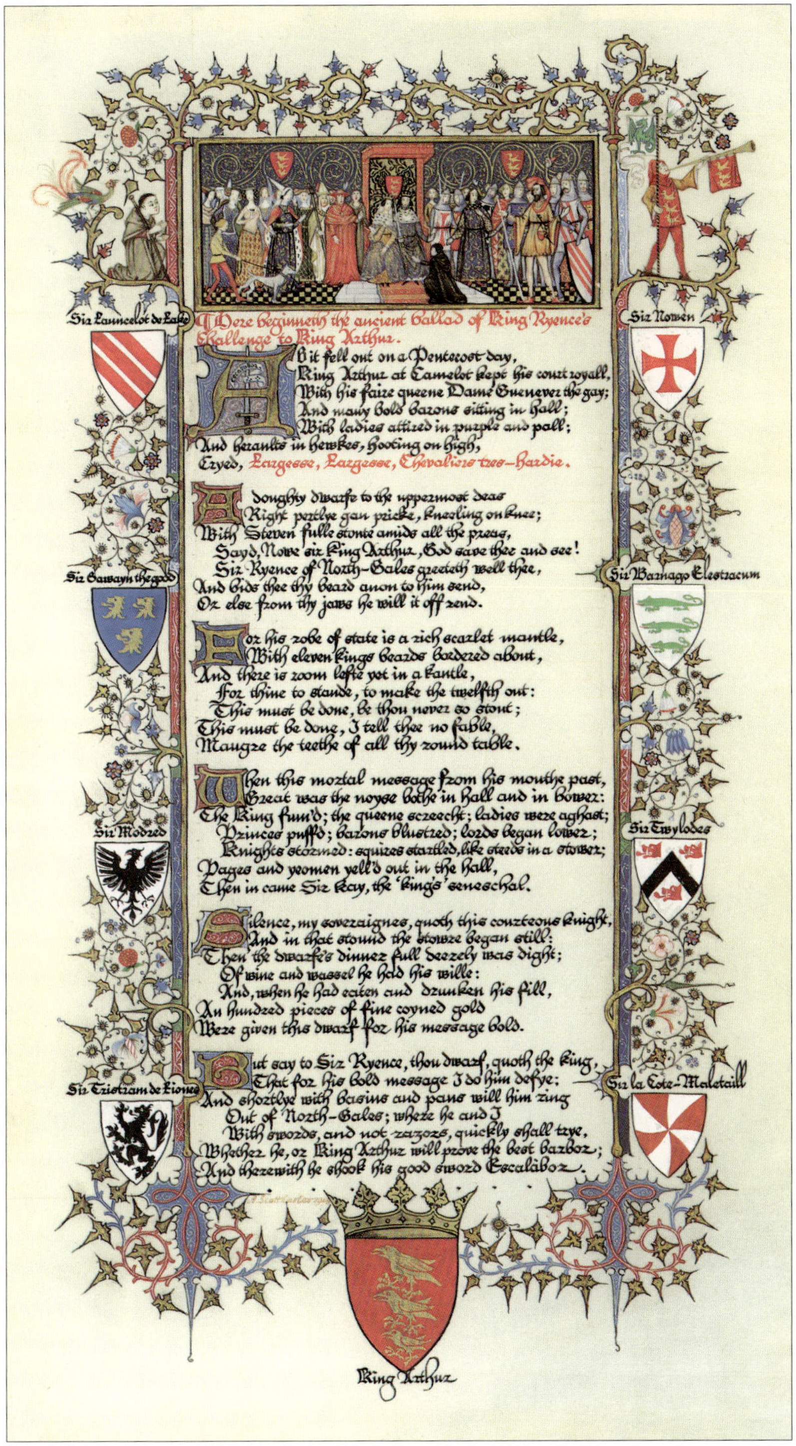

Here beginneth the ancient ballad of King Ryence's Challenge to King Arthur.

As it fell out on a Pentecost day,
King Arthur at Camelot kept his court royall,
With his faire queene Dame Guenever the gay;
And many bold barons sitting in hall;
With ladies attired in purple and pall;
And heraults in hewkes, hooting on high,
Cryed, Largesse, Largesse, Chevaliers tres-hardie.

A doughty dwarfe to the uppermost deas
Right pertlye gan pricke, kneeling on knee;
With Steven fulle stoute amids all the preas,
Sayd, Nowe sir King Arthur, God save thee and see!
Sir Ryence of North-Gales greeteth well thee,
And bids thee thy beard anon to him send,
Or else from thy jaws he will it off rend.

For his robe of state is a rich scarlet mantle,
With eleven kings beards bordered about,
And there is room lefte yet in a kantle,
For thine to stande, to make the twelfth out:
This must be done, be thou never so stout;
This must be done, I tell thee no fable,
Maugre the teethe of all thy round table.

When this mortal message from his mouthe past,
Great was the noyse bothe in hall and in bower:
The King fum'd; the queene screecht; ladies were aghast;
Princes puff'd; barons blustred; lords began lower;
Knights stormed: squires startled, like steeds in a stower;
Pages and yeomen yell'd out in the hall,
Then in came Sir Kay, the 'king's' seneschal.

Silence, my soveraignes, quoth this courteous knight,
And in that stound the stowre began still:
Then the dwarfe's dinner full deerely was dight;
Of wine and wassel he had his wille:
And, when he had eaten and drunken his fill,
An hundred pieces of fine coyned gold
Were given this dwarf for his message bold.

But say to Sir Ryence, thou dwarf, quoth the king,
That for his bold message I do him defye;
And shortlye with basins and pans will him ring
Out of North-Gales; where he and I
With swords, and not razors, quickly shall trye,
Whether he, or King Arthur will prove the best barbor;
And therewith he shook his good sword Escalàbor.

Club Christmas card, 1917 (*Peter Donovan*), sent to Agar Adamson, commanding troops on the front line.

(*Left*) Illuminated manuscript, 1915. (*A. Scott Carter*) The subject is "King Ryence's Challenge," sung before Queen Elizabeth I at a grand entertainment at Kenilworth Castle in 1575.

Augustus (Gus) Bridle , undated. (*Wyly Grier*)

The Old Club, 1916. (*J. E. Sampson*) Members at the Adelaide Street Court House quarters.

1 Robt Holmes
2 George A. Reid
3 Robt F. Gagen
4 Robt W. Beatty
5 Ruthven McDonald
6 Henry Button
7 Peter O'Donovan
8 Eugéne Beaupré
9 Ivor Lewis
10 Jas Manson
11 Percy Hollinshead
12 Guy Mitchell
13 C.W. Jefferys
14 Jimmie James
15 Herb S. Palmer
16 Tom Greene
17 Bill Beatty
18 Eden Smith
19 Dr J.A. MacCallum
20 Alfred DeLury
21 Gus Bridle
22 Rufus Hathaway
23 Bob Defries
24 George Locke
25 Boris Hambourg
26 Ab Robson
27 Edwin Bell
28 Will Alexander

Handmade postcard, 1910. (*J. E. H. MacDonald*) MacDonald mailed this card to his colleague at Grip Limited, T. W. McLean, on vacation at Deerhurst.

Falling Leaves Meadow Vale, undated. (*J. W. Beatty*)

(Left) *Artist's Studio*, 1919. (*Frederick Challener*)

Banners. (*J. E. H. MacDonald*) MacDonald designed a series of seventeen of these banners to decorate the Great Hall, punning on the names of the members of the 1920–1921 executive and the earliest presidents. In the sixties, owing to the banners' deterioration, they were replaced with meticulous reproductions by members Robert Hubbard and his son Jim.

(Left) Christmas Scene, 1927. (*A. J. Casson*) This silkscreen was designed for the 1927 Christmas dinner program.

(Far left) Winter Scene, undated. (*Franklin Carmichael*)

Nativity, 1924. (*Fred Varley*) This mural in St. Anne's Anglican Church, Toronto, features a self-portrait of the artist (left).

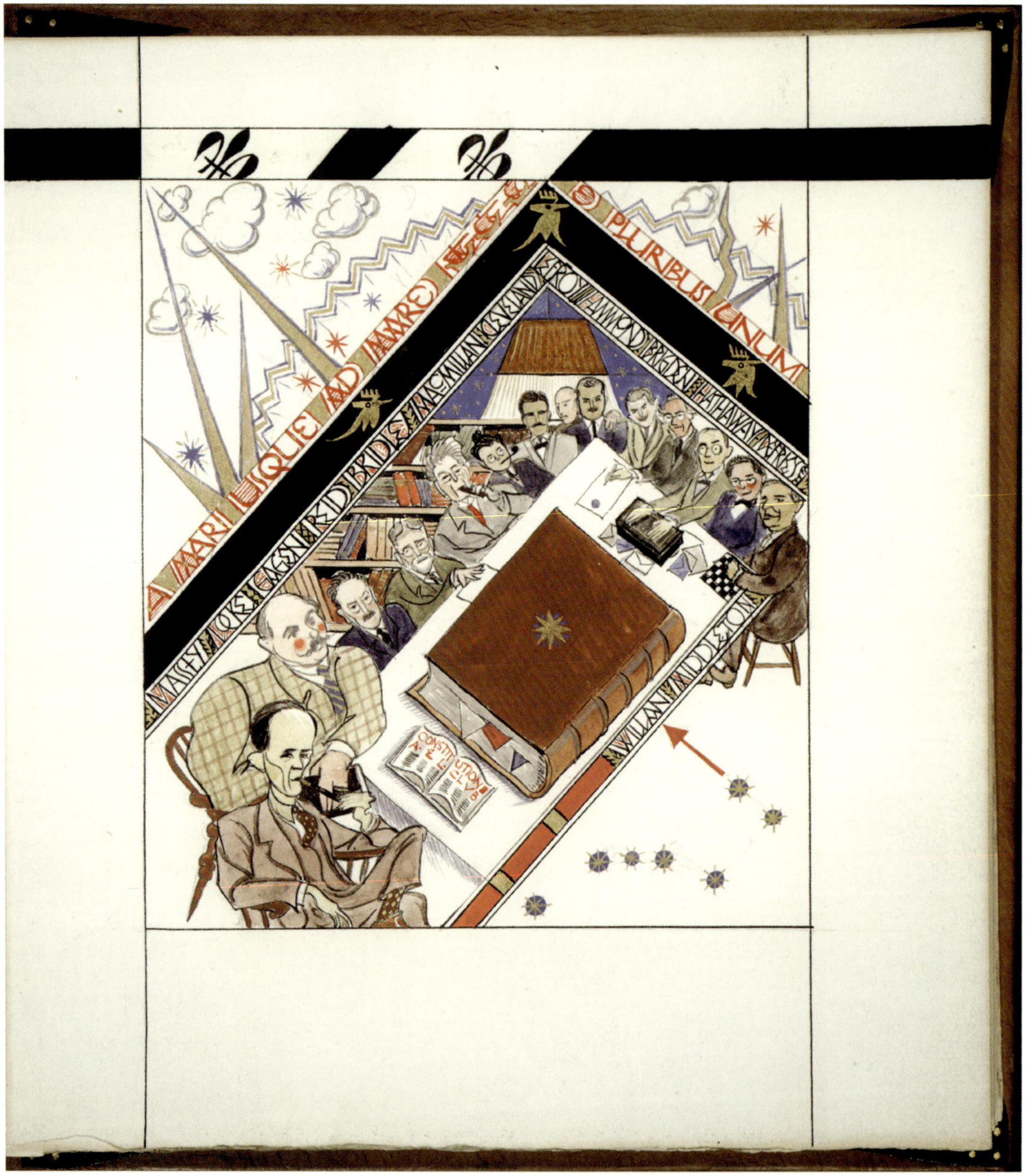

1921–1922 Executive Committee, 1927. (*J. E. H. MacDonald*) From left to right: President Vincent Massey, George Locke, Robert Gagen, George Reid, Gus Bridle, Ernest MacMillan, Barry Cleveland, Harold B. Lefroy, M. O. Hammond, Fred Brigden, E. J. Hathaway, Bob Defries, Healey Willan, and Jesse Middleton.

The illustration is from a book presented by the club to Massey on his appointment as Canada's first diplomatic representative to the United States. Note the club scrapbook in the centre of the table.

(Above) *Desjardins Canal*, undated. (*Leonard Hutchinson*)

(Above left) *Medicine Lake*, undated. (*Fred Banting*)

(Left) *The Bridge*, 1953. (*Franklin Arbuckle*) This painting appeared on the cover of *Maclean's*, March 1, 1953.

Trees Eastern Ontario, undated. (*Fred Haines*)

(*Above right*) *Old Beech Trees in Carnarvon*, undated. (*Joachim Gauthier*)

(*Right*) *Boreas* (*North Wind*), c. 1959. (*Nicholas Hornyansky*)

(*Above left*) "Come on, d___n you!" 1922. Treasurer Defries struggles with members over unpaid fees (*Fergus Kyle*)

Doug Hallam as Nellie McClung, 1922. (*Arthur Lismer*)

presence of women in the club made some members uncomfortable. A few days later, at a members' dinner, they staged a mock debate about women as authors. In the midst of the debate there was a noisy interruption from the gallery, where Doug Hallam, in drag, was impersonating McClung and attempting to hang a banner over the railing. A "sergeant-at-arms" rushed up to arrest "her." He brought "her" downstairs, and forced "her" to take a drink. The evening ended with great hilarity. As the saying goes, "I guess you had to be there."

One irritation that year caused members much distress. Maestro Giuseppe Carboni, an Italian vocal coach who had joined the club in 1916, was renting the room at the southeast corner of the main floor and using it as a studio. The soaring voices that emanated into the hallway and the Great Hall were very disturbing. In the end, his lease was not renewed. It may also be that his politics were unsettling to the members, since he was known to be involved with a fascist organization in the city.

There was continued enthusiasm for the club's new quarters, but ongoing financial concerns cast a shadow. The building was in poor shape and renovation costs were soaring. Paying the rent continued to be a challenge. There were difficulties as well with members who chronically couldn't or wouldn't pay their fees—Treasurer Defries deserved a medal.

Despite the continual woes, Massey soldiered on into 1922. He honoured charter member George Reid, who had recently completed a mural on the north wall of the Great Hall, at the members' dinner in January. After officially unveiling the mural, Massey launched into some of his humorous doggerel, written for the occasion. Here it is, in part:

Upon this wall I ask you all to see
In all its freshness—done recently
A scene that has been generously painted
By one with whom we all are well acquainted,
Who to this club has long since given his heart;
Who was the founder of a school of art;
Who for this year by common vote has been;
Chosen to hold the honoured post of dean
Of painters in this club—and, well, indeed,
You probably have guessed; George Agnew Reid.

The placid beauty of the situation
Suggests that test of one's intoxication
But now the hour has come when we're agreed
To give our grateful thanks to Mr. Reid
So Button, sirrah, seek him in the crowd!
If singers have more songs let them sing loud!
Place him upon a chair and bear him round
Accompanied by every form of sound!
This is the toast for everyone who drinks it
It's Latin, I may tell you.
GEORGIUS PINXIT.

"GEORGIUS PINXIT" was a customary way of saying "George painted it." The mural, sad to say, did not survive when a new stage was built some years later. Reid's half-round lunette of a Viking ship can still be seen above our proscenium.

In February, the theatre committee staged three short plays: *In the Zone* by Eugene O'Neil, *Fancy Free* by Stanley Houghton, and *Wurzel-Flummery* by A. A. Milne. One of the actors in the O'Neil play was Vincent's younger brother Raymond, who later wrote in his autobiography, "It was my first taste of the new realistic theatre.... I worked with a cast who had vitality and enthusiasm, with that team feeling which I believed must be part of the professional theatre." He also wrote that his brother Vincent "had always been a frustrated actor but...had to settle for being governor general of Canada." Raymond remained a member for only four brief years. He was "dropped," presumably for not paying his fees.

The highlight of the club's social season, a masquerade ball, was held at the end of that month. According to the *Toronto Evening Telegram*, the party was "notable for its novel conceits." Those with the best costumes were sketched by Arthur Lismer, Fred Varley, and Sammy Sampson. Then, in April, came a special dinner to honour Walter Allward, who had been chosen to design the Vimy Ridge Memorial and was heading for France for what would be a fourteen-year stay to supervise its construction. Allward sat at Massey's right and enjoyed watching Merrill Denison's *From Their Own Place*—a satire about backwoods trappers attempting to hoodwink a young couple from Toronto. The performance was followed by a lantern slide of Allward's monuments, the last one a sketch of his proposed memorial. This remained on the screen while Frank Blachford, Boris Hambourg, and Ernest MacMillan played a Brahms trio. "So the evening closed with an all-round glow.... Allward, in his modesty, took no part except to receive good wishes."

Walter Allward in his studio, 1922. (*M. O. Hammond*)

Not surprisingly, the annual meeting in October marking the end of Vincent Massey's highly successful presidency turned out to be a memorable event. For the second time that year Massey launched into a poetic exhortation that cleverly managed to mention, in rhyming couplets, sixty-six members of the club, beginning with Gus Bridle:

First comes our "Fellow Member Number One,"
Our own particular George Washington;
The Club's "First Cause," ordained by fate to be
Our genesis; our *premium mobile.*
Confessing that he made it all alone,
Remaining still the power behind the throne.
He wields admonition past belief,
From president to president remaining chief.

and ending with:

We've many other, if I'd time to cite 'em.
I could go on like this ad infinitum
At least I could proceed for several years;

Healey Willan, President, 1922–1923. (*J. E. Sampson*)

But here's an end with just—(suppress those cheers!)
An exhortation, if you'll pardon me.
Let's glorify ourselves less furtively!
Why sneak about in abject modesty?
We *are* the chosen people—no conceit
Is reprehensible in the *elite!*
We're of the truest esoteric line
We've imitators but none genuine.
A "tranquil consciousness" have we
Of "effortless superiority!"
Elders we have, but we can have no betters!
Your glasses, gentlemen! The Arts and Letters!

This doggerel prompted a standing ovation. Incoming president Healey Willan then took over and, for the first time, led the club choir in singing the constitution, which he had recently set to music. The crowd roared its approval, and Charlesworth moved that the constitution be sung at every annual meeting henceforth. The motion was carried with great enthusiasm. Until now the constitution had been known to only a very few, hidden by Bridle for years because he didn't want members to be unduly caught up in bureaucracy. Now Willan had outsmarted him. The evening ended with a skit spoofing prohibition, censorship, and other contemporary irritations. The choir burst into a song entitled "The Damned Police." Several verses and many laughs later, the fun concluded

Singing the club's constitution, 1928. MacMillan conducts, with incoming president MacDonald in the foreground. (*Arthur Lismer*)

with a "policeman" (Arthur Lismer) taping paper underwear to a fetching nude—a painting by George Reid. So much for censorship.

Sadly for the club, Frank Johnston—now going by the tonier name of Franz—left to become the principal of the Winnipeg School of Art. The Group of Seven became a group of six. Massey's teasing doggerel at the annual meeting had included:

> Then there's the Group of Seven's kind of art
> To prove that art and law are miles apart.
> With scant respect for truth their paints they mix;
> Even the number seven means but six!
> Critics recoil with outraged eyes to see
> Their polychromatic atrocity.
> Harris and Lismer, Varley, MacDonald, too
> Carmichael, Jackson, that's the Group's "who's who."

Sir Henry Newbolt, the English writer and poet, arrived at the club in February 1923. In Hammond's words, Newbolt was "a slight, bare-faced, ascetic looking man, small enough to escape notice in a crowd, and lacking any distinction of appearance save the intellectual lines of face." His words were, at times, hard to understand due to the rapidity with which he spoke and his English accent. This must have been one of the club's ladies' nights because Hammond, while he enjoyed hearing Newbolt, had difficulty appreciating local author Katherine Hale, who was seated next to him, "radiant with self-satisfaction... to such an extent that she ignored nearly everyone else she knew.... The event seemed to go to her head."

In March, the club's picture committee exhibited more than one hundred of Hammond's splendid photographs of Canadian statues and monuments. Jim MacDonald was in charge of the event. He and other club artists, given their positive approach to creative endeavours, were clearly encouraging photography as a growing art form. In so doing, they were a good ten years ahead of Canada's National Gallery. Certainly Hammond was happy to have *his* work recognized.

That same month, a letter arrived from Peter Donovan. He had been suspended for unpaid fees because, he said, his change of address notices had been ignored by Bridle, the "hairy, harassed but heroic" secretary. "But what does Gus care for addresses," wrote P. O'D (Donovan's pseudonym), "except the lengthy ones he makes!" By this time the membership was up to 325. Of note among the newcomers was the multi-talented

Bertram Brooker—artist, novelist, poet, journalist, and playwright. He was a great admirer of the Group of Seven and undoubtedly a fitting member for the club.

The six remaining members of the Group were still very much on the scene—and their work was still, at times, a hot topic. One evening that summer, James MacCallum launched into criticism of Fred Varley, claiming that he was being spoiled by Fairley's praise, that he wouldn't do commercial work, and that, therefore, he had not enough to live on. (Rumour had it that he had been put out of his house.) A month later, Varley's behaviour was drawing criticism from several quarters—for his drinking and because he was said to have seduced several of his female students. He had become something of a hot topic himself when club men settled down for a comfortable chat at lunch.

Soon after this, Varley did find some gainful employment. St. Anne's Anglican Church was being renovated and Varley and several other artists—Frank Carmichael, Herbert Stanfield, and Herbert Palmer—were hired to paint murals high up on the ceiling of the dome, with Jim MacDonald in charge. The murals—in Byzantine style to complement the architecture—were, and still are, magnificent. They literally glow. William Kilbourn wrote years later that "the one with shepherds adoring the Virgin Mary—including a self-portrait of young Varley, red hair, craggy nose and chin, kneeling reverently before her—is, as the Michelin guide would say, worth the journey." There was another St. Anne's story that year. Although the original architect, charter member Ford Howland, was still active professionally, the church, for motives now unknown, retained William Rae, also a member, to do the renovations. It was a dreadful slight to Howland. For whatever reasons, Howland resigned from the club the following year. Rae remained a member until his death in 1957.

While several of our artist members were busy producing murals at St. Anne's, another member, J. J. R. Macleod, was attracting worldwide acclaim. He and his research colleague, Frederick Banting, were jointly awarded the Nobel Prize for their discovery of insulin. Unfortunately, animosity soon developed between them, with Banting accusing Macleod of stealing his discovery. Shortly after the prize was awarded, Macleod resigned from the club. The animosity escalated over the next few years until finally Macleod left Canada to return to his birthplace in Scotland.

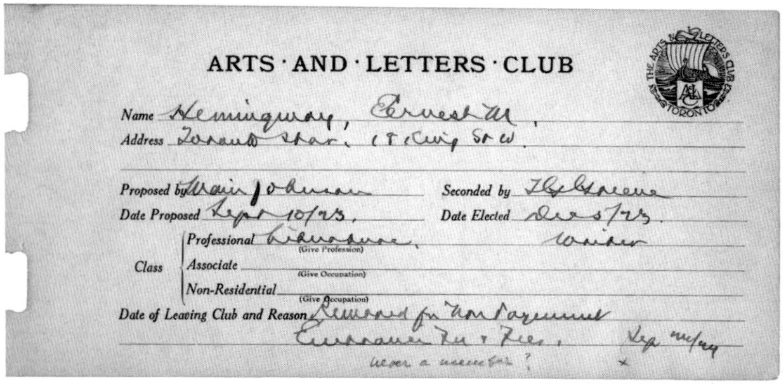
ARTS · AND · LETTERS · CLUB

Name Hemingway, Ernest M.
Address Toronto Star, 18 King St W.

Proposed by
Seconded by
Date Proposed Sept 10/23.
Date Elected

Class
Professional (Give Profession)
Associate (Give Occupation)
Non-Residential (Give Occupation)

Date of Leaving Club and Reason Removed for non payment

Ernest Hemingway's membership application, 1923.

A major disappointment in the annals of club history involved a young journalist who *almost* became a member. His name was Ernest Hemingway. In 1920, he had landed a job at the *Toronto Daily Star* and was sent to Europe as a correspondent. In October 1923, shortly after his return from Paris, he applied for membership in the club, sponsored by Main Johnson, the *Star*'s promotions manager. But, as Greg Gatenby has written, "Almost from the moment Ernest returned to Toronto...his life at the paper was hell." He was handed lowly assignments that took him out of town for days on end, the very thing he had been promised would not happen. Hemingway, his wife, and their new baby slipped out of Toronto at the end of the year, just prior to his being accepted as a member.

As the next annual meeting approached, club politics once again loomed front and centre. Charlesworth was nominated for president—despite the fact that some members wanted Healey Willan to continue for a second year. At the meeting, Willan took to the podium to lament his shortcomings and to beg out of the race. William Mulock then presented him with a loving cup "fashioned of tinfoil, and about the size of an eggcup," suitable, he announced, for libations under the Ontario Temperance Act. Finally, when it came to the vote, Charlesworth went down to defeat and C. W. Jefferys became the next president. To everyone's delight, the evening ended with the choir's enthusiastic

C. W. Jefferys, President, 1923–1924. (*Jack McLaren*)

Christmas 1924. Ivor Lewis (left) and Jules Wegman are dozing in the foreground and the chess players, recently banished from in front of the fire, can be seen to the right, bent over the board, with the top of inveterate player James Mavor's head visible. (*Arthur S. Goss*)

Healey Willan (seated) with (from left) Jack Neilson, cellist Phillip Spivak, and violinists Frank Fusco and Elie Spivak at the club fireplace.

singing of the constitution. To this day Willan is remembered not only for setting our constitution to plainsong but also for claiming "I am English by birth, Irish by extraction, Canadian by adoption, and Scotch by absorption."

That year's Boar's Head attracted about 160 members. As usual, officers and committee members wore ceremonial vestments, with the choir sporting monks' robes. The club orchestra was ensconced on stage. For the second year, several members sported colourful tabards, now a Boar's Head tradition. Entertainment was provided by Géza de Kresz and Mark Hambourg, in town to visit his family.

A new member of note in 1924 was the talented and fun-loving John Wilson McLaren. He had achieved renown as one of the Dumbells, a vaudeville group that had entertained the troops during the war with tunes such as "These wild wild women are making a wild wild man of me" and "Oh! It's a lovely war!" The group continued to perform into the twenties. Pianist Clement Hambourg, the youngest Hambourg brother, and pianist-conductor Reginald Stewart also joined that year.

March saw the English historian George Macaulay Trevelyan on hand to discuss literature. In June, Charles Currelly turned up at the club with English archaeologist Howard Carter, who had, two years previously, discovered the tomb of Egypt's King Tutankhamen. He spoke of his excavations and their accompanying difficulties. In November, Massey's guest was the novelist and historian John Buchan, author of the fast-paced *The Thirty-Nine Steps.* A decade later, he would be named the first Baron Tweedsmuir and appointed governor general of Canada.

Monro Grier, President, 1924–1926. (*Wyly Grier*)

Monro Grier, brother of Wyly, became the next president. An accomplished public speaker, he once addressed the club for more than an hour on the "Art of Talking," all without notes! He was both a lawyer and an enthusiastic amateur actor. As Massey put it,

> The brothers, Wyly and A. Monro,
> See how art and the law on one stem grow!
> Yet, now, it's true the arts both Griers engage,
> Since lawyer Grier has taken to the stage!

In December, a dinner was held to honour Beverley Baxter, back in town on his way to Vancouver to be married. By this time, Baxter was achieving considerable renown as editor-in-chief of the *London Daily Express.* He gave an enjoyable, rambling talk and seemed happy to be back with his friends at the club. He remained a member until 1926.

The architects of the club staged a dinner in February 1925 called the Architects' Revenge, which turned out to be one of the highlights of the decade. The menu appeared as an architectural blueprint—with "all work to be thoroughly smoke-tested and approved by the inspectors." Entertainment included a short skit by Fred Jacob, and a song that opened with

> We belong to a curious profession
> Which began when the earth was first made;
> For who built the Ark or the Tower
> Of Babel, save one of our trade?
> Yet we read of no public ovation,
> We don't know his title or name,
> He most probably died of starvation
> Today it's exactly the same.

As It Will Be, an imaginary Arts and Letters clubhouse, 1924. (*Jack McLaren*)

On display were two tongue-in-cheek architectural drawings. One, by Jack McLaren, shows a section through an imaginary Arts and Letters clubhouse, featuring portly lay members, "Bridal" standing high on a pedestal, money bags hidden in the basement, and a long lineup of prospective members. The other, by Jules Wegman, shows the floor plan for an equally imaginary Arts and Letters cathedral, "at an estimated cost of $4,350,000 (architects' fees not included)." It still hangs in the club today.

Charles G. D. Roberts, sometimes referred to as "the father of Canadian literature," was next on the scene. In March, he was a guest at the club to speak to the Canadian Authors' Association. About six weeks later, he was back at the club looking "a bit seedy" following an all-night party. When asked if he had ever known the Metis poet Pauline Johnson, he replied, "Oh, yes. You know we had a little romantic interest in each other at one time—just a sly wink, a squeeze of the hand and a furtive kiss." Ten years later he was knighted and came to be known, in some quarters, as "Sir Charles God Damn."

There were more hijinks in April when club artists staged an Artists' Jamboree. These creative souls discovered an organ grinder—Organ Joe—on the streets of Toronto and brought him to the club to provide musical entertainment—of sorts. When his selections

Organ Joe at the Artists' Jamboree, 1925. (*Arthur Lismer*)

came to an end, Ernest MacMillan was summoned to try his hand with the instrument, after which a sign was dangled on it reading "Pupil of Dr. MacMillan." Then recent member Fred Banting had his turn and, as he varied the speed, someone said he was treating it for diabetes! Frank Johnston (visiting from Winnipeg) and Sammy Sampson cavorted around the room dressed as girls and flirted with the men. One of them even kissed Bridle. Jack McLaren took part in the show, acting as spieler with the "girls" to summon everyone in.

On a more serious note, we opened our doors on Good Friday so that members might meet anthropologist Marius Barbeau of Ottawa and hear his associates sing a program of French-Canadian folk music. Barbeau had recently co-edited a collection of these songs, which Ernest MacMillan had reviewed with praise in the *Canadian Forum*, and now, at the club, the two men were meeting for the first time. It was the beginning of a lifelong friendship.

Not only did members enjoy hearing the Canadian folk songs, they were also developing a growing interest in the artistic integrity of early documentaries—or so it would seem, given the healthy turnout in early December for the showing of an unexpurgated version of Robert Flaherty's *Moana of the South Seas*. The film was unavailable to less-fortunate Ontario theatre patrons at the time due, no doubt, to its honest portrayal of the bare-breasted women of Samoa.

A letter from the secretary to members in early February 1926 announced that the club would take part in the opening of the Walker Court at the Art Gallery of Toronto, along with the Ontario Society of Artists and the Graphic Arts Society. It was named after Sir Edmund Walker, the Gallery's first president, who had died two years before. Our men were to be part of a grand procession—a choir, the presidents of the three organizations, candle-bearers, standard bearers, musicians, dignitaries, art characters, and a jester. Because this would be the first appearance of club members in any public way, they were advised to preserve the "best club form." This stagey midwinter jaunt, some of it out-of-doors, was undoubtedly a brisk one.

Masthead, *Hotairian Blast*, 1926.

April of that year saw the publication of the four-page *Hotairian Blast,* another attempt at in-house humour. Mercifully, its first issue was also its last. Humour that may have a place in lighthearted gatherings should not be in print for posterity.

Bob Defries was honoured in July with a small presentation book prepared by Jim

Great Hall decorated for the "Hotairian Ball," 1926. Looking south to the minstrel gallery and Elm Street door. (*Arthur S. Goss*)

MacDonald to reflect "the spirit of the Arts and Letters Club." In beautiful script and adorned with exquisite small illustrations, it told with humour of Defries' never-ending challenges as treasurer: "No one who has not been a treasurer of a club can appreciate the multiplicity of details, the unlooked for responsibilities, and the uncalled for criticisms that distinguish one's official career." The book mentioned his resignation from that post, and "the deserved rest which we somewhat reluctantly give him." This present did the trick—Defries agreed to continue serving as treasurer. The book is now safely housed at the National Gallery.

Journalist-author-poet-playwright Jesse Edgar Middleton became the club's next president. A gentle kindly man, he wrote mostly for newspapers as a columnist and music critic, but he also published a three-volume history of Toronto, in which he described the club as "the most intellectual and at the same time the most frolicsome institution of Toronto."

Plays had, by now, become a club tradition. One-act plays were often staged after monthly dinners, and several full-length plays were produced every year. In late November, the theatre committee staged a nineteenth-century temperance play, *Ten Nights in a Bar Room*, produced by Pat Mitchell, Roy Mitchell's wife, and done both as a serious morality play and as a burlesque—a device that allowed the audience to deplore drunkenness while laughing at that perennial scapegoat, the funny drunkard.

J. E. Middleton, President, 1926–1928. (*F. S. Challener*)

Bertram Brooker. (*Charles Comfort*)

The differences between the avant-garde and the more conservative members were still surfacing from time to time—usually with good humour. The conservative contingent had become know as the Knockers (!) because of the genial insults they liked to toss around. Whoever they were—we have no record—they must have enjoyed their sobriquet. In December they hosted a four-course dinner in honour of, and prepared by, the club cook, Mrs. Bessie Webster.

The highlight of the members' dinner in January 1927 was a show of abstract paintings, said to be the first such showing in Canada. With Arthur Lismer's help, the paintings had been hidden behind curtains until the meal was finished. When the works were unveiled, they were met by commotion, confusion, and dismay. There were gasps and groans. Alec Jackson remarked cautiously that the paintings "made the Group of Seven seem like old hat—it would be too bad if the public caught up with the artist." Even Jim MacDonald was puzzled. When members were asked to guess the identity of the artist, only one member, organist G. D. Atkinson, was able to do so correctly. "Oh, I know who did them," he exclaimed, "Brooker! Look, it's all music!" Yes, they were the work of Bert Brooker, inspired, he said, while listening to music. Brooker was not dismayed by the negative reception. "The artist does not aim to please," he wrote some years later. "That is the artist's function and fate—to give the world *novelty* too soon for society to appreciate it—and to be acclaimed too late."

Shortly after this event, the club staged a farewell dinner to honour Vincent Massey, who had recently been appointed first Canadian envoy to the United States. He was ordered to appear before the bar of the club and demonstrate "how the eagle swooped down upon the beaver." Fittingly, the Hart House String Quartet—Géza de Kresz, Harry Adaskin, Milton Blackstone, and Boris Hambourg—provided musical accompaniment. Hammond, as always duly impressed, noted that Massey "was human and warm in all his contacts and apparently quite touched. He used to have some detachment and has been accused of an Oxford touch and snobbery, but that was gone tonight. He sat up at the high table with Middleton, Mulock, Frank Moore, Jim MacDonald, and others, and the room was comfortably filled." Massey was given a small and exquisite presentation book designed by Jim MacDonald. It is now in the Fisher Rare Book Library, with a copy at the club for members to enjoy.

In March, the Arts and Letters Players staged four one-act plays at Hart House Theatre. The first evening featured *Low Life*, a prize-winning play by Mazo de la Roche, and *The Baker's Dozen* by H. H. Munro (Saki). On the second evening, *The Jest of Hahhabba* by

Lord Dunsany was paired with Merrill Denison's *The Prizewinner*. Dunsany's first play, *The Glittering Gate*, had been performed at the club in 1914. As for *The Prizewinner*, Alexander (Sandy) Leggatt has called it Denison's "richest play and one that deserves to be better known." These four plays, we are told, were all highly creative and successful ventures for the club. But this was no thanks to Mitchell who had by this time become discouraged with theatre in Toronto. After coping with years of resistance to his progressive ideas, he decamped to New York where he became a professor of dramatic art at New York University. Today Mitchell is still considered one of the most prophetic voices in Canadian theatre. Denison also became discouraged; he found that writing about theatre in Canada was "depressingly like discussing the art of dinghy sailing among the bedouins. There is so little to be said on the subject save to point why there is none." But Dension went on to become a successful and prolific writer for radio, with his *The Romance of Canada* series that was broadcast nationally in the thirties.

England's world-famous D'Oyly Carte Opera Company came to town two months later and arrived at the club *en masse* at eleven o'clock one evening, for a special ladies' night. The place was packed. It wasn't until 1:30 a.m. that the opera people trooped up to the stage and happily launched into various choruses, duets, and solos from Gilbert and Sullivan operettas.

The club also held a dinner for Mazo de la Roche that month. She had just won an astonishing $10,000 prize for her novel *Jalna* in a contest run by the *Atlantic Monthly*. This gala event, another ladies' night, met with less-than-universal approval. Bridle was particularly annoyed—he was in the club that evening but did not stay for dinner and "went away grouching." Hammond—upset—told President Middleton that the club was too big to be dominated by one man's prejudices.

During the summer, Alec Jackson and Fred Banting, a talented artist in addition to being a renowned scientist, left for an Arctic expedition aboard the steamship *Beothic*, sailing as far north as Ellesmere Island. It was the first of three painting trips they would take together. Years later, Banting's second wife, Henrietta, donated to the club a narwhal tooth—over seven feet long—that Jackson and Banting had acquired on their Arctic trip.

Frederick Banting. (*J. E. Sampson*)

At that year's Boar's Head there was, as usual, plenty of good cheer. The entire evening was a triumph, with two boys' choirs, a lot of pranks, a French-Canadian carol, some English carols, violin music, the *Toy Symphony*, and a skit about the old club at the courthouse. Perhaps some of the good cheer centered around the fact that prohibition had finally ended after eleven long years. On a more serious note, Middleton read a long poem written for the occasion—verse that effectively summarized his love for the club. It ends with the following lines:

For twenty years this club has stood
A lighthouse in a tossing sea;
A little patch of general good
Where life is gentle, blithe and free.
Let others rave of bonds and stocks,
Pursue the dollar to its lair;
Within these walls, behind our locks
We breathe a more delightsome air.

In 1928, the executive decided the time had come to recognize acting as a real art form of interest to respectable society. Our members had after all been in the forefront of theatrical activity in Toronto since 1911, when Maeterlink's *Interior* was produced. So it is hard to understand why it took the club so long to reach this decision. In any event, it was agreed that "good actors" would be allowed in as professional members. But the S in the LAMPS acronym would, for some time, continue to stand for "sculpture," not "stage."

When it came time for the annual meeting in October, Jesse Middleton took to the podium with another poem to mark his last dinner as president:

But as the dancing years go by
Each tossing snow-wreaths on my hair
As troubles come, as pleasures fly,
As more of wrinkles must I wear,
One solace will be ever mine
One evergreen emolument;
My name is in the Royal Line
Sometime—I was your President.

J. E. H. MacDonald, President, 1928–1930. (*Charles Comfort*)

The much-loved Jim MacDonald became our next president—the only member of the Group of Seven to be so honoured. He set a lofty standard for this position, handling the job with his usual kindness and tact, and, when necessary, with firmness. He was unfailingly decent, thoughtful, and honourable. "Not to have known Jimmy," Bridle wrote, "was to miss an experience in living." Frank Johnston found just the right words. "He was a gentle man with a spine of steel," and Casson, called him "one of the finest people I've ever known." During his previous seventeen years as a member, MacDonald had had four one-man shows, produced dozens of illustrations for club publications, created our Viking ship logo, designed a list of members who had served in World War I, and created the punning heraldic shields for the Great Hall. He also designed eight of the early executive lists, the Defries presentation book, the Massey presentation book, and many broadsheets and programs—all exquisite works of art and all done because of his devotion to the club.

Two weeks into MacDonald's presidency, a huge crowd poured through the doors just before midnight to welcome once again the more than forty members of the D'Oyly Carte Company. Their first song began with four men on stage, then others rose from their seats to join them until eventually the entire cast was there. They sang until 2:30 a.m. No one wanted to leave. Finally, the evening drew to a happy conclusion as surprised and delighted members heard the company launch into a rousing rendition of the club's constitution. It turned out that the singers had been rehearsing it during their travels across Canada.

That year's Christmas dinner brought out two hundred members—we'll never know how or where they all fitted in—to enjoy the usual pranks and the excellent music by the club's orchestra and the Hart House String Quartet. The evening's entertainment had a Dickens theme, with more than twenty costumed members on the stage and "very old time English in the air."

In mid-January 1929, Napier Moore suggested that the club hold a "father and son" banquet, with half those attending taking the role of fathers and the other half of sons. This bizarre idea, as far as we know, failed to materialize. And *The Elm Corners Wallop*, another decidedly "unfunny" publication, surfaced the following month and died unmourned. It was the second and last newsletter published during the twenties.

On October 29—Black Friday—the bottom fell out of the Toronto Stock Exchange. The Great Depression had begun, a decade marked by fear, pessimism, and ongoing upheaval. Yet no one at the club seemed unduly concerned—in fact, a party was in the offing, this time to celebrate our twenty-first anniversary—our coming of age—on November 6. Spirits were high when about two hundred members and former members arrived at the club, ready to party. The evening was, in Hammond's words, "a big walloping success." Bridle had organized the whole affair. Campbell McInnes put in a plea for reinstatement. Our records show that this didn't happen, although he continued to sing at club events for the next few years. Percy Hollinshead, visiting from New York, was the hit of the evening. When he finished singing, "he was overcome by an emotion which he could not control. The crowd gave way to shouts and sustained applause, especially after

Percy Hollinshead, 1929. (*Arthur Lismer*)

Napier Moore. (*Jack McLaren*)

'Mother of Mine'." The whole show ran until nearly midnight, with skits, a film showing the trek from the Brown Betty restaurant to the courthouse, lantern slides of early club life, and music provided by club musicians. A telegram arrived for President MacDonald from Vincent Massey in Washington saying, "I rejoice that the brotherhood has come of age. My greetings to the faithful. My congratulations to you, sir. My humble duty to the secretary, and my respectful and continuous salutations to the treasurer." That evening, Bridle was named a life member.

By early 1930, the Depression was making itself felt even at the club. Not surprisingly, there was a drop in lunchtime attendance. Various solutions were discussed by the executive, such as having the president and executive members make a point of sitting at various tables over lunch to hear comments from members. But nothing seemed to make much difference.

The first of the club's legendary annual spring revues, "April Foolies," was launched that year with Napier Moore as director, a role he would hold for more than a decade. He once said that the revues were begun to make amends to wives whose husbands spent so many evenings at 14 Elm Street. Ever since—except for a six-year gap in the forties—spring revues have been the highlight of the club year, offering members—talented and not so talented—the opportunity to strut their stuff. It hasn't always been wonderful, but "it's club"—and it has always been fun.

On May 14, tragedy struck when wildflower artist Robert Holmes died in the Great Hall. Newton MacTavish described the scene: Holmes was speaking with praise about his young women students at the Ontario College of Art. He had just referred to them as the "flowers of time" and was confessing that they appealed to him as veritable wild flowers themselves. At that very moment, Frederick Challener, an old and intimate friend of Holmes, saw that something was wrong. He noticed Holmes falter, letting his notes fall listlessly from his hands. He fell backward into Challener's arms "and there almost immediately expired." For his funeral a few evenings later, there was standing room only. The lights were lowered as Jim MacDonald solemnly led a procession to the front of the Great Hall, the walls of which were hung with thirty-six of Holmes' wildflower paintings on loan for the occasion. The service was conducted by Reverend Frank Moore. Pallbearers included Gus Bridle, George Reid, Wyly Grier, Fred Brigden, and Alfred DeLury. Messages of condolence arrived from Stephen Leacock and Percy Hollinshead, one of Holmes' closest friends—Holmes had contributed a delicate watercolour painting for Hollinshead's presentation book.

At an executive meeting that month, the question of women at the club came to the fore yet again, this time because of English artist Violet Oakley, a member of London's prestigious Royal Academy of Arts. Her presence at lunch one day was seen as a violation of club policy and an "offense against males" and President MacDonald was called on to explain. Then Bridle allowed, "Not guilty—but don't do it again." The usually mild-mannered MacDonald replied firmly that he would make no such promise, as he felt the president had the right to interpret the rules as he saw fit. Brooker moved a resolution of confidence in the president and all hands went up.

Although little was seen of Bridle over the summer months, he turned up at the last minute for the annual meeting in October. MacDonald was ending his two years as president and his words of farewell were moving. "If I may speak personally, I may say that the club has been a church, a home, and a studio for me. It has called on me for service, it has developed my power to serve. It has often given inspiration and ideals. It has enlarged our Canada for me. It has made a blessed centre for me in this grey town." Ernest MacMillan, as the new president, took hold of club affairs with vigour and firmness, and with his usual good nature.

Ernest MacMillan, President, 1930–1932 (*J. E. Sampson*)

The Christmas dinner that year featured the club choir, conducted by Healey Willan, with the club orchestra—seventeen in all—ensconced high up in the gallery. The post-dinner program had a historical theme that included a poem by E. J. (Ned) Pratt and two skits, one recreating Christmas at Port Royale, Nova Scotia, in 1606, and the other based on a story by Charles Comfort about an 1860 Christmas at a Hudson Bay Company's post. At evening's end, "The First Noel" was sung by all in a roof-raising chorus.

Reginald Stewart.

By 1931, the Depression had wiped out entire businesses, and more and more Canadians were finding themselves out of work. At the club, financial woes continued. Along with the treasurer's ongoing laments about unpaid fees, occasional differences arose with the St. George's Society. These spats, usually about the rent, cropped up in the society's minute books as well. They were settled more or less amicably—obviously so, since we have coexisted happily under the same roof ever since. President MacMillan received a letter from one irate member, Cecil C. King, urging the club to "consider very seriously the purchase of another property where we could establish a home independent of all landlords and other annoyances." His suggestion fell on deaf ears.

MacMillan, always busy, must have been even more so at this time—he had just been appointed conductor of the Toronto Symphony Orchestra. There had been a long-standing conductors' rivalry between him and Reg Stewart, with club members lining up behind their favourite. In *The Globe*, Bridle predicted "a scrimmage, with our two chief conductors each beating time to out spot the other." MacMillan's appointment made him the clear winner. Stewart went on to a fine career as conductor of Toronto's Promenade Symphony Orchestra, and then of the Baltimore Symphony. He also served as director of the Peabody Conservatory.

A few weeks later, an announcement went out to members urging them to sign up for another Architects' Revenge. Included in the mailing was a list of excuses "to hand out to the 'ball and chain,'" to assure her that this would be a "big evening," one not to be missed because there would be a skit by Merrill Denison—"he used to be an architect, you know," an architectural menu, slides and a lecture by Arthur Lismer, sea shanties by Walter Bowles and Healey Willan, and so on. Tickets were priced at one dollar, and members could bring a male guest. In the same vein, in April, members were urged to sign up for another Artists' Jamboree. "Come and bring your guests—No ladies of course!" Women were, however, welcomed to that year's spring revue, "Spring Fever," which ran successfully for three nights in March. It was another resounding success.

What had been promised as a highly auspicious event in November, turned out to be a big disappointment when English author A. A. Milne came to the club as the guest of John McClelland. Milne's work was known to virtually everyone in the club, thanks to his *Winnie the Pooh* and other classic works for children, and almost all the literary members turned up to hear him. But when he stood up to speak, his only remark to the assembled crowd was to announce that he had managed *not* to make a speech in New York, "and I shall *not* make one in Canada either!" An editorial in *The Globe* somehow managed to find excuses for his dismissive behaviour.

In December, the executive asked Jim MacDonald, who had in recent years been in charge of the scrapbooks, if he would allow someone else to take over the responsibility for them. MacDonald was then in ill health and readily agreed. He made only one proviso—that he continue as official keeper of the records. "I look on the office as a life appointment—a senatorship due to my hoary age and services." Care of the scrapbooks was considered a major responsibility. From the club's very first days, even before minutes were kept, the club had been safely preserving its records, all of which were pasted into huge scrapbooks. The earliest of these precious volumes are in safekeeping at the Fisher

Rare Book Library. They contain programs, letters, newspaper articles, cartoons, and sketches—fascinating memorabilia covering most of the club's highlights from those first exciting years. Scott Carter took charge of them and was a fine choice. His work in the art of heraldry was gaining international acclaim. Among his many accomplishments was the design for the heraldic map and the armorial shields of the universities of the British Empire and Britain's World War I allies. They still adorn the walls of Hart House.

The club's vice-president, Barry Cleveland, wrote to the *Toronto Evening Telegram* in early February 1932 to complain about the publication of photographs taken at the club's masquerade gala a few days earlier. All the pictures were innocuous enough and Cleveland was primarily objecting to the club's name appearing in the paper. The city editor's prompt reply noted that guests had willingly posed for the photographer and that several of them had expressed a desire for copies. But the club did not complain about an article in the *Mail and Empire* that reported on the same party, naming many of the people who attended—all "quaintly costumed" and many "representing a burlesque of the gay nineties." It would not be the last time that the club was mentioned in the press.

A highly charged issue surfaced at the executive's July meeting. Jesse Middleton was threatening to quit the club if the resignation of one member (unnamed) was not demanded "on account of a public matter." Middleton's ire was likely directed at either Fred Banting or Donat M. LeBourdais, main players in a very public scandal that had surfaced at the club's New Year's Eve party several months before. The steamy scandal—in which Banting accused his wife of adultery with LeBourdais, although he himself was enjoying an affair with the attractive writer Blodwyn Davies—had hit the press. Polite society in the city could talk of little else. Michael Bliss, in his *Banting: A Biography*, wrote that "Opinion at the Arts and Letters Club...was split down the middle, with D. M. having enough support to make Fred feel not quite comfortable there." The Bantings were divorced not long after. Both Banting and LeBourdais remained members. The executive in its wisdom had deemed that "the private conduct of any member of the club is not a matter for executive action, unless and except said conduct may reflect discredit upon the club." Middleton reconsidered his resignation and remained a member until his death in 1960. In a bitter memorial notice in *The Globe and Mail* in 1994, Banting's son Robert remembered his mother (Banting's first wife, Marion Robertson Banting), who had died in 1944. She had, he said, been "sorely wronged and slandered by a society protecting the reputation and good name of its hero."

C. B. Cleveland, President, 1932–1934. (*Wyly Grier*)

Hector Charlesworth takes over as first chairman of the Canadian Radio Broadcasting Commission, 1932. (*Arthur Lismer*)

Later that year, when another annual meeting rolled around, Barry Cleveland was named the new president. He was a handsome and popular architect who had worked on some of the largest buildings in Canada. But the financial news continued to be gloomy. Members were in for a shock when treasurer Defries reported that the club's securities had fallen in value from $24,000 to $7,000 during the year. The club, he said, "had made $439 in the kitchen and lost $17,000 on the market."

A fine farewell dinner for Hector Charlesworth was held in October. Charlesworth was heading for Ottawa to take up his appointment as chairman of the newly established Canadian Radio Broadcasting Commission (CRBC), which later became the Canadian Broadcasting Corporation (CBC). As reported in the 1932 issue of *The Lamps* (the first since 1919), "Everything said about Mr. Charlesworth was in his favour and he must have departed wondering why he had not previously known what a great fellow he is." B. K. Sandwell replaced Charlesworth as editor at *Saturday Night*, bringing about a change that, in the words of Greg Gatenby, "immediately raised the journalism standard of the paper and expanded its horizon to include all of Canada, not just Toronto."

November 1932 brought yet another tragedy with the death of Jim MacDonald. His loss cast a pall over the entire club and Jesse Middleton wrote the following heartfelt tribute:

> He had treasures for all his friends; affection and intimate thoughts, sparkling epigrams, flashes of real genius; and labour as well. The time and toil he gave to the Arts and Letters Club only we older members know. This was his place of rest, where music and poetry, drama and design and colour were in the air. He never could do too much for it.... The Arts and Letters Club was honoured by having Jim MacDonald as president for two years, and as vice-president or executive member for twenty. We bid him not adieu, but *au revoir*, remembering with admiration and affection the work he did for the club and for Canada, the cunning of eye and hand, the sweetness and light of his personality. And so he walks with each of his friends today and will walk until the soft distant trumpet-call sounds for us.

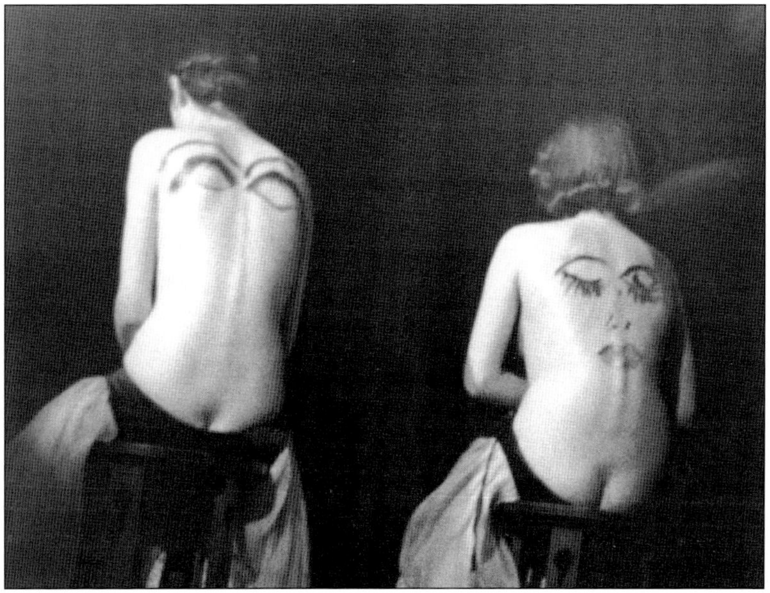

One of several "living pictures" at the Artists' Jamboree, February, 1933.

In January 1933, Chuck Matthews showed a film he had produced that featured many club members. Although they all appear to be relaxed and speaking freely, there is no soundtrack so it is impossible to discern what they were saying. Some sixty years later, one bright soul at the club, Rod Austin, took the film to an organization for the deaf, thinking that lip-reading might help. But it was not to be. Virtually every man featured had either a pipe clenched between his teeth or cigarette smoke wafting gracefully around his face. Deciphering their words was impossible. The original film now rests in the National Archives in Ottawa, although the club still has a copy.

By this time, three years into the ever-worsening Depression, 30 percent of Torontonians were jobless and club finances were in dire shape. Some members, unable to pay their fees, were forced to resign; others simply disappeared and had their names crossed off the membership list. At its February meeting, the executive reduced the salary of the club's cook, the redoubtable Mrs. Webster. But in spite of these difficulties, the club went ahead with its annual Artists' Jamboree. More than a hundred members turned up to enjoy the evening—quite possibly because they had heard of the plan to have "living pictures" featuring groups of men and women posing in compositions by Watteau and other famous painters. According to reports, "One group of figures in half light included a girl in a light robe, which she threw off and revealed her nude form." The members loved it.

Late one evening in March, the entire cast of Marc Connelly's *The Green Pastures*—a Pulitzer Prize-winning all-black drama loosely based on biblical themes—showed up at the club. The play was in town for an engagement and the entire company of sixty-five was welcomed for a midnight jamboree. After dinner, the players marched down singing from the third floor through the Great Hall and up to the stage, where they sang, and sang, and sang. An enthusiastic crowd was on hand to enjoy it all—and remained well into the early morning hours. Adding lustre to the program was Canada's great Metropolitan Opera tenor, Edward Johnson, who had been singing at Eaton Auditorium that evening. Reg Stewart was at the piano and the Hart House String Quartet also performed. It was an exhilarating evening. The crowd rose and shouted in satisfaction. This was not the first time the club had hosted black singers—in 1929, a troupe of jubilee singers had been similarly entertained.

Birds of a Feather group (B.O.F.), 1930. From the left: Arthur Goss, Ivor Lewis, Jack McLaren, Edgar Stone, Walter Bowles, Chuck Matthews, and Pat Mitchell. (*Arthur S. Goss*)

This year saw the formation of a members' inner circle known as Birds of a Feather, or B.O.F. for short—or to some, Bloody Old Fools. It all began on a weekend in September when Ivor Lewis, a top executive with the T. Eaton Company as well as a fine sculptor and an acclaimed actor, was feeling very despondent about current business conditions. Jack McLaren happened along and suggested a weekend at his Lake Simcoe cottage. Twenty or more other members also turned up and each was assigned the name of a bird—Lewis was the High Cockalorum, McLaren was the Ruptured Duck, Napier Moore was the Dodo, Charles Comfort was the Tomtit, and so on. And so the B.O.F. was born. It gradually grew to about sixty members and the old "birds" met once a month at various weekend retreats to play poker, smoke, and drink—to forget about ruffled feathers, empty nests, and flying south for the winter. Guests such as Fred Banting, Ernest MacMillan, and others were occasionally invited—they were known as the Hard-Boiled Eggs.

In October, the executive, faced with continuing financial losses, discussed raising revenue by having "ladies at dinner." Defries and Bridle firmly opposed this suggestion and moved that "ladies be not privileged to attend *any* dinner of the club." But the motion went down to defeat. By the following month, it was agreed that ladies would be invited to attend a dinner in January. And so the debate continued.

Meanwhile, there was always something going on to raise the spirits. This time it was the club's twenty-fifth anniversary—yet another celebratory banquet. And so, one evening in November, members trooped to the club and raised a toast to our first quarter-century. The entertainment featured skits about charter members (several of whom were in the audience), a costumed MacMillan at the piano, and Bridle waxing lyrical as he recalled the club's early days when the "slanderbund" met for the original "gathering of the arts." He spoke with affection about our first president, William Langton, who had signed the lease "for a garret as the only fit habitation of a club so dented to things of the soul as expressed in art and so scornful of shekels." It was pure "Bridle-ese." The evening came to a happy end with Jack McLaren leading the crowd in popular hits from those early days—"Sidewalks of New York," "Daisy, Daisy," and others. "The dinner was spiced by a bit of steaming punch, which helped spirits."

Over the winter of 1933–1934, five issues of *The Bulletin* appeared, each a slight one or two pages. The fourth, in January 1934, reported that the first "bi-sexual" dinner had taken place, at which "Noel Coward's *The Marquise* was capably performed...and the ladies particularly enjoyed the risqué parts. The few members who were shocked were reassured by their wives."

That was the year the club had the honour of being the venue for weekly orchestral concerts aired by the CRBC for the enjoyment of Canadians across the country. Since Hector Charlesworth still headed the broadcaster, staging these concerts in the Great Hall may not have been entirely coincidental. In March, the fifth spring revue, "Round the Corner," began a five-night run. As an outreach venture, the club had invited more than one hundred homeless men to the dress rehearsal. In a letter the next week, the Toronto Men's Hostel expressed its thanks to the club and to Mr. Ivor Lewis "for generously supplying our men with tobacco." It was a kindly gesture indeed, but we can be sure that Lewis had not purchased the tobacco at Eaton's, where, by decree, tobacco was never sold.

Members were understandably delighted when Fred Banting was knighted in June. It was an honour that he professed to dismiss, correcting anyone who attempted to call him Sir Frederick. But it was one of only a few bright moments for club members as the Depression continued its unrelenting pace. Each treasurer's report became more dismal than the last, which was why, no doubt, the executive decided that "the privilege of purchasing tickets for the annual Christmas dinner be extended to members who had resigned during the last three years"—anything to fill the hall for the holiday celebrations.

Adding to the ongoing despondency, we lost a universally admired member when M. O. Hammond died suddenly in October at the age of fifty-seven, apparently of a heart attack. Sandra Gwyn wrote glowingly of him, "The earth has seldom produced a more honourable and upright character." His last journal entry ends in mid-sentence suggesting

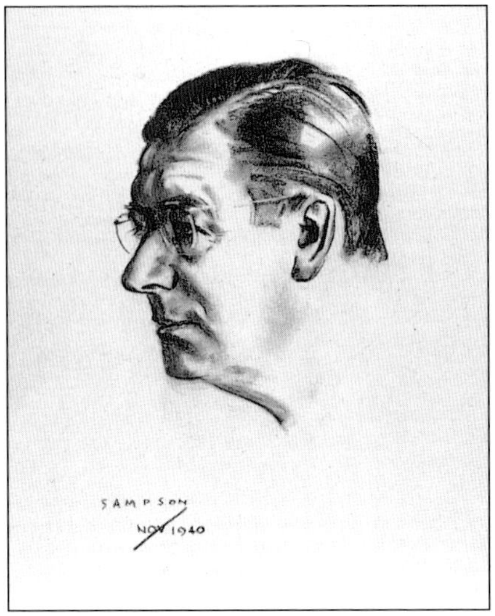

H. Napier Moore, President, 1934–1936. (J. E. *Sampson*)

that the pen had fallen from his hand as he wrote. Having read his daily journals covering twenty-six years, when I reached that last entry, I too felt a sense of personal loss.

But life at the club went on. At the annual meeting that month, Napier Moore was named the next president. The hot topic had to do with acquiring a beer and wine license at a cost of $100. Speeches were limited to two minutes, but unfortunately, no one had thought to place a limit on the number of times a member might speak. The chairman of the house committee stated firmly "that he would rather see members drink beer openly than go to the cellar and drink something much stronger." His approach carried the day. A motion that the club should apply for a license was carried by an overwhelming majority. It would be another twenty-one years before a liquor licence was obtained.

One of the more useful gifts to the club was acquired in 1935: a fairly large round oak table, intricately carved with symbols of animals around its border donated by member Jack Ridpath of Ridpath's Fine Furniture. To this day, it is a focal point at the club—a place of choice when looking for somewhere to sit with a drink before dinner. As one new member was told, "If you're feeling shy, just sit down at the round table, listen to the conversation for a minute, and then state firmly 'I disagree.' You'll be fine."

A long-standing problem resurfaced that year and was finally put to rest, albeit uneasily. It had all started in 1922, when Roy Mitchell proposed the purchase of a valuable set of six magnificent baroque viols. This was duly done with the help of several club members and the viols were placed under lock and key in the club library where, as Defries noted, "moth and rust doth corrupt." But Hart House was also claiming ownership and many adversarial letters were exchanged on the matter over the decade. By 1932, the viols turned up at Hart House. Its warden, Burgeon Bickersteth, claimed that they had been given to the House by the Massey Foundation, although he acknowledged that the club was part owner. He asked the club to pay a portion of the insurance, which it did for a time. He then offered to buy the club's share for $800 and the club, "with sniffs," agreed. The viols are still at Hart House, safely ensconced in a proper display case and now valued, some say, at over $100,000. Bickersteth's role in the affair has an interesting aside. According to club records, he was a member for three years in the early twenties, although decades later he claimed in a letter to Defries that he had never been one. Perhaps the unpleasantness of the "viol affair" had left him with a memory lapse.

Club members had made some use of the viols when they had access to them. Members of the Conservatory String Quartet—Elie Spivak, Harold Sumberg, Donald

Fred Housser (centre) with Lawren Harris (left) and Judge Frank Denton, 1934. (*Arthur Lismer*)

Heins, and Leo Smith—had played on them at a special concert. Leo Smith, according to his biographer Pearl McCarthy, loved the collection's viola de gamba, and played it frequently. Sometimes he would take it home and keep it protected in a bedroom of its own, "with curtains drawn to prevent drafts and a very light eiderdown plus a Shetland shawl ready for changes of temperature and humidity."

In early June, Canadians learned that Ernest MacMillan and Wyly Grier were to be knighted by King George V, joining members Sir William Mulock, Sir Edmund Walker, and Sir Frederick Banting who had preceded them in receiving this honour. The granting of royal honours to Canadians had been dropped by the federal government in 1919 but revived in 1934. Knighthoods, not surprisingly, gave these men added prestige and more clout in their respective disciplines. There is an amusing story—possibly apocryphal—that has been handed down in the club about the honours. According to artist Franklin (Archie) Arbuckle, a member phoned Grier's home not long after Grier was knighted, and asked for him. His wife answered, saying with distinct formality, "Wyly is busy, but Lady Grier will take a message."

President Moore sent a circular to members later that month telling them he had received a letter from a friend who had sailed to England with the D'Oyly Carte and related how the company had sung the praises of the Arts and Letters Club. "It isn't the hall. It isn't the fireplace. It isn't the dingy-curtained stage. It's the spirit of the members that warms them." Then, having softened up his readers, Moore went on to remind them that the club is unique in all ways but one. "The exception is in the matter of financial worry. We shall end the current club year with a heavy deficit on operation costs."

Adding to the ongoing gloom of the Dirty Thirties was the death of journalist Fred B. Housser, an art critic who had been a member since 1922. Four years after he joined, he published *A Canadian Art Movement: The Story of the Group of Seven*, a book that created quite a stir in the art world, as did Newton MacTavish's *The Fine Arts in Canada*, published about the same time. Charles Hill has written that both exemplify "how the debate about art in Canada was transformed into a debate about Canadian art." Housser and his wife, Bess, were ardent theosophists, as were Arthur Lismer and Lawren Harris. Scandal had ensued two years before Housser's death when Bess divorced Housser to marry Lawren Harris, who had also been recently divorced. Fortunately there was no bitterness on Housser's part since he was then in love with painter Yvonne McKague, whom he married. But it was all too much for Toronto's prim society. MacCallum, one of the Group of Seven's most ardent supporters, was particularly vehement in his disapproval and told Harris not to even *think* of setting foot in Toronto again. So, the Harrises left for the United States and then Vancouver. Housser was mourned by a heartbroken Yvonne and a host of friends. John D. Robins said that anyone who has been honoured to know Housser "cannot despair of humanity."

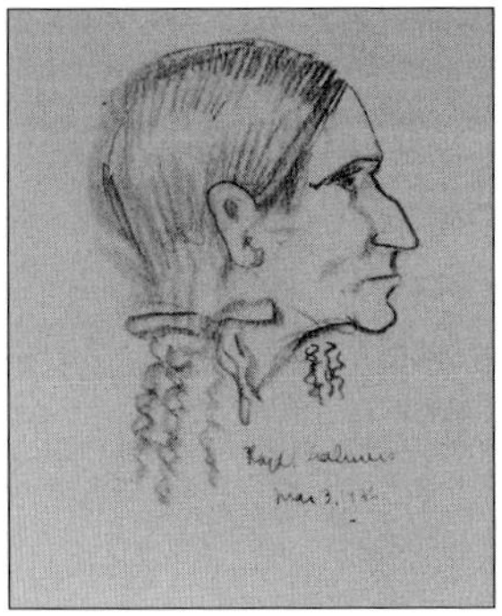

(Above) Grey Owl. (*Floyd Chalmers*)

(Right) Grey Owl at the club, 1936. (*Arthur Lismer*)

In March 1936, a rather famous Englishman—perhaps infamous is a better word—arrived at the club: Archibald Delaney, otherwise known as Grey Owl, a Metis identity he had adopted after arriving in Canada. He had been touring through this country, the US, and England speaking to fascinated audiences about his Beaver Lodge in Saskatchewan. Gordon Snell, in one of his *Hysterically Historical Rhymes*, described Grey Owl as follows:

> He dyed his hair the deepest black
> And with a hide thong tied it back
> He tried to walk the Indian way
> And learned to speak in Ojibway.

Grey Owl, then in his late forties, was the guest of his publisher, Lovat Dickson. Our members were delighted to meet the much-publicized visitor and three of them produced quick sketches of him, copies of which hang near the front door. One was by publisher Floyd Chalmers, who, for an amateur sketcher, managed to produce a pretty fair likeness. Hugh Eayrs noted Grey Owl's visible discomfort that day, perhaps because his false identity was about to be revealed. Grey Owl died two years after this visit to Toronto, and then the story of his deception was made public.

So Grey Owl's pose as man of mystery
Was very soon consigned to history.

"Smells Nice," *Maclean's*, May 1, 1936.

There is a club in Toronto composed of artists, literary men, musicians and actors. In addition to meeting daily for lunch, they put on shows for their own amusement.
The other night, the artists gathered to paint scenery. They had been told that a pail of sizing would be left for them in the basement cooler.
For an hour they worked frantically, sizing flats and canvas.
But the paint wouldn't "take."
They found out why when the housekeeper went down next morning to get the day's supply of soup.
They had picked up the wrong pail.

It was about this time that a few artists met to paint some scenery for an upcoming stage production. They had been told that a pail of sizing had been left for them in the basement cooler. For an hour they worked frantically, sizing flats and canvas, but the paint wouldn't "take." They found out why the next morning, when the housekeeper went downstairs to get the day's soup. They had picked up the wrong pail! It's likely that the painters were working on sets for that year's spring revue, "Date Pudding."

Charter member Ivor Lewis was named club president in October. Earlier that year he had won an award at the Dominion Drama Festival for the club's entry, *The Poacher*, a Welsh play by J. O. Francis. He went on to win the best actor award the following year for the club's production of *Napoleon Crossing the Rockies* by Percy MacKaye. As for his sculptures, his best-known work is the massive bronze seated figure of Timothy Eaton that sat for many years in Eaton's downtown Toronto store where passing shoppers could rub his bronze toe for good luck. This well-loved sculpture has since been moved to the Royal Ontario Museum where it rests in relative obscurity. Sammy Sampson's portrait of Lewis hangs just outside our Great Hall. Vincent Massey summed up Lewis in a delightful rhyming couplet: "There's Ivor Lewis—art and business blent. Sweet are the uses of advertisement."

Ivor Lewis in *Napoleon Crossing the Rockies*, 1936 winner of the Dominion Drama Festival. (*Karsh*)

(Right) Ivor Lewis sculpting the Timothy Eaton statue, 1919.

As that year's Boar's Head drew to a close, Sir Ernest launched into a new and brilliant rendition of "The First Noel," adding sparkling improvised interludes between each verse. It was the beginning of a hallowed club tradition. "The First Noel" has since become a highlight of every Boar's Head and Christmas celebration, and many club pianists have tried, with varying degrees of success, to emulate Sir Ernest's musical meanderings.

Trouble lay ahead in 1937. In February, Bob Defries resigned as treasurer, a post he had held with distinction for twenty-nine long years. The minutes suggest that this was entirely his choice. The executive regretted the development, stating that their interpretation of the wishes of the membership differed from his. In any event, they were "distressed to have his resignation." He was asked to reconsider, but declined to do so, although he agreed to continue on the executive for the remainder of the year. In June, in an extraordinary session, the executive discussed a shortage in the spring revue fund—a hefty $842. The treasurer for the fund, a local bank manager, resigned from the club in August, while discussions with the club's bank continued. By October, the club had "accepted the bank's offer of $500 as a settlement." We'll never know exactly what transpired, or why. Defries' devoted service as treasurer ended on this unhappy note.

John Coulter's play, *Father Brady's New Pig*, which the club premiered at the end of the year, helped to lift the club out of its depression doldrums. It was described by Coulter's biographer, Geraldine Anthony, as a short but delightful comedy, "written for the annual New Year's Eve party of an elitist group of the Arts and Letters Club." Coulter, an Ulster native who had recently arrived in Toronto, joined the club the following year and remained a member for forty-one years. With an Irish talent for making friends, he and the club seemed meant for each other. He became the most important playwright in mid-century Canada.

Ivor Lewis, President, 1936–1938.
(*J. E. Sampson*)

Early in 1938, Bert Brooker was named editor for a new issue of *The Lamps*. With the help of twenty-nine of the club's leading writers, architects, musicians, and painters, he produced an elegant, well-written magazine. It had a large format with twenty pages of essays, poems, paintings, and drawings, and a handsome cover designed by Eric Aldwinckle. The issue contained one particularly amusing note announcing that a second ping-pong table had been installed in the basement, in what is now the space occupied by St. George's.

The club lost a valued member in September when Arthur Lismer left for New York City to head up the Fine Arts Department of Teachers College, Columbia University. A farewell dinner was held in his honour. An active, always enthusiastic member since 1911, Lismer's sketches of club events and his fellow members—more than sixty—are his priceless legacy to the club.

When it came time for the next annual meeting, Sammy Sampson became president. The English-born lithographer and painter had arrived in Toronto in 1913 and later linked up with fellow member Chuck Matthews to form Sampson Matthews Ltd., a firm well known as innovators in colour printing and design, especially in the silk-screen process.

From left: Distinguished visitor Noel Coward with Napier Moore and Gus Bridle, 1937.

Within the club, Sampson's most important legacy was the magnificent painting of twenty-eight members enjoying themselves during an afternoon in the club's courthouse quarters. Sampson also produced eight of the presidential portraits—including his own.

The next issue of *The Lamps*—the last for many years—appeared early in 1939, again edited by Brooker, who also designed the cover and contributed the partial script of a play. There was a particularly amusing piece, "On Being Clubbable," by the redoubtable Hector Charlesworth. "Those clubs more pretentious than ours," he wrote, "those enjoying large, impressive establishments, eventually become more and more like mausoleums. The modesty of our resources has saved us from that fate, has banished exclusiveness." Other contributors included Eric Aldwinckle, Sir Ernest MacMillan, and Jesse Middleton.

The club entered two plays in the Ontario Regional Drama Festival trials that year. One was Campbell Duncan's *The Dark Orchard*, which won two awards for the club—best Canadian play and best-acted play. Duncan, a journalist, had by then been a club member for nineteen years. The other entry was Bert Brooker's *The Dead Should Sleep*. That play must have died on the vine soon afterward, but Brooker's multifaceted career was succeeding in several other directions—as an abstract painter, lecturer, editor, novelist, and highly successful advertising executive. He seemed to do everything well. (Three years earlier, his novel, *Think of the Earth*, had won the first Governor General's Award for Fiction.)

All this faded into relative insignificance as the country teetered on the brink of yet another war. A difficult decade was drawing to a dreadful close. For a few weeks in May we celebrated our ties to Britain as we welcomed the shy young King George VI and the radiant Queen Elizabeth to Canada. But in June, as a quiet forewarning of horrors to come, Ottawa turned away from Canadian shores 907 German-Jewish refugees fleeing persecution in Nazi Germany on the liner *St. Louis*. When asked how many European Jews should be granted asylum in Canada, a senior Canadian official declared, "None is too many." Most of the passengers gained temporary sanctuary in Europe until the Nazi take-over, when many became victims of the Holocaust. On September 10, 1939, three months after these refugees had been refused entry, Canada declared war on Germany. The first convoy of troops and supplies left for Europe six days later.

J. E. Sampson, President, 1938–1940. (*J. E. Sampson*)

Architecture

The A in LAMPS stands for architecture. Professional organizations such as the Toronto Society of Architects and the Ontario Association of Architects existed in the club's earliest days, but architects also needed a social setting to meet kindred spirits, enjoy varied interests, and make business contacts. Architects could enjoy music while musicians could argue design.

Architects played a formative role in the founding of the club; architect William Langton was its first president. He would open meetings with beer in hand and "call for an opener"—hence the corkscrew in his coat-of-arms.

Eden Smith established innovative arts-and-crafts-style homes in Toronto. He also renovated the courthouse clubrooms—the jury room became the library and the judges' chambers became the kitchen. In 1911 he, with other club architects, created a fifty-ton Ohio sandstone fireplace on the south wall, converting the courtroom into a great hall that became the focal point of club activities. The members' entrance was on the south side of the building "near the manure heap of the adjacent stables of No. 1 Police Station"—now a sculpture garden commemorating the site of Toronto's last hanging.

Other architect members had successful careers in a fast-growing city, including Henry Sproatt, Ernest Rolph, Jules Wegman, Ford Howland, Allan George, and Walter Moorhouse. Howland's greatly admired St. Anne's Anglican Church opened its doors the year the club was founded. Moorhouse joined the club in 1912 and remained a member for sixty-five years. He and Allan George were responsible, in 1937, for the design of the Toronto Stock Exchange on Bay Street, a structure noted for Charles Comfort's dramatic seventy-four-foot carved stone frieze across its facade.

Sproatt and Rolph found us our new home at 14 Elm Street. Both belonged to the St. George's Society and both were charter members of our club, and they had just completed Hart House for Vincent Massey. With Eden Smith, Sproatt, and Rolph all on our executive, renovations were soon underway—from basement washrooms, to the kitchen, to the splendid Great Hall. The building has been designated by the city as "historically significant."

By 1920, thirty of the 150 club members were architects. Alfred Chapman was one. With Robert McGiffen he designed Knox College and the Princes' Gate, and also designed the handsome east wing of the Royal Ontario Museum. Professor Eric Arthur, who inspired three generations of students, joined in 1924. His masterpiece book, *Toronto: No Mean City*, established him as the city's leading preservationist whose dedication helped prevent the wanton destruction of some of Toronto's finest early buildings. He and fellow architect Tony Adamson established the Architectural Conservancy of Ontario.

One of the club's highlights came in February 1925 when the architects organized a special dinner, nicknamed the Architects' Revenge. Members were asked to wear "a blue tie, navy blue suit, an old temperance badge, anything else that would approximate the colour of a blueprint." The evening's menu was a "building permit" on a "blueprint" initialled by W. R. The following are a few choice items from it: Mock turtle soup to be poured while hot thoroughly coating the inside surface; roast veal and dressing to be filled in, with the layers to be not over twelve inches in depth; Virginia ham, hot baked, free from sap, shakes, or other imperfections; brown gravy, first quality, Cabot's stain; and green peas, to be separately placed and carefully embedded in mashed potatoes.

To cap this tongue-in-cheek amusement, Jules Wegman presented a blueprint for an Arts and Letters Club cathedral at an estimated cost of "$4,350.00 dollars, plus architect's fees." It included a twenty-five-by-fifty-foot office for Gus Bridle, with library and private street entrance.

Martin Baldwin joined the club in 1927 and collaborated with artist members on numerous Toronto buildings. Art deco motifs designed by J. E. H. MacDonald and his son, Thoreau, graced Baldwin's iconic skyscraper, the Concourse Building on Adelaide Street. The MacDonalds also designed the lobby of Baldwin's Claridge Apartments, with what architectural historian William Dendy called "the most beautiful reception hall in the city."

After World War II, young architects eager to establish themselves were joining the club. Robert Fairfield stands out for his design of Stratford's Festival Theatre—first the tent in 1953 and, four years later, the permanent building—for which a Massey Medal was awarded. Other members who pioneered a new Canadian modernism included William Fleury, John Layng, George Robb, Ronald Dick, Howard Chapman, Ernest Annau, and Gordon Adamson.

A memorable dinner was held in 1995 to honour town planner, heritage activist, and author Tony Adamson. The Great Hall was packed. Members, friends, and colleagues came to thank him for a lifetime devoted to the preservation of our architectural history. Tony was then a spirited eighty-nine. His co-author Marion McRae sat at the head table. Adamson was a member of the club from 1934 until his death in 2002. In 1998, the late Eric Arthur was similarly honoured at another jam-packed dinner.

Throughout the club's first century, several architect-designer members have served as president. Following Langton was Barry Cleveland in 1932; Alfred Chapman in 1940; Walter Moorhouse in 1949; and Norman McMurrich in 1980. In 1998, designer Margaret McBurney, co-author of several books on social and architectural history, became our first woman president. Eight years later, another designer and Ryerson professor Lorna Kelly became the second.

Scott James, recently retired managing director of the Toronto Historical Board, joined the club in 1997 and soon assumed the duties of club archivist. Rollo Myers, a committed heritage activist, won the Arts and Letters Award in 2001. He later became Ontario's governor for Heritage Canada and now serves as manager of the Architectural Conservancy of Ontario. In 2006, architect and heritage activist Catherine Nasmith became the Conservancy's president. She also won Heritage Canada's Journalist Award for her electronic newsletter, *Built Heritage News*.

Professional disciplines under the architecture umbrella now include heritage conservationists, architectural historians, urban planners, landscape architects, and interior designers. Many have played significant roles in club life—chairing the architecture committee (Hugh Westren, John Sullivan, Mark McBurney, and others) and arranging lectures for LAMPS week. Most recently, Robert Glover served as vice president (house).

John Blumenson

CHAPTER 3

Another War—Another Peace

1940–1958

Heading to war again
Support for the arts
Celebrating fifty

When Germany invaded Poland in September 1939, Canada found itself once again at war. It would be a war unlike any other. As they had done in 1914, young men lined up to enlist at the the armoury on University Avenue, but this time there was no cheering, no assumption that it would all be over by Christmas, no colourful parades, no choruses of "Rule, Britannia!" The last war was still fresh in everyone's memory. This one was being met with quiet resolve.

As the forties began, the city settled down to business—the business of the war, which was, of necessity, at the forefront of everyone's mind. The cultural life of the city proceeded quietly. *Saturday Night* stated in 1940 that "visiting the ROM's Chinese collection and attending the Anglican Church of St. Mary Magdalene to hear Healey Willan's two choirs were the only things worth doing in Toronto." But that was not entirely true. Contradicting the old adage that when the cannons roar the muses are silent, a great deal was going on in all the arts, although seldom making headlines. This was the first war to be waged in the age of broadcasting; as radio and film conveyed its actuality, artists quickly converted its sounds and images into creative work. There was a demand for new music, significant literature, and meaningful theatre, all of which produced a creative confidence and an unprecedented sense of the importance of culture.

Jack McLaren painting a war scene c.1940. (*John Fleetwood-Morrow*)

Within the club, however, it was business as usual. The executive discussed membership categories and other somewhat mundane matters, and the usual lament about arrears in fees surfaced once again. The treasurer, now

George Pepall, announced another bitter blow, "a dash of aloes in the cup"— the CBC's decision to discontinue its rental of the Great Hall would deprive the club of extraordinary revenue that had amounted to more than $3,000 the previous year. (The juice of the aloe plant is "a nauseous bitter purgative" or, in this case, "a bitter experience.") This loss, coupled with that "hardy annual" fees arrears, presented a bleak picture. But the good news was that the spring revue, Napier Moore's "Old Skit Bag" had brought in a welcome $1,000.

An unusual guest at the club that fall was William Patrick Hitler—the Liverpudlian son of Adolf Hitler's half-brother whom his Uncle Adolf referred to as "my loathsome nephew." William Patrick served in the US Navy during the war and changed his name after he was discharged. In 2005, his life story was aired on the History Channel, acknowledging publicly for the first time his relationship to the dictator.

William Patrick Hitler, November 1939.

Charter member Alfred Chapman was named the next president. Known as "Chappy" to his friends, he was a gentleman of unfailing courtesy, devoted to the club and its traditions. His architectural legacy included the Princes' Gates, the Harbour Commission building, Havergal College, Holy Blossom Temple, and the handsome east wing of the Royal Ontario Museum, now somewhat overwhelmed by the recent addition on the north.

In all likelihood, the bottom line improved after the club staged John Coulter's *Holy Manhattan,* a sentimental look at an Irish immigrant in New York. Coulter had lived in New York briefly before settling in Toronto. The play reflects nostalgia for his Belfast roots. He wrote that "emigrants who leave their own country after they reach, say, twenty"—

(*Above*) Alfred Chapman, President, 1940–1942. (*J. S. Hallam*)

(*Left*) Royal Ontario Museum east wing, designed by Alfred Chapman, c.1933. (*William James*)

John Coulter, 1941.

Hugh Eayrs, 1928.

he was now fifty-two—"are likely to remain exiles rather than immigrants to the end of their days." *Holy Manhattan* became the basis of his novel, *Turf Smoke*, and, in 1955, CBC-TV's *Come Back to Erin.*

The club lost one of its leading literary lights that year when Hugh Eayrs died of a heart attack at the age of only forty-six. Bright, charming, and enthusiastic, he had worked hard and played hard. As president of the Macmillan Company of Canada for the previous nineteen years, Eayrs had become the best-known book publisher in the country. He had been president during the scandal in 1924 when Florence Deeks, one of the company's authors, sued H. G. Wells for plagiarism in his *Outline of History*—a suit that dragged on for years. On a more personal note, A. B. McKillop, in his engaging book about the Deeks affair, *The Spinster and the Prophet*, claims that Eayrs "had an affinity for the bottle, and in the end the bottle bested him." He had "often relaxed over more than one drink at the Arts and Letters Club—a place where minds could meet, and, when it suited their fancy, men could be boys."

Throughout the forties, the club continued to be a place where musicians gathered with publishers and writers, and a good mix of painters, architects, and theatre people, to chat, to relax, and on occasion to perform. Cellist Marcus Adeney joined in 1940, as did the twenty-two-year-old Godfrey Ridout, who went on to forge a career as a composer, teacher, writer, and conductor. Rex Battle, best known for his CBC radio show *Singing Stars of Tomorrow*, joined three years later, as did Lucio Agostini, remembered for his music in the National Film Board's *Canada at War* series. Composer-educator Arnold Walter, who was immersed over the next quarter century in building the Conservatory's Opera School and the University of Toronto's Faculty of Music, also joined at that time. Other new members included organist David Ouchterlony, voice teacher Ernesto Vinci, Leslie Bell—founder and director of the famous Leslie Bell singers—and Sammy Hersenhoren, a Toronto Symphony Orchestra violinist and CBC conductor for *The Wayne and Schuster Show.*

In February 1941, our Nobel laureate, Sir Frederick Banting, died in the crash of a Hudson bomber over Newfoundland. He had been on his way to England to look into the state of medical research there. Sadly, his celebrity status as co-discoverer of insulin had weighed heavily on him. It turned out that his role had actually been a minor one, and living with this discrepancy led him to lead a turbulent and unfulfilled personal life. Banting's sketching trips with Alec Jackson and convivial dinners at the club during his sixteen years as a member were among the few times he seemed to be truly happy. He died a frustrated and bitter man.

The club's theatre activities continued apace with that year's spring revue, "Never Again," so named because these words had been heard from the director after every dress rehearsal for the past decade. It was booked for a six-night run, with a seventh show added later, the proceeds of which were devoted to the war effort. One of the most popular skits was "Gone With the Wind"—a six-minute version with Napier Moore and Jack McLaren.

Later that year, Mavor Moore's one act comedy, *I Know You*, opened at the club with Lieutenant Governor Albert Matthews in attendance. As Moore later recalled, his play caused "a merry scandal." The action on stage included an "actor" and a "director" engaged in a dispute about the interpretation of the script. Another actor, Alex McKee, had been planted in the audience. As McKee made his angry way to the stage, President Chapman rose in alarm and was already muscling him out, to McKee's gleefully improvised protests, when the "director" (Bob Christie) strode out to assure him it was all just part of the play.

That autumn, with the death of the club's fourth president, Bill Beatty, the club became a quieter place. He had been a colourful, opinionated, and argumentative man—the clenched fist in the Beatty banner reflects the belligerent side of his temperament. But he was also a talented painter and fiercely loyal to his friends at the club.

In November the club held a dinner honouring violist Milton Blackstone, who was retiring from the Hart House String Quartet due to ill health, and Vincent Massey sent a warm tribute to the last of the original four quartet members to leave. Since its founding in 1924 membership in the quartet had changed from time to time, but, with two exceptions, all the musicians were also members of the club. In its earlier years, the quartet had achieved recognition as one of the finest on the international scene. According to Godfrey Ridout, however, while performance standards during the late thirties were rising generally, those of the Hart House String Quartet were not, and in the forties "it finally sank into oblivion."

The war, of course, was in the forefront of everyone's mind. On December 7, Canada declared war on Japan following the attack on Pearl Harbor. Well in time for Christmas, the club sent parcels of food and tobacco to members and to sons and daughters of members in the armed services, and also to our colleagues at the Savage Club in London. These parcels were continued every year throughout the war—a major endeavour, usually under the guidance of the indefatigable Chuck Matthews.

One day in January 1942, a notice signed by Alec Jackson, chairman of the picture committee, was posted at the club announcing another splendid outreach venture by club

Sir Frederick Banting, February 22, 1941, less than an hour before he left on his fatal plane journey to England. (*Dr. F. W. W. Hipwell*)

Carl Pemberton as Marshal Petain, Head of State in Vichy France, 1941 spring revue "Never Again." (*Arthur P. Holden*)

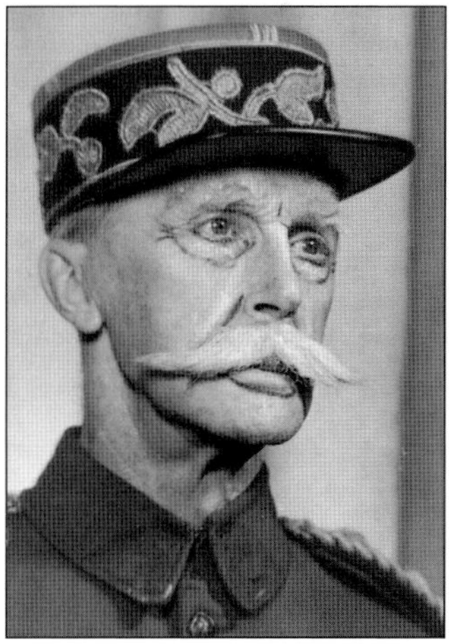

Original Hart House String Quartet, (from left) Geza de Kresz, Milton Blackstone, Boris Hambourg, and Harry Adaskin (*Allan Sangster*)

members. England's wartime government had rounded up German and Austrian "enemy aliens" as a security measure and shipped them off to various Commonwealth countries. Some of the internees at a camp in northern Ontario managed to send a request for art materials, a plea that was answered by club members who used the proceeds from the sale of a donated picture to provide them with paints, brushes, and other items, enough to help the internees cope with their enforced isolation. In thanks, some of their art work was sent to the club and displayed for everyone's enjoyment. What eventually happened to those pictures, however, is anyone's guess.

Versatile musician Bob Farnon joined the club that year, not long before heading for England with *The Army Show*. A genial giant of a man, he was already famous in Canada because of his daily appearance with *The Happy Gang*, then the country's most popular radio show. Earle Grey, an Irish actor and director, also joined the club in 1942, four years before he introduced the Earle Grey Players—and Shakespeare—to Trinity College. In fact, we continued to attract a stream of talented and enthusiastic theatre men, since by this time the club was well known for its adventurous approach to amateur theatre and for its appealing stage facilities. The Great Hall was, of course, another attraction, with seating for a fair-sized audience.

Mavor Moore also joined during the year, thus becoming a third-generation member. His maternal grandfather, James Mavor, had been a well-known professor of political economy at U of T and a man of eclectic interests and great enthusiasms. In fact, George Bernard Shaw was so impressed by him that he named one of the leads in his play *Candida* after him. Mavor Moore's father, Frank Moore, was a curate at St. James Cathedral. Probably his best-remembered antecedent, however, is his mother, Dora Mavor Moore, a pioneer of Canadian theatre for whom the Doras—a series of annual awards in theatre, opera, dance—are named. The young Moore—cut from the same eclectic cloth as his grandfather—went on to become a noted stage and television actor, playwright, professor, TV host, and journalist. He died in 2006.

The first issue of *The Monthly Letter*, in November 1942, announced that the club would close at 5:30 p.m. for the duration of the war. *The Letter*'s title suggested the promise of a regular publication, which indeed it became, although it was not published *every* month. The December issue mentioned the CBC's performance of *Marche Heroique Dieppe*, composed by Thomas J. Crawford "in gratitude to an immortal company" whose men were lost in the single most costly day in Canadian military history, and conducted by Sir Ernest MacMillan. *The Letter* also reported that by this date, twenty-nine members were on active service, seventy-four had sons or daughters serving, and six had lost sons. After going to press, member Flying Officer G. Stevenson Cartwright was killed. A graduate of U of T and a Rhodes Scholar at Oxford, he had joined the club in the mid-thirties.

George Pepall, President, 1942–1945. (*J. E. Sampson*)

The Monthly Letter reported in February 1943 that Bob Chapman, RCAF, had also been killed in action. Although never a club member, he was the son of recent past president Alfred Chapman and the brother of Howard, Francis, and Chris. Howard was a conscientious objector who served his country by driving ambulances through the war zones of Europe and the Mediterranean.

One morning in May, John Coulter came across an article in *The Globe and Mail* describing how the British Council was spending large sums on the arts and promptly decided that Canada could well do the same. The very next day, he headed off to the Arts and Letters Club where members gathered around to discuss his ideas. There were cries for "action, action!" But building up enthusiasm was one thing—getting action was another. First he met with our president, by now George Pepall, and our secretary, Harry Tedman, who suggested that he appear before the executive, which he happily did, urging that the club sponsor a gathering of all the arts to press for government support for their activities. Such a step, however, warranted a special meeting with the executive, which eventually led to a special general meeting of the entire club at the end of June. By this time the "old guard" had stirred up considerable dissent. The club's cherished privacy would be destroyed! Public funds should *not* be used to spoon-feed the arts! And so on. In the end, an advisory council of twelve was set up with Marcus Adeney in the chair—and this became the next hurdle.

The advisory council pondered this weighty matter for almost a year. In the meantime, interest in the project was beginning to stir outside the club's walls. Newspapers and magazines featured the debate, public lectures were held, letters to the editor were published, and panel discussions on radio were aired. Coulter, with difficulty, held onto his patience. Today, when one reads his memoir, his exhausted sigh seems almost audible.

Meanwhile, life at the club continued quietly. Napier Moore and Chuck Matthews were busy lining up volunteers to greet visiting servicemen arriving at Union Station. Those who expressed an interest in the arts were warmly welcomed at the club or at the homes of members. On another front, Squadron Leader Dr. Harvey Doney, then in charge

Artist airmen on arrival in UK, c. March 1943. In front, left to right: Edwin Holgate, Charles Comfort. Standing, left to right: Paul Goranson, Carl Schaefer, and Eric Aldwinckle.

of a convalescent hospital on Bayview Avenue, appealed to his fellow members to donate books for his patients. One of the newsletters mentioned that Eric Aldwinkle, then stationed in England, was lamenting the lack of letters from home—a vacuum that members promptly filled.

During that year, the Canadian War Art Program was set up by the federal government. Thirty Canadian artists—including Eric Aldwinckle, Donald Anderson, Leonard Brooks, Charles Comfort, Charles Goldhammer, Edwin Holgate, Rowley Murphy, William Ogilvie, and George Pepper—were hired to record the story of Canadian forces during the war in pictures. Paintings dealing with the war by other members—A. J. Casson, Syd Hallam, Peter Haworth, and Sydney Hollinger Watson—were also added to the country's fine collections.

By mid-April 1944, the club's advisory council was, at long last, ready to release its report on Coulter's proposal. The report recognized the need for long-term planning of post-war "recreational, educational, and cultural services" and recommended that the club use every means possible to press its claims for the arts upon the federal government. At the suggestion of Edward (Ned) Corbett, the club sent a group consisting of George Pepall, Marcus Adeney, Herman Voaden, and John Coulter to Ottawa to hear what advice Walter Herbert, director of the Canada Foundation, had to offer. Herbert was sympathetic and suggested that they approach the House of Commons Special Committee on Reconstruction and Re-establishment, known as the Turgeon Committee after its chairman J. Gray Turgeon, MP. Three weeks later, back in Toronto, Pepall and the others, along with Nicholas Hornyansky, met at the club with fifteen professional art societies. There was a question as to whether the Arts and Letters Club would become a sixteenth member. "We knew the answer of our old guard would be an emphatic 'No,'" Coulter recalled, "but, fortified by the advisory council's recommendation, our answer was an equally emphatic 'Yes'."

Herman Voaden, c.1950.

But the old guard had not given up. Before long, the "wily saboteurs" struck. They met with a few members of the executive and the advisory council to decide whether "the club, being a social body, could properly be associated with the fifteen professional organizations in visiting Ottawa and presenting a joint brief." And so another meeting was arranged, this one held on a summer evening when, it was assumed, most members of the "yes" faction would be out of town. Twelve men arrived at Pepall's house, and they argued for hours. When the vote was finally taken, five were for supporting the Ottawa venture, five were against, and one member abstained. Pepall cast the deciding vote—against the old guard. He then led everyone to his dining room and his whiskey. On the whole, Coulter wrote, members usually got along. "Apart from differences of opinion and policies—and in my own case with the exception of a few members for whom I had indeed immitigable dislike—we tolerated each other in our quirks and oddities and even managed to convert all into the bantering leg-pulling amenities of civilized intercourse and pleasant club-fellowship."

At last, on June 21, after more than a year of hard work and dogged determination, Coulter led a group of sixteen major cultural organizations from Toronto on their great "march" to Ottawa (no doubt by train), bringing "the battering ram of their combined briefs" to the federal government. The briefs made a remarkable set of documents that outlined the strengths and weaknesses of Canada's cultural life. Pepall, with Voaden, Adeney, and Garnard (Rick) Kettle presented the club's brief. Ernest MacMillan spoke for

George Pepall, 1942. (*Arthur Lismer*).

(*Below left*) Paul Robeson lunching with Bridle at the club, 1944.

(*Below right*) Yousuf Karsh at lunch, February 1944.

Canadian music and musicians, and Forsey Page for the Royal Architectural Institute of Canada (RAIC). Meetings and discussions to further this initiative continued at the club.

In September, the internationally renowned actor and bass-baritone Paul Robeson was a guest at the club, introduced by Alfred DeLury. Robeson had just completed a highly successful two-year run as Othello and was in town to sing with the Toronto Jewish Folk Choir at Massey Hall. Racial bigotry was still all-too prevalent at the time—black soldiers, for instance, had rioted in 1941 at Toronto's Palais Royale dance hall when they were refused admittance to hear Earl "Fatha" Hines' black swing orchestra. But the club welcomed Robeson warmly. Other private clubs of the day would not have done so.

Vincent Massey was at the club that year, home from his post as high commissioner in London. "I went back with joy to my old haunt," he wrote in his memoirs. When lunch was over, George Pepall rose to say, "Gentlemen, I introduce you to the tenth president of the Arts and Letters Club, and the first Canadian in Great Britain." Massey found it difficult to respond. "I had to get myself under control before I could say how touched I was at the welcome."

On May 8, 1945, the war in Europe finally came to an end with Germany's surrender. There was a mixture of great joy and profound sorrow around the world. In Toronto, at Yonge and Queen, an ecstatic crowd burned Hitler's effigy, while others, equally excited, surged through the streets, singing and waving as they piled onto any vehicle that moved. The liquor control authority had attempted to keep the lid on celebrations by closing liquor stores and beverage rooms, but celebratory drinks were undoubtedly unearthed by the determined. No one, however, forgot what this victory had cost. The *Toronto Daily Star* of the previous day had estimated "forty million casualties on both sides—in killed, wounded and captured...after five years, eight months, and six days of strife that overspread the globe." Then, on August 6, the United States unleashed the nuclear age by dropping an atomic bomb on Hiroshima, followed by another three days later at Nagasaki. An estimated 300,000 people were killed by the two bombs that led to Japan's surrender on September 2.

Of the fifty-one club members who had served in the armed forces, two had lost their lives and one, James Meikle, had been a prisoner of war. Most of the others found their way back to 14 Elm Street, sure of a warm welcome and hoping to enjoy once again the camaraderie and comfort offered within its walls. They found that the club had changed very little. Randolph Macdonald, after enlisting in the photographic section of the RCAF and serving with the invasion forces in Germany, stepped through the front door on his return to be greeted by one fellow who said cheerfully, "Hello there, Ran! Been away?"

By this time, the club had already attracted an impressive lineup of young radio actors, writers, interviewers, and producers, many of whom had been producing work of remarkable quality throughout the war years. Among them were Andrew Allan, Bernard Braden, John Drainie, Bud Knapp, Fletcher Markle, Lister Sinclair, Vincent Tovell, and Tommy Tweed. This influx of talent continued after the war, but few remained members for long. While they all shared an unbridled optimism and energy, many eventually became impatient with the slow—some thought stodgy—pace of the club. Others were just too busy.

Meanwhile, Marcus Adeney, John Coulter, Earle Grey, and Herman Voaden were busy trying to put theatre on a national and professional footing by creating a Canadian theatre council. According to Maria Tippett, however, this venture never got beyond meetings at the Arts and Letters Club and the preparation of a manifesto written by Voaden.

At that year's annual meeting, Ettore (Mazz) Mazzoleni became president. A prominent Toronto musician who had just been appointed principal of the Toronto Conservatory of Music, he was also MacMillan's brother-in-law. Post-war ebullience abounded. The singing of the constitution under the direction of Fred Silvester and George Lambert was particularly "spirited," and Gus Bridle signed copies of his just-published *The Story of the Club*, in which he had modestly omitted his own biographical sketch from those of the other past presidents. A copy was given to each member and additional copies were available for $1.50.

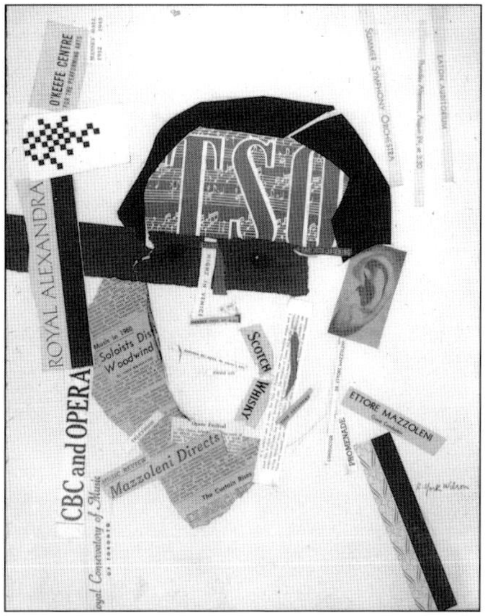

Ettore Mazzoleni, President, 1945–1947. (*R. York Wilson*)

Things began looking up in December for the broader cultural initiative. The discussions that had been continuing since the summer of 1944 finally came to fruition with the formation of the Canadian Arts Council (CAC), created expressly "to win governmental recognition of the arts." Herman Voaden was its first chairman, and Rick Kettle, D. M. LeBourdais (Banting's *bête noir*), and J. Murray Gibbon (enthusiastic general publicity agent for the Canadian Pacific Railway) were named members at large.

The club's theatre contingent was still going strong and, as always, attracting members who wished to take part in or simply enjoy whatever appeared on the club stage, be it a spring revue or a new play. In March 1946, the club produced John Coulter's *Oblomov*, an adaptation of an Ivan Goncharov novel. The play went on to receive international acclaim but garnered little notice in Canada. In the meantime, Coulter and others were still hard at work promoting the idea of a Canadian National Theatre. Representatives

Scene from John Coulter's *Oblomov*, 1946. Eric Aldwinckle as Stolz and Mary Ericson as Olga. (*W. E. Humphreys*)

from local theatre groups invited by the club to discuss this ambitious proposal packed the club lounge one day that spring. Coulter had also invited his friend, legendary British director Tyrone Guthrie, to play a role in the project. Although Guthrie did offer to bring his production of *Peer Gynt* with Ralph Richardson to Canada, nothing came of it. An incensed Dora Mavor Moore wrote to Mavor about the club's initiative. "Such things make me mad," she fumed. But, according to Mavor, what really angered his mother was Guthrie's "wasting his interest in Canada on the chimerical notion of a national theatre, sprung fully armed from the brow of the Arts and Letters Club." Dora certainly hoped for a national theatre for this country, but she didn't think it was likely to happen with the club in charge. She was a feisty cultural activist—Lister Sinclair described her as "an amiable steamroller"—who later founded the New Play Society, directed, produced, and raised funds for new Canadian plays, and became a legend in her own time.

At the annual meeting in October 1947, painter Fred Haines, principal of Ontario College of Art, became president. He was then at the height of his career, having recently shaken the foundations of the seventy-five-year-old Royal Canadian Academy of Arts—then seen by many as "a creakily venerable institution"—by resigning as its president and thus attaining a moral victory that led to the rewriting of its constitution. But he was less adventuresome when it came to his own paintings and other social issues. His art would be considered decidedly conventional today, and his attitude to women painters was sexist in the extreme. Doris McCarthy, having tried unsuccessfully three times to be admitted to the Ontario Society of Artists, approached Haines for help, but he seemed only amused at her temerity. Surprisingly, it was Alan Collier who came to her assistance; finally, she was able to "proudly sign OSA after her name and attend the monthly meetings at the Arts and Letters Club with all the greats."

Fred Haines, President, 1947–1949. (*J. S. Hallam*)

No sooner had Haines taken office than the club embarked on its annual outreach endeavour in aid of the Savage Club in London, whose members were still coping with shortages of food and other necessities. Food rationing during the war had been bad, but after the war it was terrible—even bread was often unavailable. With the country in a shambles and its economy shattered, Britons as a whole were overcome with a tremendous war weariness. Small wonder that the men of the Savage Club were overjoyed to receive bounty from Canada. It was no small achievement to assemble all these delicacies—"everything from soup to nuts"—along with soap and towels, which were still scarce throughout Great Britain. All this was done with great enthusiasm and good cheer, and shipped to England in dozens of packages, each sent to an individual recipient, since regulations forbade sending foodstuffs in large containers. In all, 125 "Savages" enjoyed a marvellous Christmas dinner that year.

In April 1948, members turned out in droves one evening to celebrate the club's fortieth birthday. Gus Bridle, "Fellow Member Number One," was master of ceremonies. He was in top form as he summed up forty successful years "from nomadism to the garret, to the defunct Assize Court behind Police Station No.1—then to Sproatt's transfiguration of old St. George's Hall, Elm Street." Contented members lapped it all up. Of course, no one could foresee that for the next several decades the club would settle into a comfortable but somewhat lethargic existence. Whom the gods wish to destroy they first send forty years of success.

The club remained very much a man's world, but within this masculine sphere it was exceptional for its egalitarianism. One went to the club to say hello to the men at the round table in the lounge and then, after a while, saunter into the Great Hall and settle in at one of the long oaken refectory tables for a chat and to catch up on the news, or

Owen Staples, July 1932. (*M. O. Hammond*)

perhaps to make a business contact—but generally it was just to have a pleasant time. The calibre of the meal was of secondary importance. "One went to the club for the wit not the vittels." A businessman might find himself deep in conversation with a musician, an artist, or an academic who had wandered over from the university. There were even a few lawyers, doctors, and engineers in the company. No one knew, or even really cared, if his luncheon companion was renowned, or rich, or accomplished, just as long as he could manage an intelligent conversation. That was key. But there was always one lurking hazard, as one member cautioned: "It is the better part of wisdom in the Arts and Letters Club never, during the lunch hour, to agree to anything, and more particularly, never to agree to do anything that you are suddenly asked over the shoulder to do."

Certainly egalitarianism was evident when it came time for the annual spring revue and, with little enticement, writers, actors, painters, and musicians all showed up to lend a hand. The 1948 production—the club's fourteenth—was directed as usual by the talented but often irascible Napier Moore. It would be his last. This being the year of Toronto's conversion from 25-cycle to 60-cycle electricity, the revue was aptly titled "Sixty Cycle; a Sort of Hydro-phobia—or Light Entertainment." A favourite tale is told of one difficult and noisy rehearsal—whether it was for this production or another of the many revues that Moore directed—when he suddenly roared, "How many sons-of-bitches are directing this show?" In the silence that followed, Carl Pemberton's voice was heard from back stage, saying, "Only one, Napier, only one."

Walter Moorhouse, President, 1949–1951. (*Adrian Dingle*)

The efforts of the CAC and others nationwide were finally rewarded in 1949 with the formation of the Royal Commission on National Development in the Arts, Letters, and Sciences—usually referred to as the Massey Commission after its chairman, Vincent Massey. That year, too, highly respected journalist Willson Woodside joined the club. He had sounded early warnings on the rise of Nazism in Germany in the thirties. During World War II, he had served as the foreign editor of *Saturday Night* and had broadcast every weeknight on CBC radio with his analysis of the war news and political affairs. But we lost Owen Staples, "painter of Canada's past," who died that year. A few months after his death, the club mounted an exhibition of thirty-five of his pastels. For more than sixty years he had been an artist for the *Toronto Evening Telegram*, but was retired without a pension, having rarely been allowed to sign his work. (In 1917, the *Telegram*'s founder, John Ross Robinson, had donated hundreds of Staples' historical pictures to the Toronto Public Library.) The works in this club show had all been produced in the last years of his life, incredibly, after a stroke had paralyzed his right arm and he had taught himself

Boar's Head procession, 1953. (*Alan C. Collier*)

to use his left. All were sold. Those works that remained in his studio were given by his family to public museums and galleries, to be enjoyed by everyone. "There are so many things more important than money," said his daughter.

In October, architect Walter Moorhouse was named president. He had begun his career with Sproatt and Rolph, the pair who had so skillfully designed the club's Great Hall thirty years earlier. In no time, he and others were happily following Chuck Matthews' lead in putting together yet another Christmas package for the Savage Club. When the ecstatic Savages learned that turkey, roast ham, mince pies, Christmas cake, Christmas pudding, chocolates, apples, and cheese would soon arrive, they cabled Matthews to express their "joy, glee, delight, thankfulness, and gratitude.... God bless you all."

Arts and Letters men also enjoyed a fine Boar's Head feast that year. They "sang merrily, ate sumptuously, and then said hail and farewell" to Bessie Webster, the club's cook and "mother emeritus," who was retiring after twenty-five years of devoted service. "Under Mrs. Webster the club has enjoyed peace, prosperity, and honour, even among the Philistines." Members presented her with a purse holding a generous $2,000. Mrs. Webster later donated to the club a handsome silver ladle, engraved with the club logo. It is still used to dish out the legendary manhattans at the yearly Boar's Head. The decor for Mrs. Webster's last dinner was, fair to say, unusual. Walter Coucill, a man never short of bright ideas, had decorated the Christmas tree that year. Then, in a burst of silliness, he had hung it upside down in the Great Hall. In his words,

> Let's paint it pink, and tie a bow
> And then string pretzels in a row
> Or, better still, upend the thing
> Suspend from ceiling with a string
> When friends come in, won't they look neat
> With suction cups tied on their feet?

During the fifties, Toronto became one of the fastest growing cities in North America. With this growth came tumultuous cultural change—rock and roll, jazz, folk music, Elvis Presley, and television. On the classical side, Glenn Gould arrived on the scene, along with renowned singers such as Lois Marshall, Jon Vickers, and Maureen Forrester. Art galleries were popping up throughout the city showing works by exciting young artists, while theatre-lovers welcomed the Crest, where *Spring Thaw*, an annual revue similar to the club's, became wildly popular. The city was offering limitless possibilities for everyone who loved the arts. "Toronto the Good" was becoming "Toronto the Interesting."

Television, of course, was new and exciting, with many creative Arts and Letters men leading the way. At the club, however, life continued on its comfortable, quiet, and private path, remaining a haven from all that was happening outside its doors—which was just what its members wanted. Not that it didn't offer enticing amenities as always, but it was no longer the only show in town.

The club continued to attract new members, including some of the country's leading musicians. Opera director Herman Geiger-Torel joined in 1950, as did band leader Horace Lapp, who was often heard on CBC radio. His writings included a music column for *The Monthly Letter* during the sixties. Within the next few years orchestra conductors Boyd Neel, Mario Bernardi, and Walter Susskind also became members. Given the number of fine musicians who might walk through the club's doors on almost any day and the frequent formal and informal musical performances during these years, it's perhaps not surprising that one of them, a teacher at the Conservatory, was occasionally heard to mutter grouchily, "I have to deal with music all day—why do I have to listen to it at the club?" But most members counted their blessings.

Highlighting the theatre scene as the fifties began was John Coulter's *Riel*, the first published work, Coulter said, that showed Riel in a good light. Produced by the New Play

Society with Mavor Moore in the title role, it was a huge success. Merrill Denison called it "the first Canadian play of genuine stature." Gordon Alderson, in a tribute to Coulter at the club, said that it would be "impossible to estimate the impact *Riel* had upon the Canadian people, so powerful and so subtle has it been."

In March 1950, the *Toronto Daily Star* ran a lengthy article by Gus Bridle that, in true Bridle fashion, dealt with several disparate club topics. He discussed at great length an event at which Chuck Matthews had demonstrated "colour-camera pictography" to "an audience of art-goers.... He showed his personalizations to a club that chronicles many arts." Within the next few paragraphs, Bridle managed to drop the names of at least a dozen other members, then continued with a rambling discussion of "Ivor Lewis, Eaton Co. director, now retired; only artist in Canada ever a big store director...and bubbling over with arts when he joined the ALC." After more of the same about other members, Bridle ended his article with an obituary for Richard Tattersall, one of the city's leading organists and piano teachers. Few men have had as extensive—and certainly as incongruous—an obituary as did Tattersall, thanks to the incomprehensible Bridle.

Northrop Frye, the renowned Biblical scholar, consummate essayist, and authority on Shakespeare and symbolism, attended the club's monthly dinner at the end of April. He had been a member for only a year or so, his sponsors being Ned Pratt and Barker Fairley. But Frye seemed unimpressed with what he found there, recalling in his journal that "most of the Arts and Letters membership is just a lot of overweight Babbitts. Very few university people belong, not that that's a bad thing." Nonetheless, he maintained his membership for another five years.

While cultural life in Toronto was becoming more enticing daily, the world outside our Canadian borders had yet to settle down. In June, the Korean War began, and within five days, Canada sent three destroyers to join the United Nations forces. In July, the country sent an air transport squadron. And there was more to follow....

Gilbert Jackson became president in 1951. A respected economist, "he had an acute and penetrating mind which nonetheless found humour, even in economics." He served as advisor to the governors of the Bank of England some years later, almost certainly the only Arts and Letters member to do so. When he died in 1959, his funeral was held at the club. Decades later, during one of the club's frequent financial crises, someone was heard to exclaim, "Gilbert, thou shouldst be living at this hour. The building committee hath need of thee!"

Gilbert Jackson, President, 1951–1953. (*Cleeve Horne*)

Lunch at the club, October 1, 1952, with Scott Carter in the right foreground.

John D. Robins. (*Arthur Lismer*)

In January 1952, Vincent Massey became the first native-born governor general of Canada. Not everyone in the country approved of the appointment, but Prime Minister Louis Saint Laurent vigorously defended it, as did Massey's fellow club member, B. K. Sandwell, who composed some memorable doggerel to mark the occasion:

> Let the Old World where rank's yet vital,
> Part those who have and have not title.
> Toronto has no social classes
> Only the Masseys and the masses.

Two months after this event, music was the main attraction for a special ladies' night. *Opera Back-Stage* featured scenes from familiar operas done "first in the modern manner of restrained gesture and fidelity to the score, and then in the exaggerated style of conventional performances of a few decades ago." It was staged by Nicholas (Niki) Goldschmidt, Herman Geiger-Torel, and several guest artists.

In the September *Monthly Letter*, an item entitled "Below the Belt" reported that "public enemy number one, alias high cost of living, dealt the denizens of the club a sock on the jaw...when the lunch tariff was raised from 70¢ to 75¢." The October *Letter*, on a happier note, announced that, thanks to Alan Collier's creative energy, club artists had presented a show of "Members by Members," and its success had prompted a ladies' night, arranged so that "fair visitors" could also enjoy these portraits. John Robins, who had been a member since 1918, "personally conducted the ladies from picture to picture with felicitous comments upon both artist and subject. The only time when he showed any embarrassment was when he came to his own portrait and then he did seem to be at a loss for adequate words." Robins was a remarkable man, according to Frye's biographer, John Ayre. Part black, he had "worked his way out of a poor family in Kingsville, Ontario, as a railway porter and labourer, eventually earning a PhD from the University of Chicago in German philology.... He had a fascination for folk literature which was then considered academically eccentric in North America." Robins did not publish many scholarly papers and was looked down upon by professors at other colleges. Not so by Barker Fairley, who counted Robins among his many friends. Fairley's daughter, Ann Schabas, remembers evenings in the forties when Robins would entertain informal gatherings at their home, telling Uncle Remus stories from the deep south—in dialect. "But despite fits of gloom," Ayre goes on, "he was probably the most popular teacher at Vic."

Gus Bridle with Ernest MacMillan, 1944. (*John Fleetwood-Morrow*)

Just five days before Christmas, Gus Bridle died. He had been in hospital for a month after being hit by a truck while crossing Bloor Street. Anthony Stephenson wrote of his death, "Something strange and colourful and spontaneous has disappeared from the world." And from the club. He had devoted his life to supporting artists and artistic endeavours. His writing style was—to put it kindly—uneven. Novelist Wilfred Eggleston described it well: "Sometimes it would soar into the empyrean, sometimes it bogged down into almost formless sentences. But it had character." For his columns in the *Toronto Daily Star*, Bridle would fill endless pages of paper with cryptic hieroglyphics that only one linotype operator could decipher. On instructions from the *Star*'s publisher, Joseph Atkinson, his columns were never to be edited—and they never were. Sometimes that was very evident! (His more incomprehensible sentences occasionally appeared in the *New Yorker* as comic filler.) Eggleston remembered Bridle as "a legendary figure, with a crown of unruly white hair framing a lined and wrinkled face." His funeral was held at his beloved club. Music for the occasion was the slow movement from one of Healey Willan's violin sonatas, played by Elie Spivak with Willan at the piano. In his eulogy, Jesse Middleton said,

L. A. C. Panton, President, 1953–1955. (*R. York Wilson*)

Robert Fairfield, architect of the Stratford Festival Theatre. (*C. A. G. Matthews*)

> One man had the vision, the energy and the determination to bring this club into being. In all the highlights of achievement in this club over forty and more years, one man stood in the shadowy background seeing his most fanciful dream come true: Augustus Bridle. And to the grief of us all, this eminent friend of all dreamers, this noble spirit beloved by all his associates, is struck down in the wild traffic of this crazy time, while still young in heart—at eighty-three.

L. A. C. (Alex) Panton, an English-born artist and "a jovial companion at the club's long tables," became the next president in April 1953—the first year that the annual meeting was held in the spring. He too had come to Canada as a young man and established himself as a painter. In time, his works hung in the National Gallery and the Art Gallery of Ontario (AGO), and he became an inspiration to artists and art students. In the words of Paul Duval, his landscapes were "some of the most remarkable in Canadian art."

That spring, the Stratford Festival was planning its first season. A young architect, our own Bob Fairfield, designed the immense tent that was needed to cover the thrust stage. There is an interesting story about how he was engaged. The Festival's director, Tyrone Guthrie, asked Ned Corbett if he knew any architects, and Corbett replied, "My son-in-law." When Guthrie met Fairfield he asked, "Have you ever designed a theatre?" "No," said Fairfield. "Good," said Guthrie, who had been looking for a fresh unbiased architect and decided that Fairfield was the one. Fairfield also designed the Festival's permanent theatre, which opened four years later. This magnificent building received the 1958 Massey Gold Medal for Architecture and, in time, became an icon recognized worldwide. More than forty of our members have been actively involved at the Festival over the years. Bob Christie played important roles in the early years and Lou Applebaum made a lasting contribution with his fanfare that still heralds the start of each performance at the Festival Theatre.

At the end of March 1954, Toronto's first subway opened—from Union Station up to Eglinton—making the trip to the club easier for members living in the far reaches of north Toronto. At about the same time, the southern stretches of Yonge Street were becoming known as the "sin strip."

In April, the club happily—and no doubt surprisingly—found itself the beneficiary of an unusual bequest from the estate of Mabel Shaw. Her will instructed that two-sevenths of her estate (which amounted to more than $22,000) be paid to the club "toward the purchase and erection of a new club house." Today this bequest would be worth almost eight times as much. Since it wasn't spent as directed, and since there is no record of how it was spent, one is left to assume that it went into the general coffers. And one wonders why this unusual bequest at all? Shaw's husband had never been a member of the club, and she would not have been allowed inside club doors, except on very special occasions.

As Alex Panton welcomed members to that year's annual meeting in May, he announced, "This is a shareholders' meeting," and then proceeded to elaborate:

> A shareholder's meeting is a democratic device to allow every member of an organization to actively participate in its management by listening once a year to a recital of decisions and events which it is too late to undo, and presenting criticism and instructions for the future, which it is the secret intention of the executive to ignore. The Arts and Letters Club has followed this pattern religiously for many years and I have too much regard for tradition to attempt to change its habits. Now...it is the duty of the president and the officers to render an accounting of their stewardship in such terms of humour and guile as will delude the shareholders into believing that what has been done was for their sole benefit and delight. Time has hallowed this practice of embalming the dullest and driest facts of prosaic achievement in a shroud of evasive witticisms so that members are deceived and seduced into a state of inert and silent admiration and respect for a dead and empty past for long enough, at least, to allow the officers and executive to escape unscathed. I trust that they and I are able to do so again tonight.

To the present day, Panton's words ring a bell with every member who has loyally and, with varying degrees of enthusiasm, attended the club's often lengthy annual meetings.

That fall, Chuck Matthews brought members together once again to pack and mail parcels of Christmas cheer for the Savage Club, including two "goodly Canadian hams." (Even nine years after war's end, England was still suffering shortages.) Their secretary, George Baker, wrote an effusive letter of thanks that was published in *The Monthly Letter*. In it, he launched into a discourse on the meaning of the word "ham," from Ham, son of Noah, down through the ages to the ham actors who have done Hamlet to death in the twentieth century. The club rejoined with "Only a Savage Chief with the imagination of a Chef steeped in Bacon could wax lyrical about the homely ham of culinary commerce.

Cleeve Horne, President, 1955–1957. (*R. York Wilson*)

Vincent Massey with President Cleeve Horne, monthly dinner, November 24, 1956. (*John Fleetwood-Morrow*)

We should like to send a royal haunch of Canadian venison to this accomplished Baker to see what sort of a dainty dish of poesy he would serve us by way of Grace after Meat!"

Cleeve Horne, a well-known portrait painter, was named president somewhat sooner than anticipated, due to Panton's sudden death at the age of sixty. So it was Horne who applied for a liquor license for the club. According to Ontario's Liquor License Act, this application allowed for objections from concerned citizens. Two weeks later, one such objection was received: Two ministers at Carlton United Church pointed out that,

> within a stone's throw of this club, there are a variety of outlets for liquor, such as Steele's Tavern, Zanzibar Tavern, Bassel's Restaurant.... It would seem to us that the character and atmosphere of the club will not be improved by the granting of this license, and the tendency of persons to join for the sake of the privileges made available, not associated with the original purposes of the club, will eventually be detrimental to it."

Despite this objection, the license was granted. As one member later remarked, "Perhaps the ministers who made the objection were unaware of the original purpose of the club. As the license board files plainly record, the object of the club shall be to promote intercourse."

A defining development for Canada in 1957 was the establishment of the Canada Council, thanks in large part to the Massey Commission. This brought to fruition the earlier efforts of Herman Voaden, John Coulter, Ernest MacMillan, Marcus Adeney, and others. It favoured supporting high culture over low, the professional creator over the amateur, and homegrown culture over foreign imports. In 1958, the CAC became the Canadian Conference of the Arts (CCA). (Its membership now represents more than a quarter of a million artists and cultural supporters across Canada.) Canadians have, to this day, been the beneficiaries of those far-sighted and determined efforts.

Years later, Coulter recalled with gratitude the significant role that President George Pepall had played in the early days of the campaign to get federal support for the arts:

Let us recall the trumpetings,
The callings-together of people
(Of which came expectation

Of Canadian Theatre, Tyrone Guthrie heard,
In unexpected ways
Expectation became accomplishment.)
Trumpetings, comings-together:
Which begat the "Artists' Brief"
Which begat the Massey Report,
Which begat the Canada Council, Which begat
Begetting enough to please
Old midwife George. Take him for all in all,
My man. Businessman!
President of The Arts and Letters Club.

James Wardropper, President, 1957–1959. (*Fred Finlay*)

James Wardropper became president that year. Well-liked and hard-working, "he had slaved on and behind the stage under the genial tyranny of Napier Moore in the club revues," so he was just the man to organize the club's upcoming fiftieth-anniversary celebrations. Membership had reached 355 by this time, including forty-seven life members—men who had been members for at least forty-five years.

In preparation for the celebrations, it was decided to restore Jim MacDonald's tongue-in-cheek coats of arms. These banners, produced in relative haste in 1920 just in time for the club's first dinner at Elm Street and treasured ever since, were in very poor shape. The task of restoring them was given to Bob Hubbard who set to work with the help of his son Jim (not yet a member) and Irwin Forster, a glass manufacturer. Forster, who had no fear of heights, climbed carefully up the thirty-foot ladder and took down the crumbling beaverboard panels. They were found to be beyond repair, so the Hubbards made copies by tracing the original designs and transferring them to new masonite panels. The work took months. Finally, again with the prowess of Forster, the new banners were installed where the originals had been, just in time for the jubilee celebrations.

Leading off the festivities in March 1958 was a week of five special luncheons, one for each of the LAMPS disciplines, and each chaired by a past president from that discipline. For the first four, there were no designated speakers, just talk and reminiscing. On Monday was the writers' luncheon with Jesse Middleton presiding. Joining him at the head table were Floyd Chalmers, John Coulter, Willson Woodside, and Ned Corbett, all chatting happily about the club's early days. On Tuesday was the architecture lunch, chaired by Walter Moorhouse, with a head-table lineup of some of the country's leading architects, including Anthony (Tony) Adamson (son of Agar), Eric Arthur, and Forsey Page. Wednesday was the artists' day, presided over by Fred Haines. At the head table were A. J. Casson, Fred Challener, Alan Collier, Charles Comfort, and Gustav Hahn. The musicians' luncheon on Thursday featured Healey Willan in the chair, flanked by Horace Lapp, Ettore Mazzoleni, and Geoffrey Waddington. Willan reminisced about the days when membership fees were ten dollars and luncheons cost twenty-five cents, then paid tribute to Carl Pemberton, a banker who had been his sponsor and who "had kept more musicians out of gaol for debt than he would like to say." The highlight of the week was the stage lunch on Friday. Bob Christie read John Coulter's "Fellows of Infinite Jest: a Scribble of Personal Regrets," a moving look at the remarkable men who had founded the club—beginning, of course, with Bridle:

> When I think of them
> I think of Gus, the twister
> Of words. He could not bear
> To write or speak the unadorned simple word:
> Could not forbear to fantasticate
> The word, heaping, festooning, entangling
> The word with words, words, words
> Till he lost himself at last
> In a trackless wilderness of words
> Wandering among his stars.
> But this was the public Gus fabricated by Gus.
> I shall remember instead that other Gus
> Who sat at the end of the board-room table
> At executive meetings. Old Father Gus,
> Silent, unsmiling, far away
> In a room above a court house
> Alone, forlorn,
> A straight old jack-pine
> Stark in winter.

These five luncheons became the model for what has now become an event celebrated every year in February and known as LAMPS week.

The final event in this week-long celebration was a grand dinner on Saturday. Given our members' love of fanfare, their admiration for the club's founders, and their enjoyment of a good party, it's not surprising that nearly two hundred of them streamed through the front doors that chilly March evening to look back with satisfaction on a half-century of remarkable achievements. Even a number of charter members were on hand as Wardropper took to the podium. "Our founders wanted a club different from all the other clubs in Toronto," he claimed. "These other clubs had seemed and even looked more or less alike, rather institutional and sticky, as indeed they remain today." He concluded with the following wise and prophetic words: "Those who come after us may do it better or do it worse but we can be sure of one thing—they will do it differently.... Dynamic leadership is required, tolerance to new and different ideals is essential, but we look forward to the future with confidence that the essential characteristics will be preserved and enriched." As George Locke had prophesied in his first address as president in 1910, the Arts and Letters Club had not, even after fifty years, become an "upholstered" club—nor was it likely to become one. Looking ahead fifty years with the club's centennial in mind, Ned Pratt summed it all up nicely with:

"The End," sketch celebrating the club's fiftieth birthday, 1958.

A CLUB INVENTORY OF HADES

Composers and apothecaries,
Poets, plumbers, antiquaries,
Bankers with their secretaries,
Home and foreign missionaries,
And writers of obituaries.
Mystics in perpetual trance,
Painters with their disputants,
Philosophers in baggy pants,
Ministers to whom the chance
Had never come in life to dance
Save when the dreadful circumstance
Of death removed their maiden aunts.
Doctors, auctioneers, and bakers,
Dentists, diplomats, and fakirs,
Architects and undertakers.

Baritones and pacifists,
Tenors and evangelists,
Publishers and atheists,
Puritans and classicists
Scrapping with the modernists.

Journalists who slanted news,
Actors who forgot their cues,
And those who never paid their dues.

Landscapers in dungarees,
Chronic luncheon absentees,
Scholars, saints, and Ph.D's.

Rich men, poor men, sages, sots,
Lawyers tying shades in knots,
Pagans, Christians, and what-nots,
Musicians good and bad in spots,
Ruralists and wyandots.

And others not easily classified.

Music

At the initial gathering of the club at the St. Charles Hotel on March 23, 1908, the Toronto String Quartette performed and violinist Frank Blachford played. The importance of music for this nascent organization was thereby clearly established. Twenty of the charter members were in some way allied to music, including Gus Bridle, Hector Charlesworth, Robert Stuart Pigott, Richard Tattersall, F. H. Torrington, J. D. A. Tripp, Augustus Vogt, and Frank Welsman. Other early members include Leo Smith, the Hambourg brothers, Ernest Seitz, Luigi von Kunits, Healey Willan, and Ernest MacMillan. There were teachers, composers, organists, choir masters, singers, instrumentalists, critics, and music patrons. Monthly musicales began in 1910 and, that same year, a boys' choir sang at the first Boar's Head. A thirty-piece orchestra was formed in February 1911 and performed Haydn's *Toy Symphony* under conductor Paul Hahn. Francis Coombs was the first of our many club choral leaders and visiting international musicians such as pianist Arthur Friedheim and violinist Mischa Elman were welcomed. The pattern and quality of musical performance was firmly established.

There were many performances by amateur and professional musicians—often jointly, until the Toronto Musicians' Association forbade such interaction in the early forties. Club members were also well represented in Toronto's performing groups—the Hambourg Trio, the Academy String Quartet, the Adanac Quartet, the New World Chamber Orchestra, the Hart House String Quartet, and the Conservatory String Quartet, all of which played at the club on occasion.

Healey Willan set our constitution to music. He also composed and arranged more than a dozen works—carols, marches, and incidental pieces—specifically for club events. Two of his ballad-operas, *The Order of Good Cheer* and *Theatre of Neptune*, were performed several times. He also composed incidental music for several of the Chester Mysteries—nine performances were staged by the club between 1931 and 1955. Willan was our president for one year (1922–1923), and for over fifty years added illumination to music's place in this "cave of harmony"—a sobriquet for the club coined in 1938 by Hector Charlesworth and Arthur Duncan. The club held a month-long tribute to Willan in 1980, the centennial of his birth. Other musical presidents were Gus Bridle (1913–1914), Ernest MacMillan (1930–1932), Ettore Mazzoleni (1945–1947), David Ouchterlony (1959–1961), Jack Yocom (1967–1969), David Franco (1986–1988), and Ezra Schabas (1996–1998).

There was always a piano at the club. In the first few years it was a rented upright. In 1914, because of the quality and quantity of performances, the club decided to rent a Steinway grand from the Nordheimer Piano and Music Company and, a year later, with the help of Ernest Seitz, wisely purchased it for $1,000. This piano was performed on for more than ninety years by members and visitors alike. It was finally retired in 2005 and replaced by a magnificent nine-foot Steinway concert grand. A smaller Steinway grand (built in 1903) had been donated to us by Clarence Hassard in 1973 and resides in our lounge. In 1995, Jack Yocom gave the club his Baldwin electric organ, which has pride of place in the gallery of our Great Hall. The third floor is home to an electronic keyboard and an old upright.

The club has always been blessed with great pianists for its special events and annual spring revues: Sir Ernest

MacMillan, Reginald Stewart, Scott Malcolm, Reg Godden, Clifford Poole, Gordon Hallett, Horace Lapp, Jack Yocom, Wilf White, Malcolm McGrath, and Ruth Morawetz. Some are composer-arrangers as well. Club choirs have been directed by Francis Coombs, Healey Willan, John Cozens, Malcolm McGrath, Edward Moroney, and Roger Hobbs.

Some post-war special events stand out. The 1947 "Variations on a Theme" featured Willan's *Suite for Fiffle Flutes*, Harry Somers' *Suite for Percussion*, and the Godden-Malcolm piano duo—their final appearance. In April 1950, there was a concert with violinist Sammy Hersenhoren, pianists Gordon Hallett and Bela Boszormenyi-Nagi, and baritone-pianist Niki Goldschmidt accompanying himself as he sang German lieder. In the mid-eighties it was the Arts and Letters String Quartet—violinists Frank Fusco and Gerald Kantarjian, violist Jacob Loft, and cellist Marcel Ray—accompanied as required by pianist David Franco. In 1978, *Faust and Lucy*, by Jim Parr and Malcolm McGrath, was performed, the first of seven opera bouffes. Their last, *The Rivals*, was staged in 1995. Lou Applebaum composed a club fanfare that was premiered in November 1992 by the University of Toronto Brass Ensemble.

Music committees wax and wane as does musical interest, but enthusiastic chairs have ensured a plentitude of musical events by members, visitors, and visiting groups (such as *Les Amis*), throughout the eighties and nineties. Weekly music tables and monthly music club nights became standard fare under John Lawson's fine leadership. These varied programs often showcase young artists or club musicians. Again thanks to John Lawson, the committee commissioned composer Srul Irving Glick to write a song cycle, *South of North*, based on a set of poems by Richard Outram. This fine work was premiered as part of our ninetieth anniversary celebrations before a full house on December 6, 1998, with baritone James Westman and pianist Albert Krywolt.

The club has always been ready to introduce new ways of bringing music to members and there have been two firsts in the very recent past. We have extended our performers to include a member of our serving staff—Todor Kobokov recently gave two fine piano recitals in our Great Hall, and during the LAMPS week in 2006, Stuart Hamilton recorded for future broadcast CBC's *Saturday Afternoon at the Opera Quiz*. The panel—Jim Norcop, Iain Scott, and Stephen Ralls—ably fielded questions from knowledgeable members.

William Krehm, a ninety-year-old visitor to a 2004 music table, remarked that during the twenties and thirties the club was regarded as a "musical Parnassus" because of the crucial influence its members had on musical development in the city, province, and country. Over the past forty years, twenty of our musical members have earned the Order of Canada. Although our Parnassus' peak may be lower in this era of media, technology, and mass entertainment, the club's musical tradition of excellence continues. Krehm had come to the club to hear his clarinetist son Jonathan and his soprano granddaughter Rachel perform in a recital—purely for the joy of making music.

Pat Wardrop

CHAPTER 4

The Comfortable Middle Years 1959–1985

Fun, games, and outreach
Becoming an "old man's club"
Picketing at 14 Elm Street!
Worries, worries

David Ouchterlony, President, 1959–1961. (*Alan C. Collier*)

As the fifties drew to a close, the club settled in to enjoy its comfortable middle years. The conviviality remained, with friendships nourished and business liaisons quietly established, but it was no longer the centre of the city's cultural life. The action was moving elsewhere.

Yet it was still fun to drop in at the club, where spirited discussions were the norm. Annual spring revues remained a tradition; plays were produced periodically; art shows appeared on the walls; members continued to be honoured. In April 1959, the club's leading musicians—Healey Willan, Eli Spivak, Geoffrey Waddington, David Ouchterlony —and a host of others turned out to pay tribute to popular past president Sir Ernest MacMillan. He was then serving on the Canada Council, and was heading off for an extended holiday. That send-off dinner was one of the last events to be presided over by Jim Wardropper.

The next president, David Ouchterlony, took over in May, declaring, as he was sworn in, "This club has never housed the orthodox," a remark that met with a roar of approval from the assembled members. Ouchterlony had an elegant, bone-dry wit—as Ned Corbett found out at lunch one day when he sent a note to Ouchterlony across the table. "What's the name of the fellow sitting beside you?" he asked. The note was shoved back with a scribbled reply: "How the hell would I know? I don't even know your name!"

The members' dinner in November began on a serious note with Charles (Chick) Hendry, a professor of social work, describing the political situation in China. When asked if China minded its lack of recognition by the United States, Hendry replied, "They couldn't care less." Then the entertainment took a lighter tack. Sid Johnson, known professionally as "Sid Lorraine, the Magician's Magician," took to the podium to conduct an auction with the help of our earnest and dedicated archivist Hunter Bishop. On sale were what appeared to be current worthy periodicals such as the *Architectural Review* and *Theatre Arts.* But behind their respectable covers were hidden recent issues of

Hunter Bishop, club archivist (seated) with Raymond Peringer, Archivist Emeritus, 1983. (*John W. Scott*)

(*Far left*) Sid Johnson, aka Sid Lorraine, magician, performing in the spring revue, 1969.

various pornographic magazines, which, to no one's surprise, attracted fantastic bids. The proceeds, of course, went to the club—a noble cause, indeed.

Entertainment at the Boar's Head, held on Boxing Day that year, featured Healey Willan's ballad-opera *The Order of Good Cheer*, about a society founded by Samuel de Champlain at Port Royal in 1609. Decor included moose heads and bear skins hanging in the Great Hall. After the traditional verbal jousting between our president and the president of the St. George's Society—for forty years presidents of St. George's had been honoured guests at Boar's Head celebrations—our esteemed poet Ned Pratt took over and, to the delight of his audience, read his *The End of the Depression*.

By the time the sixties arrived, the membership had reached close to five hundred, and even the financial situation was looking better. At the annual meeting, treasurer Philip Clark reported with a grin that the bar, somehow, had made enough money to make up the deficit of the catering account. Also helping the bottom line were proceeds from that year's spring revue, "Haut Beaux Arts"—otherwise known as "Hobo's Art." A young Jim Hubbard, now a member, was perched high up to the right of the stage throughout the show, pretending to be an Eskimo carver and surrounded by fake Eskimo carvings made by Cleeve Horne out of Plasticine. The next year's revue was "The Magnificent

"The Magnificent Klondike Party," 1961. (*Philip Clark*)

York and Lela Wilson at the opening of the O'Keefe Centre, 1960, in front of York's mural *Seven Lively Arts*.

Klondike Party," directed by Bob Christie with sets by Walter Coucill. Phony hundred dollar bills—"miners' mazuma"—were passed around and the club was decorated as a saloon. Members' wives dressed in skimpy costumes served drinks, and nude paintings by Alan Collier, York Wilson, and other club artists hung on the walls. Pierre Berton and his wife were guests for one performance, with Berton reciting *The Cremation of Sam McGee*. The menu? Small pots of beans, sourdough bread, and champagne.

In May 1961, Ian Cameron, a businessman with a love of singing, was named president. He was "in many charming ways a Highland laird straight out of Sir Walter Scott." There was some memorable fun at the Boar's Head, with a new twist to the jousting between presidents. In reply to Cameron's toast to St. George's, its president, Robert Onions, suggested that all would be well if members of the Society joined the Arts and Letters Club and vice versa. At this point, one of our members, a kilted Scotsman, stood up and, in rich Aberdeen, proposed a toast to the St. Andrew's Society.

Ned Corbett became president in 1963. An educator of note, he had taught for many years at the University of Alberta and played a major role in the founding of the Banff School of Fine Arts. He was also a superb raconteur, "his table talk meatier than the menu," according to *The Monthly Letter*, "and liberally laced with salt and vinegar."

(*Below right*) Ian Cameron (left) and artist-designer Walter Coucill, c.1965

Ian Cameron, President, 1961–1963 (*Alan C. Collier*)

Later that year, Napier Moore died. Members recalled his legendary spring revues, his ongoing advocacy for all things British, and his sense of fun. They also remembered a ditty penned by Christopher Morley after, according to Greg Gatenby, "a healthy night of male ribaldry and excess with Ned Pratt and Moore."

If I don't get drunk in Toronto
It's not because I don't want to
For Napier and Ned
Will put me to bed
So give me another drink pronto!

Ned Pratt died in 1964, only a few months after that bit of fun, and with his death the club lost one of its most popular members. A distinguished professor of English at Victoria College, he had been a club member for more than forty years. Northrop Frye, another distinguished professor of English at Victoria College and one of Pratt's former students and greatest admirers, said of him, "As long as Canada's culture can remember its origin, there will be a central place in its memory for the poet in whom it found its tongue." Pratt had often been in demand as a speaker, in part because he could make people laugh. His favourite pre-prandial grace was "Lord grant us capacity, longevity, elasticity, avoiding obesity."

That spring, an art fraud was uncovered, prompting headlines in the press proclaiming, "Great Canadian Art Fraud." There was much discussion about it at the club, in part because it involved a new member. It all started when a painting purported to be the work of Jim MacDonald was up for bids at a Ward-Price auction. Elizabeth Kilbourn, then an art critic with the *Toronto Daily Star*, rose to demand that auctioneer Ben Ward-Price reveal whose collection the work had come from. Her friend, collector Sheila Mackenzie, shouted, "Those are not J. E. H. MacDonald's, and you know it!" During the resulting chaos, two Ward-Price employees "pushed their way to the troublemakers and demanded their names which were refused." Ward-Price, on the defensive, claimed the disturbance was caused by Communists. But a few days later, the painting was taken to the Art Gallery of Ontario for authentication and proved not to be MacDonald's work. Inspector Jim Erskine of the Ontario Provincial Police, with the help of A. J. Casson, Arthur Lismer, Alec Jackson, Fred Varley, and Charles Comfort (director of the National Gallery), eventually seized ninety-one other paintings purportedly by members of the Group of Seven or by Tom Thomson. All were found to be wrongly attributed. They were being

E. A. (Ned) Corbett, President, 1963–1964. (*Alan C. Collier*)

Poet E. J. (Ned) Pratt at the Boar's Head, 1958.

Marshall McLuhan, 1975.

sold by Ward-Price on behalf of Leslie Lewis, who operated a studio gallery at the back of the auction house, and another dealer, Neil Sharkey, a member of the Arts and Letters Club—albeit for only three brief months. His membership was terminated when he was found guilty and sentenced to one year in prison. Lewis was sentenced to two years.

This was the year that another new member, Marshall McLuhan, communications theorist and professor at the University of Toronto, published his *Understanding Media*, coining such phrases as "the medium is the message," and "the global village." His influence became worldwide, even extending to popular media such as *Playboy* and *Wired*, with the latter proclaiming him its "patron saint." It was also the year that the Beatles arrived in Toronto, to be greeted at the airport by 10,000 Beatlemaniacs. More than 32,000 screaming fans packed their two shows at Maple Leaf Gardens.

But despite the arrival of McLuhan with his startling new ideas, the Arts and Letters was now, it seemed, becoming an "old man's cough of a club"—this according to Mordecai Richler in an article in the *New Statesman*. John Coulter fired off a cheerful rebuttal to its editor. "The jibe has truth—too much for my comfort," he acknowledged, "but would also be true of any club that has existed long enough for once-young members to have grown old. Admitted. Yet, as an elder member of the club, I would like Richler to admit that the coughing old men of the A&L have in their time coughed up a few very important contributions to the emerging artistic life of Canada." Coulter went on to outline many of the club's successful initiatives during its fifty-six years. "But surely I've cited enough," he said in conclusion. "Old man's cough! Surely it deserved a fairer response than a young man's derisive fart!"

Sadly in late November, Ned Corbett died by his own hand from a gunshot wound. He was eighty-two. In failing health for some time, he had been troubled by increasing memory loss. His presidential duties were taken over by Oswald (Oz) Stacey, a successful commercial artist who "carried enthusiasm with him like a banner." He had been holding the fort for Corbett for some months.

Oswald (Oz) Stacey, President, 1964–1966. (*Adrian Dingle*)

The club was quiet for most of 1965, although happenings outside its walls provided much to talk about. One was a police raid in May on the "Eros 65" exhibition at the Dorothy Cameron Gallery on Yonge Street, after which Cameron was fined a steep $350 for displaying obscene pictures. The following year, she lost her appeal at the Supreme Court of Ontario and, in due course, at the Supreme Court of Canada. Other topics of interest in the art world at that time included the debate about the country's new maple leaf flag; the opening of Toronto's spectacular city hall; and Robert and Signe McMichael's gift to the province of a number of paintings and sketches by the Group of Seven, Tom Thomson, and Emily Carr, along with a home to house them—a log cabin located on six hectares of woodland northwest of Toronto. The McMichael collection and the gallery were expanded by the government in subsequent years, and a cemetery was created adjacent to the gallery where five of the Group are buried. Bob McMichael, who joined the club in 1970 and died in 2003, is buried with them. Jim MacDonald and Frank Carmichael are interred elsewhere.

Robin Strachan, President, 1966–1967. (*Tom McNeely*)

In the spring of 1966, Robin Strachan, a leader in Canadian academic publishing, was named the next president. Someone said of him, with tongue in cheek, that "he was trained for the rigours of the Arts and Letters presidency—by having served as aide-de-camp to the Governor of Aden and resident advisor to the Sultan of Hadhramaut in southeast Arabia." His term as president was cut short when he moved to Montreal. Bob Christie described Strachan as "one of the shirtsleeve members, a doer, one who would have pleased not only Augustus Bridle but even Vincent Massey!"

Jack Yocom, President, 1967–1969. (*Cleeve Horne*)

Jack Yocom became president in 1967. He was a man of considerable accomplishment, who carried his academic laurels—an MBA and a PhD—with modesty. He had been a successful editor with *Saturday Night* who left the magazine, along with B. K. Sandwell and John Irwin, at about the time it was sold to Jack Kent Cook. As he was leaving the offices on his last day, Yocom spotted a bust upended in a wastepaper basket. He stopped, took a closer look, and found that it was of the magazine's redoubtable former editor, our own Hector Charlesworth. Serendipity! Yocom picked it up, cleaned it off, and brought it to the club where it now resides atop the mantel in the club library. In his next career, Yocom was soon in the forefront of the public relations field in Canada. At the piano, he always had a hundred tunes at the ready. One of the highlights of his military career with RCAF Intelligence during World War II was the opportunity to accompany the legendary Josephine Baker at an impromptu concert in Brussels. He brought all his talent to the club where—among other things—he became a leading light in more than thirty-five spring revues.

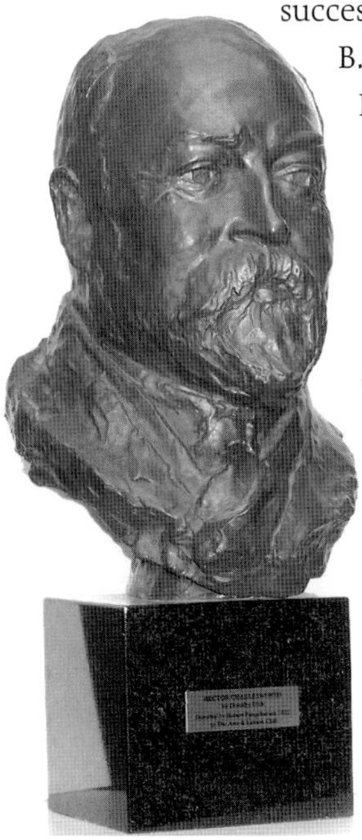

(*Far left*) Bust of Hector Charlesworth. (*Dorothy Dick*)

Jack Yocom playing piano for Josephine Baker in Brussels in the fall of 1944, after the liberation, "with no rehearsal."

Merchant and show biz promoter Ed Mirvish also joined that year. His bargain store, Honest Ed's, had at the time the world's biggest neon sign, and was well on the way to becoming a major Toronto tourist attraction. But he was a theatre owner as well, having bought and restored the crumbling Royal Alexandra Theatre in 1962. He later bought London's venerable Old Vic and restored it, too—for which Queen Elizabeth honoured him with a CBE. Ed claimed that it stands for "Creator of Bargains Everywhere."

At the end of December, Vincent Massey died. According to historian Donald Jones, Massey spent his younger days "cavorting on the stage and spending most of his evenings at the Arts and Letters Club," until a life of public service beckoned. During his fifty-six years as a member, the club was his refuge from the public gaze, where his ready wit and good humour were always welcomed. For two of these years he had served as president. A memorial service was held at Massey College, with a eulogy offered by its master, Robertson Davies:

> He was a man who made an art of life, and had given shape and finish to the seemingly intractable stuff of experience. It was in this, if in anything, that he would have liked to provide us with a personal example. What we do with our lives is in our own care, but he was, by his fostering of this College, putting out a hand toward us, to encourage and to point a way. We, and all who come after us in this place, are the heirs of his spirit.

Horace Lapp, 1955. (*C. A. G. Matthews*)

(*Above left*) Ettore Mazzoleni, Healey Willan, Herman Geiger-Torel, and John Coulter, 1966. (*C. A. G. Matthews*)

Not everyone, of course, saw Massey in this light. Michael Bliss, writing in *Saturday Night*, said that Massey "was one of the more disliked public figures in Canada," and, as some thought, "he could claim privileges and power by virtue of his Masseyship alone." Perhaps. But our members will remember him for his engaging doggerel, his love and support for the club, his spearheading of the endowment and construction of Hart House, his chairmanship of the landmark commission on the arts in Canada, and his help in establishing Massey College.

There were two losses for the club in 1968, both from the music world. Healey Willan died in February, and then, four months later, Ettore Mazzoleni. Mazz was killed in a traffic accident, and, as his friend Horace Lapp wrote, "with no one near to say goodbye except the car ruthlessly bearing down on him." Lapp also recalled how he, Willan, and Mazz had always sat together at the southwest table in the Great Hall. "The old table will never be the same. I'm sure it will understand."

In May, the club celebrated its sixtieth birthday at a dinner entitled "Gus Bridle Memorial Night." Among those present were Bridle's sons, George and Paul. The menu featured "Bridle of Beef, Viking Shiploads of Potatoes, Green Beans Langton, and Bob

Bill Swinton, President, 1969–1970. (*Gerald Sevier*)

Defries Pie with Iced Wyly Grier Cream." Highlighting the evening was the screening of Chuck Matthews' movie, produced in the early thirties and featuring sixty-six early members.

For several reasons, 1969 turned out to be a difficult year for the club. Finances were once more in poor shape, and this motivated an immediate levy of twenty-five dollars per member, along with an increase in bar prices. It was also decided to raise annual dues for resident members from fifty to seventy-five dollars. At the monthly dinner in March, a discussion about finances went on for so long that the evening's speaker, the crusty architecture professor Thomas Howarth, refused to give his prepared talk on Scottish architect-designer Charles Rennie Mackintosh despite a spirited introduction. Howarth's fellow members were not amused. And all this within the first three months of the year.

Still, by the end of May the situation was looking somewhat better. At the annual meeting, President Yocom, in a graceful farewell address, acknowledged that while money was still a problem, it should not be a preoccupation. The incoming president, Bill Swinton, replied in kind. Swinton, a professor of zoology at U of T and a director at the Royal Ontario Museum, was a man with a prodigious knowledge of dinosaurs. As president he introduced the club tie and blazer crest—innovations described by one grouchy member as "the first step on the road to Nazi uniforms." Perhaps Swinton had good reason to see them as dinosaurs too.

Once again, however, the finances took a turn for the worse. In a letter to members that fall, Swinton revealed that the club was, for one reason or another, nearly $10,000 in arrears, and that an astonishing thirty-seven members had recently resigned. Equally disturbingly, he proposed that during October women be admitted to the club for lunch, to help replenish the coffers. "There will be objections, no doubt," wrote Swinton, "to the idea of a woman's foot in the Arts and Letters door—at lunchtime." But he promised that at month's end members could decide whether to continue or abolish this practice. A special general meeting was called for November—and the gloves came off.

It took only a brief discussion at that meeting before the admittance of "ladies to regular club luncheons" was decidedly turned down. As one member said firmly, "I cannot believe that this will add substantially to our funds, and I can see no other reason for admitting them." A second said, "Surely the discovery of new men, their ideas and aspirations, has not given way to mini-skirts, mini-steaks, and mini-smatter-talk." Yet another asked, "Why try to compete with the sin-strip, the topless supper clubs, and the taverns around the corner?" By contrast, members were in favour of another item on the agenda, the proposal of a new club history, "provided it cost no money!" But things got out of hand when the possibility of raising fees took centre stage. The ensuing uproar, due in part to "too much of a mixture of sauce and oratory," prompted the treasurer to suggest that, in future, the bar remain closed when business was to be discussed. Swinton called his friend Jack Yocom the next morning to bemoan the animosity that he felt had been directed at him. He was saying, in effect, "Who needs it?" and decided against serving as president for the customary second year.

John Irwin, President, 1970–1972. (*Cleeve Horne*)

By the time the next annual meeting rolled around at the end of May 1970, life within club walls had settled down. *The Monthly Letter* reported that "the great experiment of sobriety paid off—business was conducted with quick dispatch. A closed bar produced the desired results." Bill Swinton was thanked by the incoming president John Irwin, a well-loved English-born journalist who had been chief reporter for the *Statesman* in New Delhi. After wartime service in the Middle East, he had come to Canada where he worked first for *Saturday Night* and then as associate editor of the *Financial Post*. The club's monetary problems, however, continued. As late as the following October, forty-five members were still in default of paying their dues.

But there were also some bright spots that year. A National Forum on Cultural Policy was held at the St. Lawrence Centre in September, with more than three hundred delegates from across Canada, including seventeen from the club. Mavor Moore was the keynote speaker, with Arthur Gelber and Herman Voaden playing prominent parts. Bridle would have approved.

Another memorable event that year was the appearance at the club of guest speaker Margaret Laurence, one of Canada's finest novelists, who was then serving as writer-in-residence at U of T. In order to deal with the ever-troublesome question of allowing women in the club, she was named an "honorary man for the day." Her topic? "On not being a lady novelist." There are those who say it was her lunch at the club that prompted her remark for *Saturday Night*: "It makes me wild with rage to be described as a female novelist.... You never hear people referring to gentlemen novelists. I'm a novelist and I'm a woman."

From left: Barker Fairley, A. J. Casson, and John Irwin celebrating the fiftieth anniversary of the first Group of Seven exhibition and the club's occupation of 14 Elm Street, October 1970.

Irwin's Executive Committee, 1971. At the table, clockwise from the left: John Irwin, Bob Christie, Fred Kemp, Philip Clark, Peter Teeson, Lou Hartley, and John Gallilee. In the back, clockwise from the left: Pat Hume, Hunter Bishop, Frank Carrington, Elmer Phillips, Gary Hall, Garth Haines, Bill McCoy, and Jack Yocom. Standing at the back on the right: Brent Rowe and John Snell. (*Ron Vickers*)

In May 1971, the club staged Merrill Denison's *Brothers in Arms*, celebrating its fiftieth anniversary and its more than 1,500 performances. First there was a gala dinner, with the author, then in his late seventies, front and centre, enjoying tributes from many members and guests, including Mavor Moore, Dora Mavor Moore, Jack McClelland, Walter Gordon (a former federal finance minister), and several of the original Hart House Theatre cast. After dinner the curtain went up for a fine performance directed by Bob Christie. It was described by Herbert Whittaker in *The Globe and Mail* the following morning as "the greatest tribute paid to Merrill Denison—a provocative writer with a good sense of theatre."

October saw the demise of the *Toronto Evening Telegram* (known to locals as the Tely) after nearly a century as one of the city's leading dailies. Described by Greg Gatenby as "Anglo-philiac, conservative, and down market," the paper had been home, off and on, to several club journalists, including William Deacon, considered one of the most influential book editors in the city's history; Ralph Allen, a war correspondent and novelist; Scott Symons, a reporter and novelist whom Gatenby called "the bad boy of CanLit"; Nathaniel Benson, a poet and playwright of the day; and Burton Richardson, who had served as editor of the paper and would later be an aide to Prime Minister John Diefenbaker. The

(*Above right*) Merrill Denison (left) with Arthur Beemer.

day after the Tely's demise, the first issue of the *Toronto Sun* appeared, staffed by many former employees of the defunct *Toronto Evening Telegram.*

To start off 1972 on a high note, the January members' dinner celebrated the club's fifty-seven years with its much-loved Steinway concert grand. Some of Canada's leading pianists had performed on this wonderful instrument, among them Ernest Seitz, Reginald Godden, Alberto Guerrero, Horace Lapp, Mark Hambourg, Scott Malcolm, and Reg Stewart. Of course, several past presidents—Healey Willan, Ernest MacMillan, Ettore Mazzoleni, and David Ouchterlony—had also been at its keyboard on many occasions, as had virtually every talented pianist in the club. That evening, Jack Yocom played several of the hit songs from earlier spring revues. *The Monthly Letter* reported that "Jack then stroked the Steinway and would have kissed it—had he not been faced with a bunch of philistines." A year later, the club was given a second Steinway grand. This one, built

A. Y. Jackson's eighty-ninth birthday celebration, October 4, 1971. From left to right: Dick Blue (on piano), Spencer Clark, Bob Christie, Chuck Matthews, A. Y. Jackson, Robert McMichael, Garth Haines, and Eric Heathcote. (*Ron Vickers*)

Reg Godden and the club Steinway, 1972

in 1904, was a gift from Clarence Hassard, who had been a club member since 1944. He generously refused the club's offer to purchase it and, as a gesture of thanks, he was named a life member.

The March *Monthly Letter* carried a ditty by Wilf White, who was then serving as house committee chairman, dealing with ongoing concerns about washing the windows in the Great Hall. Some thought it sacrilege to remove the "patina"—which other members recognized as dirt.

I will not rest in this my quest
Until my term is through,
To find the ass who cleaned the glass
And submit his name to you.
His punishment should fit his "grime"
From the club be he ejected,
Or as house committee chairman
May the bastard be elected!

Robert Christie, President, 1972–1974. (*Alan C. Collier*)

At the annual meeting in May, members were greeted with another depressing report from the treasurer. The gloom dissipated, however, when the choir launched into the singing of the constitution, which, no matter how well—or, for that matter, how poorly—it was performed, always managed to cheer the assembled crowd. John Irwin then turned the president's chain of office over to Bob Christie, one of the country's finest actors—and certainly one of our best-looking presidents. His work with the Dominion Drama Festival, the CBC, the Stratford Festival, Ryerson's theatre department, and Canadian Actors' Equity was unequalled, and he is perhaps best remembered for his portrayal of Sir John A. Macdonald in a CBC television documentary. In fact, his career constitutes a history of professional theatre in Canada. Christie also became director of the club's annual spring revues that, according to legend, he agreed to undertake just as long as he could do so without using men in drag. He insisted that women actors be cast for women's roles.

A few days later, the club received an unusual gift—twenty-five long-stemmed clay pipes, framed, mounted, and signed by their original owners. The pipes, presented by the irrepressible Jack McLaren, had been enjoyed during the Depression years by the "inner circle" Birds of a Feather. Gradually, over time, each "bird"—among them Ned Pratt, Fred Banting, Sammy Sampson, Napier Moore, and, of course, Ivor Lewis—had been given one. The pipes can still be seen in the manager's office.

Later that year, members enjoyed "an enchanting evening," with the staging of John Coulter's award-winning *The House in the Quiet Glen*, a light comedy first performed in 1937. Coulter was on hand to introduce the play. They also enjoyed an exhibition of fifty-five charcoal portraits of Pierre Trudeau, the work of Irma Coucill, wife of member Walter Coucill, who was also an artist. At first, Irma, being a woman, was not allowed into the club to see her own show. Then, as an experiment, the executive decided that women would be allowed to come for lunch for one week only. A few members repaired to the Albany Club and other male bastions in protest. This gave Irma the opportunity to have the last laugh. Walter, knowing just which men would not be on hand, invited their wives—and Irma—to be his guests. They gladly accepted and as Irma later remarked, "We had a wonderful time."

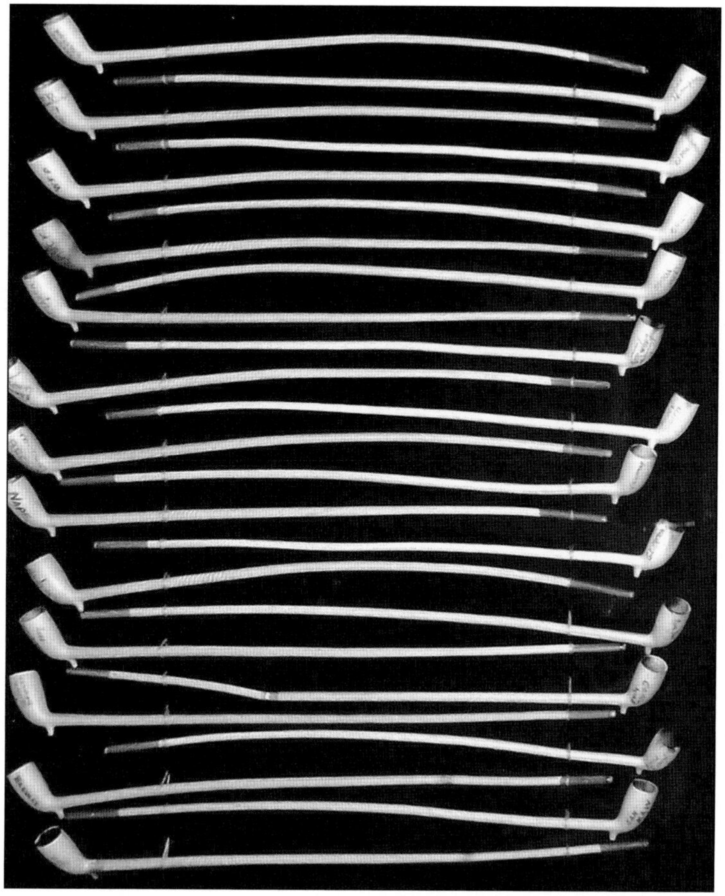

Birds of a Feather clay pipes.

John Kenneth Galbraith once wrote that "meetings are indispensable when you don't want to do anything," so he would not have been surprised that in April 1973, the thorny question of admitting women to membership surfaced yet again and another committee was promptly established to study the question. Committee members were told that because this was an inflammatory topic, the subject was not to be brought up at the annual meeting in May. And so, a leisurely six months later, the committee brought forth its report. To no one's surprise, they had found that admitting women "would not improve the financial position and would irrevocably change the nature of the club." Despite the fact that admitting women would have improved finances, no action was taken. Otherwise, all was relatively quiet on the Elm Street front. Discussions about rent with St. George's surfaced once again during the year. Another committee was set up to discuss changing the lease and, if necessary, retaining legal counsel.

By January 1974, the executive was embroiled in ongoing legal disputes with our landlord. In his report to the members, Bob Christie wrote, "so now our solicitor, having

From left: Paraskeva Clark with Bobs and Peter Haworth, 1963.

The Ontario Society of Artists Jury meets at the club, February 1974. Clockwise from the top: Gerry Sevier, Syd Watson, Cleeve Horne, Al Collier, Doris McCarthy, and A. J. Casson.

written a reminder to their solicitor, is prepared to enter in the Supreme Court of Ontario a motion asking for the landlord's defence to be thrown out, and for judgment to be given. God save the Queen; and bless us every one! Except the lawyers of course."

In March, the club mounted a two-person show of works by Paraskeva Clark (wife of our esteemed treasurer) and her son Ben. In addition to being a talented artist, Paraskeva was also, to say the least, a colourful personality. She had cut a wide swath through Toronto society ever since her arrival in the early thirties—with Ben—as the bride of Philip Clark. Clark had fallen in love with Russian-born Paraskeva Plistik in 1929, while on a trip to Paris to cram for his forthcoming chartered accountancy examinations. (In Paris? To study chartered accountancy?) It's unlikely that anyone who met the outspoken Paraskeva ever forgot her. Certainly her occasional forays to the club on ladies' days and for spring revues were memorable, as were her pithy remarks, recounted by members for years to come. Her paintings now hang in the National Gallery. At the club, the mother-and-son show was described in *The Monthly Letter* as "a fine exhibition that was a tribute to the club"—a surprising remark, since neither was a member.

Philip Clark, in contrast, was quiet and reserved. As comptroller for the Government of Ontario, he had been the architect of the province's retail sales tax, first imposed in 1961. Known as Mr. Three Percent—the tax rate then—he was credited with its success. He also served as club treasurer for fifteen years. It was to thank him for this loyal service that a testimonial dinner was held two months after the mother-and-son show. A big crowd was on hand for the occasion and the mood was upbeat, with Bob Christie in the chair and six past presidents lined up to sing Clark's praises. Jack Yocom lauded with great affection the treasurer's unique skills in dealing with delinquent members. Clark's approach was, according to Jack, along the lines that the guy was still a member and/or had ceased to be a member, providing (a) he paid his fees now, or (b) he didn't pay until next April Fool's Day; or (c) if he stayed out until, say, Christmas, and then if he would consider moving to another city, or (d) if he left his wife, or (e) if he just stayed away—far away. Whatever, it was always a fast shuffle, sort of a "don't-call-us, we'll-call-you" technique—and it worked.

Philip Clark, 1967.

Jack went on to say that he and Philip got really tired of members like that. "In fact," he said, "I nearly invented a president's drink—tomato juice, vodka, and Geritol. We would have called it a Tired Bloody Mary!" Yet, in spite of all these light-hearted reminders, the September-October *Monthly Letter* reported that $4,860 was still owed by the fifty-one members who had not yet paid their dues. By the next month, however, things were looking up, thanks to "the three Johns—Scott, Irwin, and Ingram—who 'hit the JACK pot' with their telephone blitz to collect dues."

At a dinner that fall, the speaker was humourist W. O. Mitchell, author of the *Jake and the Kid* short stories. Mitchell, from High River, Alberta, joined the club that year—to everyone's delight. A born storyteller, he could entertain virtually anyone, on virtually any subject, at virtually any time. He was introduced as an expert on "the sex life of the wild orchid." But he spoke mostly about censorship and about a letter he had recently written to Alberta's Premier Ernest Manning. The premier had publicly declared J. D. Salinger's *Catcher in the Rye* to be immoral, pornographic, and evil, so Mitchell was demanding equal time for local talent. He was sure that much of his own work would top Salinger's in all those dangerous "dirty" thoughts that had so upset Manning and his ministers, and he pointed out that it was grossly unfair for a native son with such qualifications to be so ignored. He insisted that the injustice be remedied. His audience loved it.

Elmer Phillips, President, 1974–1976. (*Joachim Gauthier*)

Elmer Phillips became president at that year's annual meeting. As a singer he had toured widely throughout Canada and Europe with *The Navy Show* during World War II. His post-war training and experience in personnel and business management stood him in good stead in tackling the club's ongoing landlord-tenant frictions. He was, of course, well known on the club's stage where he loved to sing.

Minds on the Move—a series of monthly lunches with speakers (some members, some not)—began that September and continued for many years. This bright idea was the brainchild of Chick Hendry, who soon had members filling the Great Hall. Ian Macdonald, the

Anne Lazare-Mirvish pickets the club, 1975, with (from far left to right) President Elmer Phillips, Ed Mirvish, and David Mirvish.

new president of York University, launched the series with a discussion of his concerns about decreasing academic grants. Bob Christie had collected a number of enticing handouts from the neighborhood for the occasion and mounted them on a poster, which he titled "What a Man Has to Go Through to Get into the Arts and Letters Club." It was a fascinating and wildly amusing reminder of what Yonge Street's sin-strip was before civic "beautification" took over. According to *The Monthly Letter*, Macdonald had arrived at the club after being "safely piloted through the sex jungle of the club's environs." These noontime talks were the forerunner of today's weekly literary and music lunches.

In late February 1975, the club made front-page headlines in the local press—all thanks to Anne Lazare-Mirvish. Her husband, Ed, was to speak about his Royal Alexandra Theatre for a Minds on the Move event. Although Ed had by this time been a club member for eight years, Anne was unaware that the club was a males-only sanctum. She phoned to reserve for lunch. She was brusquely advised that "Women are not allowed." "Who's waiting on tables?" she asked. When she found out that women would be serving, she leaped into action. First she enlisted the help of her daughter-in-law Audrey, and a woman friend. Then she called Honest Ed's department store and lined up one of the store's sign-painters to produce, on short order, three picket signs—all in time for Anne and her two cohorts to picket the club while Ed was talking. When he, son David, and others in the audience walked out the front door they were met by three smiling but determined women bearing placards. Anne's read "Unfair to Speaker's Wives." Another read "Get with it! It's 1975," and "A Man's World. What a Mess!" claimed the third. Not surprisingly, the media were on hand and loved it. But not all club members were amused. *The Monthly Letter* couldn't resist drawing attention to the sign-painter's inadvertent grammatical error. But, when the story hit the front page of the *Toronto Star*, the rest of Toronto had the last laugh.

The November Minds on the Move that year featured Northrop Frye discussing Ned Pratt and his work, and the December one featured Roy Thomson (Lord Thomson of Fleet) telling his audience that "life begins at sixty," or it did for him when he flew to Edinburgh to purchase the *Scotsman*. Thomson also recalled a trip to Moscow, where a dour customs agent asked him the nature of his visit and he promptly replied, "I've come to buy *Izvestia* and *Pravda*." The members' dinner that month celebrated the thirtieth anniversary of the Canadian Conference of the Arts. Some club members were upset to discover women present, including Pauline McGibbon, lieutenant governor of Ontario. Herman Voaden and Arthur Gelber, both of whom were past presidents of the CCA, took part in the proceedings, as did Marcus Adeney, who, had urged our initial participation as chair of the club's advisory council in the mid-forties. Looking back, he mused, "It was a marvellous thing this Canadian Conference of the Arts did for men."

By the end of January 1976, the executive was again exploring outreach ventures. The Toronto Transit Commission (TTC) was threatening to postpone its Art in the Subway project scheduled for the new Spadina line. President Phillips wrote to the chair of the TTC in support of the project, stating that "the arts add substance to man's existence and should be part of his every day life." By that summer the TTC's art project had been reactivated. Three months later, Phillips was writing to Toronto's mayor David Crombie to support another venture—the construction of a new Massey Hall (now Roy Thomson Hall) on Simcoe Street.

J. N. P. (Pat) Hume, President, 1976–1978. (*Cleeve Horne*)

But outreach wasn't the only thing on the minds of the executive. The treasurer estimated an operating loss for the year of $8,000 and suggested a hefty fee increase of 50 percent. Pat Hume, our new president, was embarking on stormy seas. He was an esteemed professor of physics at U of T, with exceptional communication skills. In the late fifties, he had co-presented a series of highly successful programs for CBC-TV, demonstrating and explaining phenomena in physics for the general public. As club president, he had "traded the tranquil world of scholarship for the noisy arena of rent disputes and landlord-tenant squabbles," all of which he handled with dispatch while at the same time encouraging members to savour all the fun and camaraderie that was still to be found within club walls—a *carpe diem* approach to life and arts and letters. No one, however, thought to improve the menus—the usual menu for monthly dinners consisted of nothing more exciting than tomato juice, roast beef with canned peas and, for dessert, apple pie topped with Kraft cheese.

Later that year, Lyman Henderson reported on a two-day meeting held with the Heliconian Club to explore a cultural program for Toronto. The esteemed Arthur Gelber, always a staunch supporter of the arts, chaired both sessions and Mavor Moore was the keynote speaker. "Four hours of discussion generated warmth, occasional heat, and a glimmer of light." There were three concluding observations: there had been an

John Coulter at ninety, 1978.

enormous cultural explosion in Canada reflecting a fundamental sociological change; Toronto was not keeping up its support for culture; and local politicians were still so concerned with primary needs (housing, streets, sewers, etc.) that they were not hearing the voices speaking for the arts.

In February 1978, the club celebrated John Coulter's ninetieth birthday, with the playwright himself on hand to blow out the candles. Glasses were raised and toasts proposed, after which Mavor Moore, Bob Christie, and Sean Mulcahy read from Coulter's works. The CBC filmed the event for later broadcasting to a national audience.

Also that month, Arthur Ament produced a report about the club's building fund. The fund had been established in 1914 with contributions from individual members, but was, by this time, non-existent. Over the years, from time to time, there had been some discussion of additions to this fund, but there had never been mention of its size or its use. Sadly he found that the club had been "in error when it used funds belonging to the building fund to cover operating expenses." Included in his list of donations was the substantial 1954 bequest from Mabel Shaw.

In May, John Morrow, an artist-turned-insurance-executive, became the next president. He too found that the issue of admitting women as members was not going away. Jim Parr alluded to it at the annual meeting in his rhyming report about the recent Boar's Head:

John Morrow, President, 1978–1980. (*Franklin Arbuckle*)

The Boar's Head at so early date
Oh, how can we forgive
The preordaining fist of fate
Or the executive?
But came the night, and came the feast,
And came the time to dine;
The carping and complaining ceased.
Perhaps a star lay in the east;
Perhaps it was the wine.
A proud processional swept down
The decorated hall,
Resplendently in cape and gown,
From Malabar's—the best in town;
The treasurer concealed a frown,

"Please God," he said, "that's all!"
Then song and wine. For man's delight
Is found in wine and song.
No women! Did we do it right?
Was not one voice raised in the night
To ask if we were wrong?
Then Cinderella's old appeal
Was brought to newer Arts
(And Letters), as Prince Charming's zeal
Was seen to touch on toe and heel
But not on other parts.
The evening ended! Who would dare
To shout a loud "Farewell"?
As in December's midnight air
Each prayed his optimistic prayer
To sing one more "Noel."

At the members' dinner in October, the guest speaker was the world-renowned British actor Peter Ustinov, who was on his way to the Stratford Festival to play King Lear. Everyone declared that it was the best—and the wittiest—club dinner in years, with John Sanderson's introduction every bit as memorable as Ustinov's talk, which was later published in a limited edition by Hugh Anson-Cartwright and Sanderson with the title *A Gift of Fortune*. There is a copy in the club library.

John Sanderson (left) and Peter Ustinov, October 15, 1979.

Fun was in the air for a ladies' night in mid-November, when *Faust and Lucy*, a rollicking musical with libretto by Jim Parr and score by Malcolm McGrath was staged. Elmer Phillips was a fine Faust. Bob Christie directed. The show ran for two sold-out performances and—by popular demand—was repeated for an additional two evenings the following January.

A second Parr-McGrath musical, *The Mirage of Figaro*, was produced in January 1980, starring several from the cast of *Faust and Lucy*. And Minds on the Move events continued

Cast and crew of the Jim Parr-Malcolm McGrath operetta, *Rivals*, 1995, directed by Herbert Whittaker.

Eric Arthur (right) with Joe McCulley, Warden of Hart House, 1967.

with a lineup of fine speakers. The first that year was Eric Arthur, whose *Toronto: No Mean City*, is still a "must read" for anyone interested in this city's architectural history. Arthur had chaired the committee of internationally renowned architects who chose the design for Toronto's new city hall. Next, in March, the speaker was Harry Boyle, whose topic was "Let's Deprivatize Canadian Humour and Put it in Sync." Boyle had just completed his term as chairman of the Canadian Radio-television and Telecommunications Commission (CRTC), so he had plenty to say about bureaucratic mumbo-jumbo—and the utter lack of humour to be found in Ottawa. "What has happened to us? Thirty-three cabinet ministers and a well-endowed Canada Council to encourage every vagrant whiff of creativity—and no minister of humour. We live in an age of bawds—and no bards."

The club lost one of its more colourful members that year with the death of R. C. S. (Dick) Blue. In the words of his friend Graham McInnis, Blue was "as unreconstructed a stage Englishman as you'd meet anywhere; complete with checked yellow waistcoat, tweed 'county suit,' bristly United Services Club mustache, pipe, and basset hound.... His general get-up made him about as inconspicuous as a bloodstain on a clean shirt." But he played the piano well. "Many a rye-fuelled social discussion...would be stilled by Dick's sudden slam of the piano lid, followed by a dreamy nocturne or spirited mazurka." Blue endowed a scholarship in the club's name at the Royal Conservatory of Music.

Each year the club commissions an artist to design a record of the executive committee members. This series reflects the evolution of Canadian graphic design over the past hundred years.

Executive List 1920–1921. (*J. E. H. MacDonald*)

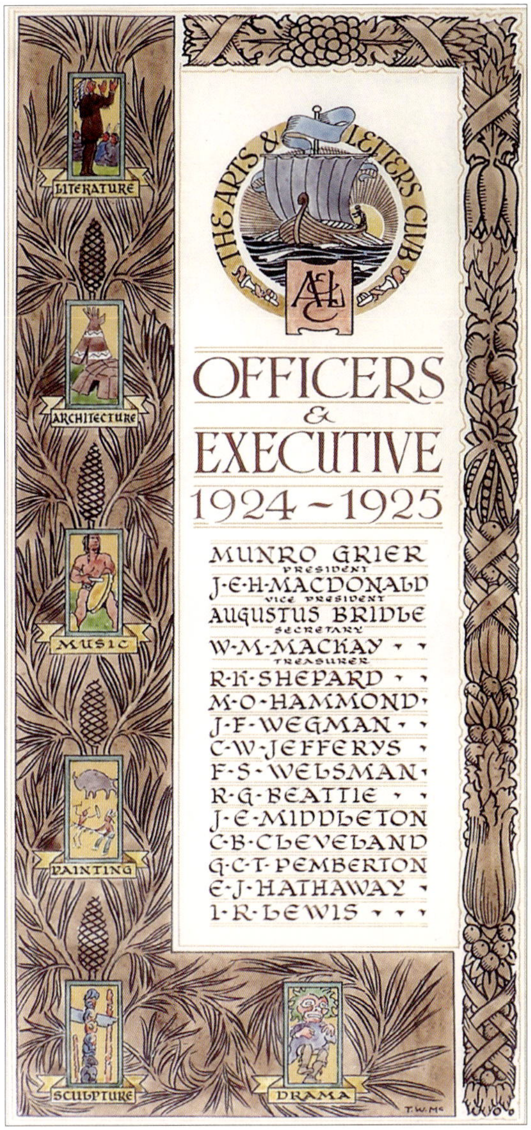

Executive List 1924–1925. (*T. W. McLean*)

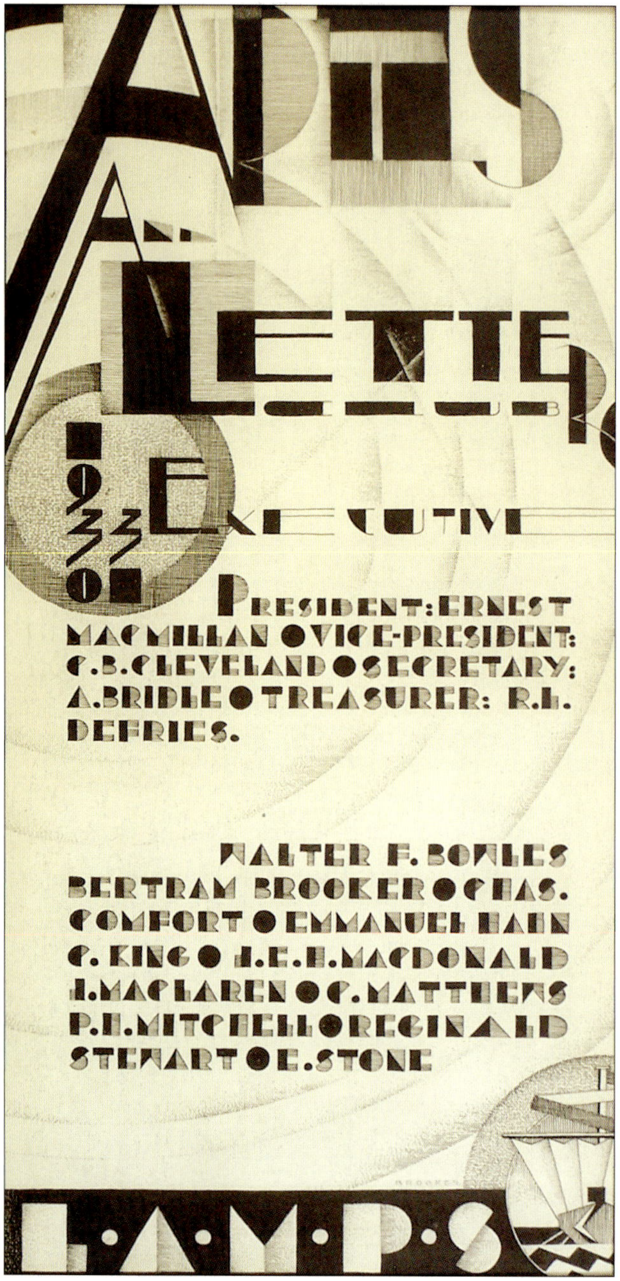

Executive List 1930–1931. (*Bertram Brooker*)

Executive List 1941–1942. (*J. S. Hallam*)

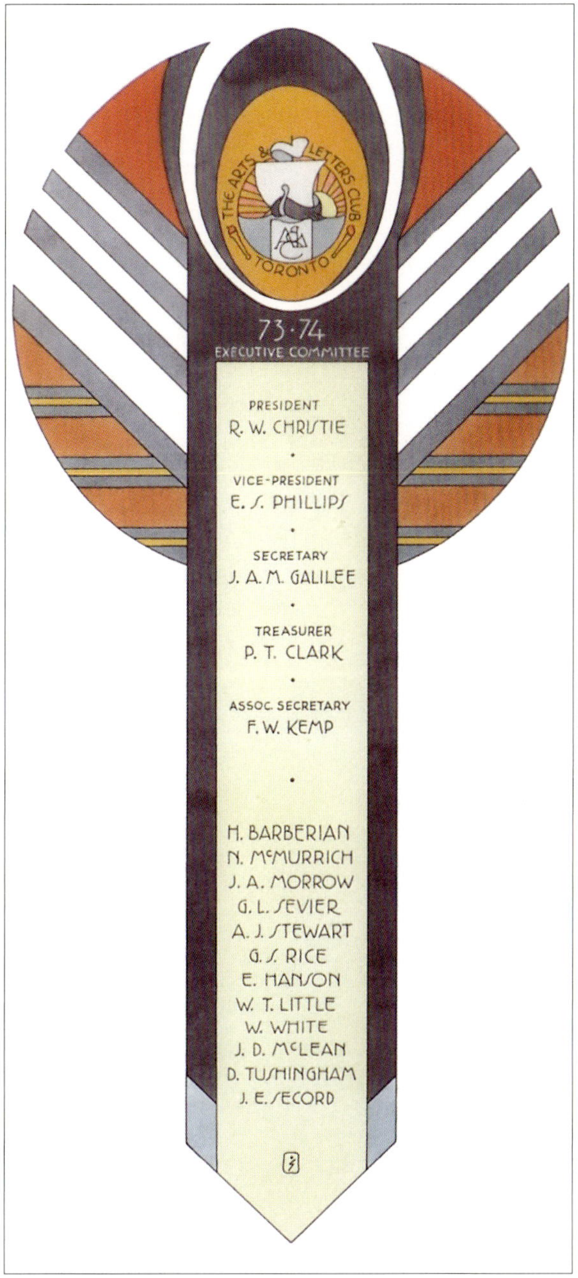

Executive List 1973–1974. (*Gerald Sevier*)

Executive List 2001–2002. (*Douglas Purdon*)

Herbert Whittaker, 1972. (*Barker Fairley*)

(Far right) Alfred Chapman in his presidential robes at the Boar's Head, c. 1940. (*Eric Aldwinckle*)

Toronto Houses, 1996. (*John Joy*)

Baicelong, undated. (*Philippa Faulkner*)

(Left) *Philippa Faulkner's Art Class*, undated. (*William Sherman*)

Autumn Arches, 1961. (*Bertram Brooker*)

Vase of Morning Glories,
undated. (*Leonard Brooks*)

(*Above right*) *A Time to Sow*,
undated. (*D. Mackay Houstoun*)

(*Right*) *Narrows at Penetang*,
undated. (*Raymond Victor Cattell*)

Log Boom, Savona, BC, 1998. (*Arthur Steven*)

(*Below left*) St. George's Hall, 1979 (*Armand Tatossian*)

(*Below right*) Artwork for *South of North* program, 1998. (*Tom McNeely*)

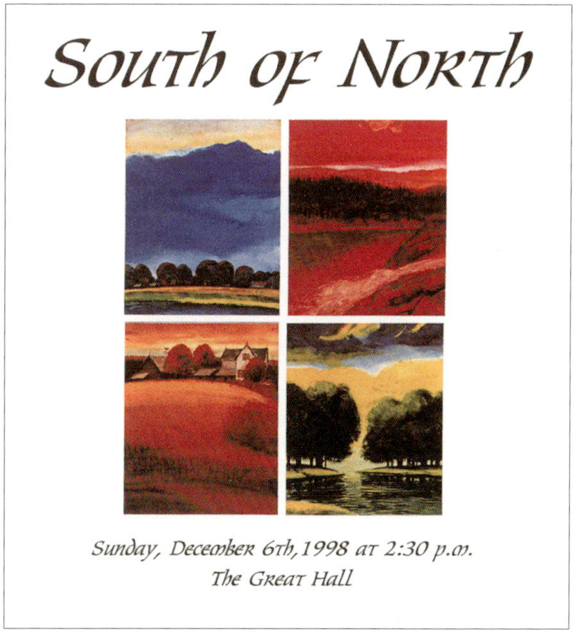

Viking Ship, 1988. (O. K. Schenk)

In May, Norman McMurrich was named president. An energetic and enthusiastic architect with a sense of humour, Norm had served as an intelligence officer during World War II, completed his degree in architecture in 1946, and later served as president of the Royal Architectural Institute of Canada.

Norman McMurrich, President, 1980–1982. (*Alan C. Collier*)

The club celebrated the centennial of Healey Willan's birth with a special ladies' night in early December. On display was a collection of Willan memorabilia, some items serious, some amusing. After dinner, the National Film Board documentary about Willan, *Man of Music*, was shown. Then Hunter Bishop outlined Willan's many contributions to the club, including, first and foremost, his musical version of our constitution. And, to top off the evening, some Willan doggerel was read. Here are the last two verses:

When I chose to accept the President's chair
Said I to myself, said I
I'll give it an odor of uplift and prayer.
Let us live in an aura of canons and cant
All cursing confine to the murmur "My aunt"
And by way of a tune the Gregorian chant
Said I to myself, said I.

But I fear that my friends will remark Dear Old Bean
Said I to myself, said I
Just leave art alone and attend to cuisine.
Sufficient the service of presidents new
If they strive for crisp pies and for boneless meat stew
Look after the eats; its the best you can do.
Said I to myself, said I.

The club was not alone in honouring Willan. Celebrations were held from coast to coast.

Late one January evening in 1981, Roland Pincoe, who often laboured long and loyally as stage manager for club productions, averted what might well have turned into a tragedy. He was alone in the Great Hall when he noticed wisps of smoke at the front of the stage. He quickly alerted the manager. By the time the firemen arrived, Roly had emptied three fire extinguishers on a growing blaze. The curtains had collapsed, blocking the stage and missing Roly by a matter of inches. He suffered from smoke inhalation, but soon recovered and returned to the club to be greeted as a hero by his impressed—and very grateful—fellow members. The fire had been caused by an overheated lamp, one of four being readied for the next musical production, *Pan*, by that remarkable duo, Parr and McGrath. Fortunately the damage was small and could be repaired in time for the performances. *Pan* featured two "delicious nymphs," a painter and a poet, both being pursued by "three lively graces, Talent, Commerce, and Grants." Delighted members and their guests considered it the jewel of the musical season.

Life-member medallion designed by Sid Bersudsky.

That spring, some radical changes were underway, changes that might encourage more use of the club. From now on, members who wished to discuss business at lunch—a practice previously frowned upon—could do so. It was even suggested that ladies would be permitted to enjoy lunch in the LAMPS Room, although the Great Hall and the lounge would be out of bounds to them. Another first was in evidence at the annual meeting in May, when life members wore brass medallions bearing the club's logo. Henceforth, these medallions were to be worn only by life members and only at designated events. Designed by Sid Bersudsky, they were the gift of journalist-philanthropist Floyd Chalmers.

At that same meeting, house committee chairman Doug Omand expressed his frustrations in rhyme:

When the Viking ship sails with a following breeze
On a sea of glittering blue
The skipper relaxes, enjoying his ease
And the same may be said for the crew.

But then when the Viking ship's running aground
And the oars are jammed in the ice
We find that there's always someone around
Just waiting to give advice.

And when there's so much to be taken to task for
It's nice, that advice, you don't have to ask for.

Early in 1982, the club held a testimonial dinner to honour Floyd Chalmers. The widely acclaimed *Encyclopedia of Music in Canada* had just been published, thanks in large part to his generous funding. In his memoir, Chalmers wrote that the Arts and Letters Club was

> a distinguished establishment of which I have been a member for more than half a century without contributing very much.... For such members as myself who sponged on the joys of the club but never wrote a skit or performed on its stage, there is a somewhat pejorative name: a "Boar's Head member." I was a perfect example of such, so I was amazed when the executive notified me of a dinner in my honour.

Floyd Chalmers (centre) with W. A. Craick (left) and Ralph Allen, past and present editors of *Maclean's*, October 8, 1955. (*Gilbert A. Milne*)

Chalmers was presented with a medal designed by Dora de Pedery-Hunt. "When it came my turn to speak," Chalmers recalled, "I was almost too moved to reply. I tried to express the depth of my gratitude for so much kindness but I'm sure my words were not adequate."

Our next president, Jim Parr, a true Renaissance man, took over in May. English-born and raised, he earned a doctorate in engineering, then came to Canada where he taught at universities in Alberta and Ontario before becoming Ontario's deputy minister of colleges and universities. He went on to serve as chairman of TV Ontario and as director general of the Ontario Science Centre. In his spare time, such as it was, he wrote several books, studied piano, wrote libretti for the club, and then tackled the various—and seemingly endless—challenges facing a club president in the early eighties.

Before long, the new president, while acknowledging the many contributions that members make to club activities, was suggesting that some might wish to donate money as well. He listed various possibilities, such as underwriting part of a spring show, putting one's name on a new dishwasher or microwave, buying a piece of furniture, or paying a month's rent. Wentworth Walker asked the president to "try the experiment of women being allowed as lunch guests on Mondays." This venture was given a three-month trial period, and was then extended, bit by bit, to the end of 1983.

Jim Parr, President, 1982–1984. (*Jack McNie*)

Yet another Parr-McGrath creation was staged in February 1983, this one entitled *The Musical Monarch*. That production had "a story line as convoluted and amusing as that of any opera ever written," and started off the year's theatrical festivities in fine fashion. It wasn't long before members were gearing up to celebrate the club's seventy-fifth birthday, which began with a week of special luncheons in September, each focusing on one

The Arts & Letters Club Quartette, 1983. From left: Jacob Loft, Gerard Kantarjian, Marcel Ray, Frank Fusco.

of the LAMPS disciplines. The first, for literature, featured Bill Swinton, who recalled his 1969–1970 presidency—specifically the controversy over the club tie and crest, and the lack of progress toward a club history. He went on to say that, although he was a member of several other clubs, he always felt most at home at the Arts and Letters, where he found a kindness that was "in short supply elsewhere." Tuesday's lunch was for architecture, which was, as past president Norman McMurrich reminded everyone, "the second oldest profession." He also mentioned that the club's first president, William Langton, had been an architect, as had four other past-presidents, including himself. The speaker that day was architect Tony Adamson, an engaging raconteur whose *The Ancestral Roof* (with co-author Marian McRae) had become one of the bibles for restoration enthusiasts across the country. The next day the focus was music, with Elmer Phillips in the chair. He outlined with humour the club's musical history, with opera singer Donald Garrard as the guest. On Thursday, Archie Arbuckle chaired the painting lunch. He paid tribute to York Wilson for insisting on juried shows—a professional approach that he applauded and which continues to the present. For Friday's stage luncheon, Mavor Moore, recently retired chairman of the Canada Council, spoke of Roy Mitchell, whose pioneering work at the club and at Hart House is part of theatre history. His *Creative Theatre*, written in 1929, is a landmark.

Wrapping up the celebrations were two evening dinners. And to top it all off, a handsome commemorative booklet, featuring all seventeen of our large heraldic banners, was distributed to everyone. It also includes an introduction in doggerel by President Parr, starting with:

> The sun smites not by day nor does
> The moon shine through by night;
> For in this Viking-vesseled club
> 'Tis better far to row, than rub
> Those leaden windows bright.

and ending with:

> Rest not your arms! Nor sleep thy hand,
> While years your lore enlarge.
> Nor hold to history so fast
> To tempt the club iconoclast;
> But rise, unbridled from our past
> To herald a future charge!

After dinner, members enjoyed *The Club*, a play written by Ken Jarvis and directed by Bob Christie that recounted the club's history in words and music from the first days at the Brown Betty restaurant to the Court House on Adelaide Street and on to 14 Elm. The play received such acclaim that it was staged again two months later for two ladies' nights.

But in spite of the high spirits engendered by all these celebratory events, the club was still waging a seemingly endless battle with financial setbacks. A special general meeting was held towards the end of the year to alert members to the worsening situation. The meeting was well attended, yet nothing much changed. Jim Parr reported in the next *Monthly Letter* that "Many members remain uninformed. You can recognize them easily. They are the happy ones." And so, yet another special general meeting was held. A hint that controversy lay ahead came when Parr informed members that an agreement had been reached for a new lease with St. George's. "However," he cautioned, "I may as well drop the first shoe and warn that the new rates, while reasonable, will call for more revenue. I'll leave the treasurer to drop the second shoe; and the chairman of house will drop the third." That meeting brought even more disheartening news. Membership was down by seventeen and the age profile was also cause for concern—60 percent of the members were more than sixty years old. One fellow, Bill Hemmerick, questioned why drinks served before dinner were free. He suggested charging for drinks, and opening the bar earlier.

Alan Collier (left) with Franklin (Archie) Arbuckle, 1982.

Rehearsal of the 1983 spring revue "Rose-Coloured Glasses." (*Ron Vickers*)

In May 1984, when it came time for the next annual meeting, Jim Parr was no doubt heaving a sigh of relief. He had recently survived a disagreement with the art committee regarding his presidential portrait. The committee didn't approve of it—but Jim did. He insisted that it be accepted, which it was. Incoming president Ken Jarvis, in thanking Jim for his hard work as president, recalled that he had taken over when the club was facing a crisis of shrinking income and rising costs. "With Jim's hand on the tiller, our Viking ship was turned around." Ken was a lawyer, at the time, secretary of the Law Society of Upper Canada, and also a sculptor of note. Several of his busts of club members can be seen atop bookshelves in the club library.

Later that month, just prior to his ninety-seventh birthday, Barker Fairley was the honoured guest at a special

Ken Jarvis, President, 1984–1986. (*Cleeve Horne*)

literary luncheon. A noted Goethe scholar and painter, he was by this time an Officer of the Order of Canada and the recipient of the Grand Cross of Merit of the Federal Republic of Germany. Also in May, the club bid farewell to Mavor Moore as he and his wife made ready to move to the west coast. Moore, a third-generation member, had joined the club when he was only twenty. Bob Christie, Harry Boyle, Jack Yocom, and Elmer Phillips all paid tribute to the man who had served as founding general director of both the Charlottetown Festival and Toronto's St. Lawrence Centre, and, with his mother, Dora Mavor Moore, had co-founded the New Play Society. He was given a parchment scroll with a tribute written by Jim Parr and calligraphy done by John Cozens.

Toward the end of October, the executive met for a special dinner to discuss continuing problems. Everyone quickly agreed that if the club was to survive in a meaningful way, it must take steps to influence the community, as it once had done. Now, they acknowledged, the club had reached the point where it "meant little or nothing to a large segment of the public." New guidelines were set up, with committees to become involved in the community and to develop connections with the media, government bodies, and other institutions. Members were to be encouraged to express their views publicly on topical subjects; the club was to provide facilities to meet committee requirements; the budget was to be balanced; and, most important, all members were to work to maintain community confidence. It was clear to everyone that something had to be done, and done quickly.

And so it came to pass that a landmark meeting of the club was called for Tuesday, February 19, 1985, to discuss Jim Parr's motion, "that the constitution of the Arts and Letters Club be honoured and that women be welcomed to all forms of membership in the club." Should the motion pass, the club would not be the first of Toronto's downtown clubs to admit women. The Albany Club, an elite Tory hangout, had opened its membership to women six years earlier because Prime Minister Joe Clark had refused to speak there until it changed its ways.

More than a hundred voting members turned up, with several nonresident members on hand just to see what would develop. Several letters from those unable to attend were circulated—most from those who felt strongly that the club should remain a males-only sanctum. Archie Arbuckle wrote to say that denying membership to women was, while an unwritten law, still a valid one. In any event, he claimed, only elderly women would be interested in joining, and, besides, while he knew several young women artists, few "could afford the fee." Chuck Matthews was simply "unalterably opposed to admitting ladies," claiming that this would have been the opinion of Gus Bridle—he was correct on that score—and other founding members of the club. Bill Duthie, in a classic case of late-life peevishness, argued that "the club has nothing to offer women members that they don't have in a variety of women's clubs, including one for lesbians that may still exist on Gerrard East." His conclusion? There was "little doubt that women's superior acumen and intuition would, in the end, take over the club, leaving the male members with no opportunities to develop their limited skills."

Without doubt the most vociferous voice weighing in against the motion came from a nonresident member, John Sanderson. His letter, read aloud by Monty Larkin, began, "Niggers-in-the-woodpile at 14 Elm Street are so numerous that the very existence of the club is jeopardized." What's more, "Men who hanker after a such a change...are always a minority, are always insecure, are always henpecked, and are always soppily nostalgic about their nannies." Women, he continued, "however artistic, and with few exceptions, are too personal; they have little veneration except for tangible objects; ideas, pure and simple, rarely interest them and they tend to lack humour. These are not clubbable characteristics." Still gathering steam, Sanderson, in the sixth lengthy paragraph of his lengthy letter, opined, "For men who have spent many years of their lives at the blunt end of war, succumbing to feminism is inexcusably gutless."

But others took a different view. Writing enthusiastically—and more concisely—in favour of the motion was the renowned historian, Jack Granatstein, who said, "We should live up to the spirit of the Charter of Rights and it would be splendid if this could be done by the time that the Charter's equality provisions come into force." Another leading historian, Michael Bliss, also came out in favour, saying that, while the club's ambiance is comfortable to many members and would be at risk, "like the Viking ship on our crest we have to strike out into uncharted seas if we are going to accomplish anything." Past president Bob Christie expressed his views succinctly: "I grew up in a setting where I always considered men and women equal in every sense. We have to accept, in the whole world, the equality of men and women, and I would favour that view in this club."

After a lengthy and generally evenhanded discussion, President Jarvis had the motion put to a vote. The result: sixty-four in favour, thirty-eight against, with one spoiled ballot. When the president announced that "qualified women would now be admitted," the irrepressible Tony Adamson leaped to his feet to say that he was volunteering to chair the qualifying committee. Everyone roared. And with that, this historic meeting came to an end. Strange to say, in the days that followed, only two members resigned because of the admission of women. The vituperative John Sanderson remained a member until his death the following year.

14 Elm St. by John Morrow.

Detail of carving on the Ridpath table. (*Peter Large*)

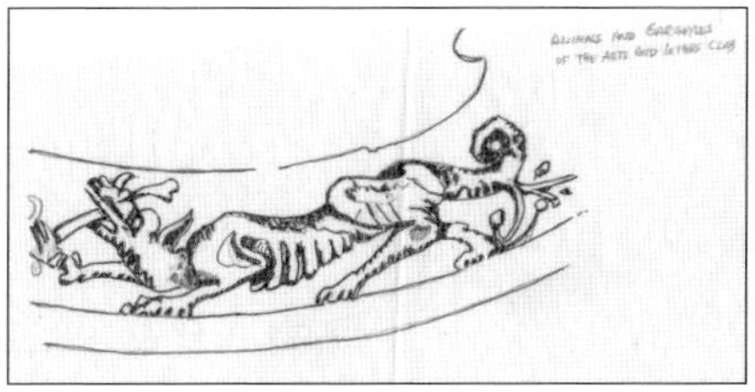

Painting

Painters have figured prominently since the club's inception. One of the first meetings was in the studio of leading portraitist Wyly Grier (later, Sir Wyly) and he suggested the Arts and Letters Club's name. Graphic design firms—Grip Ltd., Sampson Matthews, and R. G. McLean—encouraged their artist employees to join. Even today, some club painters work as commercial artists.

J. E. H. MacDonald exhibited at the club in 1911. There he met Lawren Harris, and they became the nucleus that would develop into the Group of Seven. MacDonald contributed unstintingly to the club, designing its crests, a bookplate, the mock heraldic banners, and some of the early executive lists. He served many years on the executive and as keeper of the records, and—from 1928 to 1930—as president.

Arthur Lismer and Frank Johnston joined in 1912, followed by Frederick Varley, Franklin Carmichael, and A. Y. Jackson. Their paintings focused on the bold and vibrant Canadian landscape. Sketching trips were organized to Algonquin Park, Georgian Bay, rural Quebec, and the Arctic. Until his untimely drowning in 1917, Tom Thomson was an associate, although never a member of the Group or the club. Lawren Harris and James MacCallum assisted club artists by financing the Studio Building and the Algoma boxcar jaunts. The first exhibition of the Group of Seven was at the Art Gallery of Toronto in the spring of 1920. A. J. Casson joined the Group in 1926 as "number eight." Following their eighth exhibition in December 1931, the Group of Seven disbanded. Their influence remains seminal and, to this day, provokes controversy.

Club artists met regularly over lunch for debate and camaraderie. Fifteen were official World War I artists; sculptor Walter Allward designed the magnificent Vimy Memorial.

In 1925, Casson, F. H. Brigden, and Carmichael formed the Canadian Society of Painters in Water Colour, and, in 1933, Casson and Jackson helped found the Canadian Group of Painters. George Reid, Fred Haines, L. A. C. Panton, Lismer, and brothers Emanuel and Gustav Hahn, taught at the newly formed Ontario College of Art.

Bertram Brooker held the first Canadian abstract exhibition at the club in 1927. Ivor Lewis executed the masterful bronze sculpture of Timothy Eaton, a Toronto icon. Other Toronto landmarks by club artists include Frederick Challener's proscenium arch at the Royal Alexandra Theatre and the Fathers of Confederation canvas at Queen's Park, and R. York Wilson's murals for Imperial Oil and the O'Keefe (now the Hummingbird) Centre.

During the mid-century years, club exhibitions were often on loan from other institutions and from non-members. A photographic show in 1963 was mounted at the club by the Art Institute of Ontario, followed by one of costume design from the Stratford Festival. In 1955, club painters mounted a show of their own "counterfeit" French impressionisms. Caricatures of fellow members were ever popular. Although women were not yet admitted to the club, their paintings, on occasion, were. Walter Coucill's wife, Irma, and George Pepper's wife, Kathleen, exhibited, as did the formidable Paraskeva Clark. For some years Kathleen Pepper rented space on the club's third floor.

In 1965. after considerable discussion, an art purchase fund was initiated. Two years later, for Canada's centennial, the club decided to enlarge its art collection, and members were encouraged to donate to it. As part of that celebration, the club held a major exhibition of Group of Seven paintings.

In 1969, a large Alan Collier show was organized and the club began to take a small commission on art sales. Retrospectives of York Wilson, Jim MacDonald, and Alec Jackson followed in the seventies, with ones of Casson and David Milne in the eighties.

Louis Hartley was named club curator in 1972. John Snell succeeded Hartley in 1980, followed by Karen Jacobson in 1995, Judith Graham in 1997, and Margaret Crawford Maloney in 1998. Barbara Mitchell was appointed in 2006. The club now holds some five hundred works. Most have been catalogued and securely hung.

In 1985, after long and acrimonious debate, the club voted to admit women. Among the first women artists to join were Anne Meredith Barry, Zora Buchanan, Mary Tuck Corelli, Pat Fairhead, Loi Hathaway, Barbara Howard, Anne Lazare-Mirvish, Kay Murray-Weber, and Jessica Steven. They quickly assumed active roles on committees, and their works were included in exhibitions. Soon their art was being acquired for the club's permanent collection. In 1992, following the purchase of 14 Elm Street and because of the subsequent crippling mortgage and insurance debts, the club reluctantly sold the Lawren Harris oil painting *Houses, Richmond Street*—a gift from the club's first treasurer, Bob Defries.

Over the years, club artists have designed and illustrated the club newsletters, painted stage sets, and produced event posters, menus, wine labels, and programs. They have created a century of presidential portraits (Varley did Vincent Massey's) and executive lists. In 2000, shadow boxes replaced the traditional Christmas posters for the annual silent auctions.

Wednesday, Friday, and Sunday painting sessions, sketching weekends, and vigorous exhibition and guest speaker schedules all continue. New initiatives such as Scrubbers (to clean paintings) and Inner City Kids (for art outreach) have been undertaken. A 1997 art auction raised $20,000 for new lighting and Velcro wall covering to improve the exhibition space in the Great Hall. A gala juried exhibition marked the ninetieth anniversary.

In October 2006, the club, in partnership with the Rochester Art Club, co-sponsored an international show of paintings by members—a first for both organizations. The event was held in Rochester and attended by many club members. A reciprocal exhibition is planned.

Twelve artists have served as club president: Wyly Grier, J. W. Beatty, R. F. Gagen, C. W. Jefferys, Jim MacDonald, Ivor Lewis, J. Ernest Sampson, F. S. Haines, L. A. C. Panton, Cleeve Horne, Ken Jarvis, and Julian Mulock. A thirteenth, Peter G. S. Large, will serve in 2008. Another thirteen have served as RCA president—most recently Archie Arbuckle, Clare Bice, Christopher Chapman, Ken Jarvis, Ernest Annau, and Ron Bolt.

By the turn of the millennium, a club web site was activated—a new graphic milestone. And a strong photography group has emerged among the visual artists.

Over the past century, the painting component of the Arts and Letters Club has established a vital legacy—with pride from the past and promise for the future.

Margaret Crawford Maloney

CHAPTER 5

A New Lease on Life 1985–2003

Admitting women
Buying 14 Elm Street
Celebrating nine decades

In the early months of 1985, as Arts and Letters men were bracing themselves for the arrival of women members, *The Monthly Letter* was keeping everyone up-to-date and amused. The February issue mentioned Dan Needles' delightful *Letter From Wingfield Farm* that had played for two nights in January. To add a bit of levity, the editor printed several of Frank Denton's witticisms. While handing around the salt, pepper, and mustard at the Boar's Head, he would say "Condiments of the season?" Other favourites of his were "Season's gratings" and "Time flies like an arrow. Fruit flies like a banana."

By March, the executive was back at the boardroom table involved in discussions with the St. George's Society concerning our offer to purchase 14 Elm Street. We were also looking at other premises, just in case these negotiations fell through. Otherwise club life

First Charter Women. From left: Audrey Matheson, Lela Wilson, Connie Briant, Ann Rothery, Zora Buchanan, and Pat Fairhead. Not pictured: Tyrrell Morrow.

was carrying on as usual. Arrangements to welcome women members were being made and a few women were applying. Within months, a fine new show graced the walls of the Great Hall—paintings by Tyrrell Richardson Morrow, the club's first woman member. Over four hundred people attended its opening, "the largest gathering in the memories of longtime members."

Sadly, the club's dedicated archivist-librarian Hunter Bishop died that year. He had endured the debilitating effects of hemophilia all his life. For many years he had served the club loyally and well and had brought a professional approach to what had previously been little more than a disorganized clutter of poorly protected documents. Through him, researchers—members and non-members alike—were made aware of the club's archives. In his will, he left the club a generous bequest, part for the archives and part for the publication of a club history. A smaller amount was designated "for the provision of wine at specified occasions."

Toward the end of the year, the executive appointed a special committee to study the cultural implications of the Canada-US free trade negotiations. The committee members were Ernest Sirluck (chair), Jack Carr, Arthur Gelber, Lyman Henderson, Norm McMurrich, and Rudi Stussi. Lou Applebaum asked if he could sit in and was warmly welcomed as they began their deliberations.

The membership committee was particularly busy. Thirteen women had joined and were beginning to feel welcome, although they continued to tread carefully. One woman remembers an older man who sat next to her at her first members' dinner. He said little and seemed quite ill-at-ease until finally he blurted, "I just don't know how to talk to a woman like you. My wife has always stayed at home." And then there was Alan Collier, who always made sure that his table had only men sitting at it—and that it was right under the exit sign, just in case.

Ken Jarvis, having skillfully handled the admission of women, was now occupied with the challenging venture of purchasing St. George's Hall. Members seemed pleased at the prospect, but, when they heard once again that quite a number of them had yet to pay their fees, their enthusiasm was dampened. The offenders were told that their privileges would be "suspended forthwith and their membership terminated in thirty days" unless they paid up.

Tyrrell Richardson Morrow, the first woman member, with her husband John, a former president, 1990.

(*Above*) Hunter Bishop.

(*Left*) Alan Collier.

The club's offer to purchase St. George's Hall was rejected in February 1986, but everything else was on an upswing. A LAMPS festival in April met with great approval. Comedic actor Heath Lamberts was to speak on the weighty topic of "The Role of the Arts and Letters Club in the Development of Theatre in Canada." He tried manfully to speak for several minutes, but could only come up with aaahs, throat clearing, the odd indecipherable word, an occasional "but," and strangled sounds. This, of course, was all showmanship, to get his audience on side—it worked, and he launched into his talk. In one particularly amusing part he reported that the Ontario Censorship Board had instructed actors to watch carefully for the pronunciation of such words as rapier, adulteration, cockatoo, consommé, sect, masticate, Balzac, hallucinate, penal, titular, spurn, capitulate, dickie, screwdriver, lustre, laity, and hot cross buns. Members and guests "roared with every word, nudged their neighbours, and spilled their coffee."

Lisa Lambert, a young charter woman who performed in the spring revues for a number of years, also appeared on the club stage that month. She often wrote her own material, but in the 1988 and 1989 revues, for example, she and others took part in sketches by Bob Martin and Don McKellar—both of whom shared with her the Broadway success of *The Drowsy Chaperone* in winning the 2006 Tony Awards for best book, music, and lyrics.

Heath Lamberts (left) with Bill Shelden, 1985. (*Howard Gerring*)

By the end of April, negotiations with the St. George's Society were back on track—so much so that Ken Jarvis was finally able to announce at the annual meeting on Thursday, May 29, 1986:

> This is the last time I will speak to you about the club as your president. I end my term with this tiding—at three o'clock today the Arts and Letters Club became the owner in fee simple of 14 Elm Street. We have come a long journey and now we are home. We have much to be thankful for.

The total price was $1,400,000, with generous terms to give the club time to arrange long-term financing. "Kind fortune smiled," said Jarvis, "when she put in our hands a whole year to raise the funds needed to pay for this building

Round table designed by Jack Ridpath attracts conversationalists, 1986. (*John W. Scott*)

David Franco, President, 1986–1988. (*Tom McNeely*)

of ours. What might have been a truly daunting obligation is, instead, a manageable feat." With this, another fundraising campaign got underway, and a new president, David Franco of the classical music radio station CFMX, took over.

Finally in October, after eleven meetings over eleven months, the Sirluck committee submitted its report. An impressive list of experts had been interviewed, including Curtis Barlow, president of the Canadian Conference of the Arts; Kevin Doyle, editor of *Maclean's*; Peter Herrndorf, publisher of *Toronto Life*; Lily Munro, Ontario's minister of culture; and Bernard Ostry, chairman of TV Ontario. The report listed three main conclusions:

(1) that most creative artists in Canada are significantly and inescapably dependent upon Canadian cultural industries;
(2) that the proposed trade negotiations could have serious adverse consequences for Canada's cultural industries; and
(3) that an intervention by the club would be appropriate and could be useful.

The executive accepted the report and sent it off to Prime Minister Brian Mulroney.

In the meantime, fundraising efforts were picking up steam. Our artists donated ninety paintings for an auction that month, with proceeds to go to the building fund. A members' dinner was held in November to honour Floyd Chalmers and to thank him for his generous contribution to that fund. By the time December rolled around, members who had not yet made a commitment to the fund were advised that they could expect to receive a phone call from one of forty club canvassers. Treasurer Peter Large asked that they be given a courteous hearing.

And they were. By February 1987, additional funds had been raised thanks to the phone campaign, the sale of Christmas art panels, and a highly successful "Wintertime Chautauqua," an entertaining evening produced by Michael Spence with a star-studded cast of singers, dancers, and a magician. The outcome? A handsome $2,500 for the building fund.

Another LAMPS festival in March featured Francess Halpenny discussing a "Literary Lexicon"; George Baird talking about our architectural heritage; a musical supper featuring *Les Amis*—a group of nine young musicians under the guidance of Michael Pepa; John Gould telling us about his drawings; and, lastly, Norman Campbell speaking about his career in theatre and television, and about his production of *Anne of Green Gables.* Also that month, members partied at a beaux arts ball, a costume extravaganza that would, it was hoped, start a new club tradition. In April, another successful spring revue was staged and, on a weekend later that month, members climbed onto buses that took them on a tour of the studios of eight club artists.

In the April *Monthly Letter*, members learned that Prime Minister Brian Mulroney had replied to the club's letter on the free trade issue. He wrote, in part,

> I fully agree with your comment that we must retain our right to protect and foster Canadian culture in whatever way conditions in Canada may dictate. I also recognize that Canadians have a unique cultural heritage.... Culture, however, does not flourish in our society as a dimension apart from the economy. Therefore, the trade negotiations with the United States, which are about improving Canada's domestic economy, have a critical relationship to Canadian cultural survival.

With free trade negotiations completed, it was clear that culture had been given important protections. Sirluck and his fellow committee members—and perhaps others in the club—were pleased to think they might have contributed in a small way to the favourable outcome that had been widely thought improbable. Sad to say, Mulroney's original letter, which had been posted on the club's bulletin board, disappeared—no doubt pirated by someone with a keen eye for a bit of Canada's cultural history.

The first women on the Executive Committee : *(Far left)* Zora Buchanan, 1994, and *(Left)* Pat Fairhead, 1996. (*Jim Parr*)

At the annual meeting in May, President Franco thanked Ken Jarvis, Jim Parr, and Roger Priddle for their yeoman service leading up to the purchase of our building. He also paid tribute to those members who had helped pay for it—fewer than two hundred of more than five hundred members—and hoped there would be more. He announced that the number of women members, all enthusiastic and hard working, had risen to about fifty. Zora Buchanan and Pat Fairhead were elected to the executive, the first women to serve on that body.

The club was literally humming. One evening in January 1988, we celebrated playwright Herman Voaden's eighty-fifth birthday by staging two of his earliest plays, *Wilderness: A Play of the North* and *Fragment*, both directed by Herb Whittaker. Later that month, the club's fourth Burns Supper drew an enthusiastic crowd. Many of the participants were presumably "Scotch by absorption," as the irrepressible Healey Willan had described himself. In May, Mike Spence, an electrical engineer with a love of the theatre and an all-encompassing knowledge of the club's idiosyncratic stage lighting, became the next president.

A variety of activities continued with barely a pause. In June alone, members enjoyed a day trip to the Shaw Festival, an evening of play readings, a painting weekend, a three-night run of another Parr-McGrath production, *Stonehenge*, and a talk by historian Michael Bliss on his recently published *Five Centuries of Canadian Business.*

Michael Spence, President, 1988–1990. (*Ray Cattell*)

Certainly no one could have been bored that fall. In September the club staged a fundraiser—Dan Needles' *Wingfield's Progress*, and welcomed author John Ralston Saul to the literary table. Guest speakers for Minds on the Move included Nobel laureate John Polanyi, who attracted a standing-room-only crowd, and Henry (Hal) Jackman, soon to become Ontario's twenty-fifth lieutenant governor. In October, Jim Parr—as irreverent and inventive as ever—and his son Dan staged *The Flying Trucker*, a play about a man "condemned to drive his highly toxic cargo of liquid waste up and down Highway 401 until he can find a chaste and pure woman to love him and help him dump his load."

No sooner had the curtain come down on that bit of theatrical nonsense than the champagne corks were popping for a week-long celebration of the club's eightieth birthday. Festivities began with "A Night to Remember"—a few "old boys" presenting club anecdotes, limericks, and witticisms, all accompanied by Jack Yocom at the piano. The week concluded with Doug Omand's "radio show" entitled "Eighty Years of Glorious History." Michael Bliss had written an affectionate look at our first eighty years, copies of which were distributed to all. Our founders, he wrote, ensured that the club would always be "Toronto's least pretentious.... They began great traditions such as the Boar's Head procession and the singing of the constitution at the annual meeting; and they decorated our halls with heraldic banners, presidential portraits, and memorials to all who suffered on the executive." In the same lighthearted vein, the inimitable Omand offered a tongue-in-cheek hymn, written for the occasion:

A CANTICLE FOR THE ARTS AND LETTERS CLUB

We hymn our favourite club.
Dignified and devoted to the pursuit of arts and letters
Nurturing genius for eighty years
And operating at a permanent deficit.

All praise is due our president
In whom resides valour, integrity and truth
We praise him upon the well-tuned cymbal
And upon the instrument of many strings.

Our members are all distinguished
Both professionals and those who pay their fees more promptly.
We have more Orders of Canada per cubic metre,
Than almost any place else.

All glory to this historic building
Baronial hall, minstrels gallery and defective pipes.
Abominably hot under the summer sun,
And, in the blast of winter, creaking in every beam.

The work of our artists adorns our wall,
That of our musicians, actors and singers occupies our stage.
Our architects try to keep the place from collapsing.
We give new meaning to the concept of do-it-yourself.

As it was, so it shall be.
Even from everlasting to everlasting.
The deficit will continue to grow.
And the Treasurer will continue to raise the fees.

That was all great fun, but another squall was brewing as members heatedly discussed the pros and cons of selling Lawren Harris's 1922 painting, *Houses, Richmond Street*. The art committee insisted that the painting should remain at the club as part of our collection and, in a burst of crankiness, threatened to take independent action if the work was sent for safekeeping to the Art Gallery of Ontario. Earlier that year the same committee had suggested that some items in the club's art collection should be sold "if we are unable to provide a good environment...protection, or accessibility." In any event, three artists wrote to the executive to protest the sale. After that, things settled down—for a while.

Lorne [sic] Harris. (*Jack McLaren*). The club's sale of Lawren Harris's painting *Houses, Richmond Street* was controversial.

In early January 1989, the executive discussed opening the club to the public for certain art shows, but that unprecedented suggestion got nowhere in a hurry. At a special general meeting at the end of the month, members voted overwhelmingly to embark on major renovations to our historic building, which was by then a dignified ninety-eight years old. Plans were soon underway for the installation of an elevator, the upgrading of the washrooms, a new and larger bar (the executive knew full well where a goodly portion of our revenue comes from), a renovated lounge, and the redesign of the main entrance to enlarge the foyer and bring the front door out closer to the street. Fundraising took on a new impetus. Zora Buchanan's busy activities committee barely paused for breath, attracting an impressive array of guest speakers, among them film critic Gerald Pratley, conductor Niki Goldschmidt, actors Douglas Campbell and Don Harron, architect Bruce

Reconstruction of the front door, 1990.

Kuwabara, former University of Toronto president Claude Bissell, and novelists Robertson Davies and Hugh Hood.

Everyone seemed to be having a good time, particularly Jim Parr, who was always ready to argue virtually any side of any issue, and do it well. For a debate in January 1990, it was resolved that "Government funding for the arts be discontinued." Parr and Michael Bliss supported the resolution, with John McKellar and Lou Applebaum opposing. It was "a very club-like event, enjoyable, entertaining—and a draw." By the end of the month, members were back again for another sold-out Burns Supper.

In April, the club celebrated the one hundredth birthday of Chuck Matthews. He had been a club member for seventy years and had attended every Boar's Head event from 1920 to 1987— "I'll go if I have to go on a stretcher," he'd say. He was particularly remembered for his efforts in raising funds and supervising the distribution of food parcels for Savage Club members in London throughout World War II and for several years afterward. He arrived at the club for his birthday party in a white stretch limo, as family and friends gathered round. He received best wishes from Queen Elizabeth and Governor General Ramon Hnatyshyn. It was Chuck's last visit to the club, for he died a few months later.

A gala dinner in May marked the centennial of the birth of Frank Carmichael, who had died in 1945. His daughter, Mary Mastin, was an honoured guest. Pat Fairhead, Loi Hathaway, and Vernon Mould, all former students, paid tribute, as did his old friends A. J. Casson and Alan Collier. That event was followed two weeks later by a four-day celebration of music—everything from jazz on Elm Street on one evening, to a dinner honouring opera impresario Ruby Mercer on another.

The annual meeting at the end of the month saw Ernest Sirluck installed as president. A distinguished academic of English literature, he had also served as vice president and then dean of graduate studies at U of T, and later as president of the University of Manitoba. Sirluck brought to his new post an innate ability to handle meetings—even fractious ones—with skill and a subtle sense of humour. He was also just the man to keep a careful eye on finances.

When the renovations began in June, members settled into temporary quarters at the Academy of Medicine on Bloor Street. Jack Carr, a good-humoured engineer who gave unstintingly of his time and expertise, supervised the move and the ensuing work at the club with the help of Mike Spence and Roly Pincoe. The fact that the move to temporary quarters would allow for fewer revenue-producing activities created some anxiety. And there was more financial concern about the disappointing sales of a new club publication, *The Longship Review*, which consisted of a number of essays and poems by members. It was not a roaring success. Fewer than a hundred of five hundred copies were sold, resulting in a deficit of nearly $3,000. On December 3, 14 Elm Street reopened. Members were delighted to find the new entrance, the new bar, the new elevator, new washrooms, a new archives/library office, and an updated third floor for use by members and, occasionally, for rentals.

In January 1991, President Sirluck announced that the club had been the beneficiary of a generous bequest of more than $160,000 from the will of Ran MacDonald, and that life member Alexander Fee and his wife, Betsy, had made a major donation in memory of her father, C. W. Jefferys. The president also reported that the Ontario Heritage Foundation had offered us a matching grant of $104,000, funds that would help in refurbishing the

Chuck Matthews. (*William Shelden*)

Ernest Sirluck, President, 1990–1992. (*Jim LePage*)

Randolph MacDonald, 1939.

south façade of our building, thanks to a recently signed heritage easement agreement with the city. The building had been designated of historical importance in 1975.

In spite of all this financial help, there was more to be done. A membership drive was soon underway and, within the next few months, the club welcomed fifty-two new members. Meanwhile, the question of selling the Harris painting arose yet again and discussions—lengthy discussions—ensued. There were members who were reluctant to go along with the sale, fearing that it would discourage the donation of works of art to the club in the future. By this time, the painting was at the AGO because we lacked the security and atmospheric controls needed to protect such a valuable work.

Next on the agenda was another creative endeavour, a something-for-everyone Fun Fair. A few members muttered, "We've never done this before," and that was true enough. But thanks to the energies of Zora Buchanan, Loi Hathaway, and a hard-working committee, it all came together. Several hundred members and their friends arrived at the club one Sunday in late October, ready to enjoy it all. There were clowns, fortune tellers, magicians, a silent auction, and storytelling for children, along with the sale of posters, paintings, books, and baked goods, and a white elephant table. Adding to the fun was a "Starvin' Artists' Lunch," with music provided by revered standbys Jack Yocom and Wilf White at the two pianos. The result? A handsome contribution to club coffers.

(*Far right*) St. George's Hall heritage designation plaque.

(*Below*) The commemorative plaque at the front door.

With the club still in a critical financial position, a general meeting was called for the end of January 1992. After heated arguments and with some anguish, members decided that the Harris painting must be sold. And so, in his last major announcement as president,

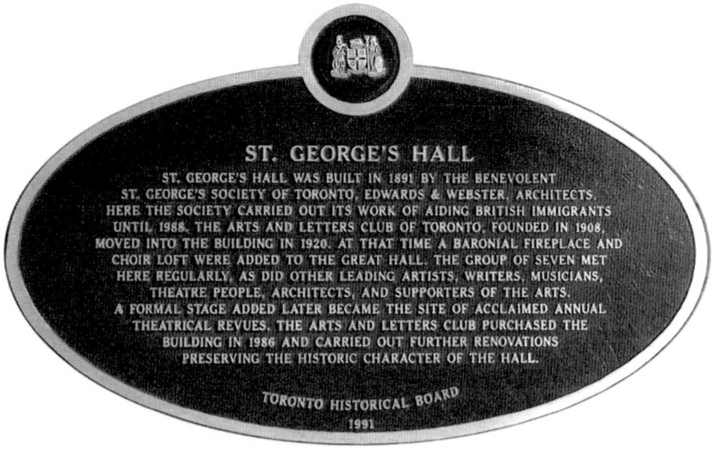

Rudi Stussi family enjoys the Fun Fair.

(Left) Fun Fair poster, 1991. (*Lesley Fairfield*)

Ernest Sirluck advised the membership that the deed was done—sold at an upscale Sotheby's auction held at the Park Plaza Hotel. It was purchased by one of Canada's wealthiest art collectors, Kenneth Thomson, for a tidy $374,000. Sirluck and his wife were at the auction, along with several other club members. Few noticed the brief, scary incident just after the hammer fell and we heard the auctioneer's firm "Sold!" Bidding had already begun on the next painting, an A. Y. Jackson landscape, as Lesley Sirluck waved her thanks to Sotheby's general manager, standing just behind the auctioneer. Lesley realized too late that she had unintentionally bid a hefty sum on the Jackson! The next few moments seemed endless, but happily, another bid prompted a sigh of relief from the club's president, who said afterward that he had aged twenty years in the interim. Some weeks later, Sotheby's presented the club with a fine reproduction of *Houses, Richmond Street*. It hangs by the elevator in the lower level of the club. There are those who still say that the sale of the Harris painting was a mistake, but hindsight suggests otherwise. Clearly the painting is in safer hands. Sirluck wrote of the sale, "It helped bring our debt down to a level which, while still burdensome, should no longer threaten the club's viability."

In a moment of inspiration that spring, President Sirluck suggested changing the name of our newsletter to *LAMPSletter.* The first issue with this name appeared in March, bearing an ingenious masthead created by Andrew Sookrah. Soon after, Ray Cattell designed the new one that has been retained to the present. That year, too, *LAMPSletter* launched a new series by Fergus Cronin entitled "Time Present...Time Past." They were biographical sketches of one, or occasionally two, of our members, personal glimpses giving us new insights into those we thought we already knew. The series continued for almost a decade.

Lyman Henderson, President, 1992–1994. (*Valda Oestreicher*)

With his presidency at an end, Sirluck settled down to writing his autobiography, *First Generation*. No doubt the next president, Lyman Henderson, was pleased to take over a club with finances that no longer threatened disaster. Henderson, a businessman with an abiding love for the arts, had vast volunteer experience with many arts organizations, including the National Ballet, the Banff Centre, the McMichael Canadian Art Collection, and a host of others. So members were not too surprised to learn just two months later that the executive was discussing whether the club should take a stand on the "perilous financial state of the arts in Canada." But they tabled that question for the time being.

At the members' dinner in November, a brass ensemble from U of T's Faculty of Music premiered a fanfare composed by Lou Applebaum especially for the club. It is still played at annual meetings and special dinners, which are, in Henderson's words, "mired with tradition" and have idiosyncrasies "amusing to many and coddled by a few." At the end of the year, to boost memberships and to address the problem of spouses as frequent guests, the membership committee recommended that the club add a spousal membership category. This was duly approved and, henceforth, fees for spouses were set at 50 percent of the regular membership.

In February 1993, the question of outreach surfaced once again with a committee set up to discuss Ottawa's $80,000,000 cut to the cultural sector. President Henderson announced in the March *LAMPSletter* that "Our esteemed member Arthur Gelber phoned and suggested to me—nay, closer to demanded—that the club take a public stand on the drastically diminished government funding of the arts. He argued that these were dangerous times for the arts and that something as prestigious as the Arts and Letters Club should stand up to be counted." With the executive's approval, the president agreed to look for "a man of experience, intellect, and drive...to investigate and report on suggested action." This elicited an immediate query from our feisty iconoclast, Jim Parr, inquiring if the executive was authorizing the president to "look for a 'man' of experience." In reply, the secretary referred to his *Concise Oxford*, which, he said, defined "man" as "human being." This didn't sit well with Parr who, "as a Canadian," quoted Gage's *Canadian Dictionary*. In it "man" is defined as "adult male person." As the man who had led the charge to admit women to the club, Parr was making a point, albeit with good humour. And that was the last heard on *that* subject.

Lou Applebaum, composer of the Club Fanfare, 1994. (*Jim Parr*)

Barely pausing for breath, Parr was on to a new cause a month or so later, and members were up in arms. This time many, if not most of them, were aghast at his latest assault on the status quo—a motion at the annual meeting in May that the club discontinue the distinction between professional and nonprofessional members. After prolonged discussion, it was agreed that a special meeting was needed. *LAMPSletter* was inundated with letters to the editor and heated arguments ensued for months. It was, as Philip Creighton said, "the best of all possible rows." At the special meeting in late October, the motion was again discussed at great length and, thankfully, with unfailing courtesy. When the vote was finally taken the motion went down to resounding defeat.

During all this ongoing angst, club activities continued to be enjoyed with enthusiasm and were well attended. By early 1994, plans were underway for LAMPS week in February—a lineup that concluded with a painting luncheon and a "Great Debate" featuring guest panelists Matthew Teitelbaum, chief curator at the AGO, and Joan Murray, executive director of the Robert McLaughlin Gallery in Oshawa. Also on the panel were Archie Arbuckle and Pat Fairhead. The topic under discussion was "Are Ontario's art galleries providing adequate exposure to Ontario artists?" The debate began with due decorum, but before long voices were raised and angry demands made by club artists and their guests. All of this may have been cathartic for the artists who were there, but little else was accomplished.

John McKellar, President, 1994–1996. (*Rudolf Stussi*)

The club was taking tentative steps to becoming better known in the community. Henderson recalled that fifty years earlier the club's membership had, according to the *Toronto Daily Star*, "touched virtually every artist in the city." "Now," he cautioned, "we could remain so secret that nobody would come to our funeral." As a step toward wider visibility, renters would henceforth be allowed to use the club's name when promoting their events.

By the annual meeting in May, membership stood at about 520—up from 450 ten years earlier. That evening we welcomed our next president, John McKellar, a lawyer with a lifelong love for the arts. John donned the president's mantle of office, a shabby red velvet robe of uncertain vintage, described by Lyman as "reeking with history, redolent with character, and resplendent with tradition." In his first column in *LAMPSletter,* John wrote, "We must be true to our history." With this in mind, the club's outreach activities continued. For the second year, artists Moya Gillett and Neville Clarke provided art classes at the club on Saturday mornings for inner city children. These kids—on average a dozen or so from nearby elementary schools—were having the time of their lives learning skills that would otherwise have been unavailable to them.

In September, members of the executive headed for Lake of Bays in Muskoka, where cottages belonging to three of our members were made available for a weekend retreat to discuss "future directions for the club." Later that year, Jim Parr announced that the Canadian Conservation Institute in Ottawa was interested in preserving our presidential portraits and executive lists that adorn the walls of our lounge. They are considered historic treasures. Reports on their condition were prepared, and then they were re-matted, re-mounted, re-framed, and re-hung, mostly at the Institute's expense. We were very grateful.

At the end of the year, the club established a special category of membership for honorary members. There would be one for each of the five club disciplines, named after five earlier members who were, in their time, leaders in the arts community. Henceforth the club would invite contemporary leaders—one from each discipline—to be honorary members, to enjoy all the rights and privileges of membership at no fee.

In January 1995, Rod Austin, chair of the membership committee, introduced with little fuss and less discussion a motion to offer spousal memberships for same-sex partners. The motion carried unanimously. We may have been one of the first of Toronto's private clubs to do this. The same month, Arthur Gelber once again asked his fellow club members to take a public stand on issues concerning the arts. That didn't happen. The art committee was meanwhile busy hanging an exhibition of women artists to celebrate ten years of membership for women. A few days later another Parr-McGrath creation, *The Rivals*, based on Sheridan's satirical comedy, hit the stage for a four-day run.

"Welcome to the Club" skit celebrating the tenth anniversary of women's membership, 1995.

Later in February, we continued to celebrate the tenth anniversary of the admission of women as members with an evening that featured a skit called "Welcome to the Club," with a script that had essentially been written ten years before—it was made up entirely of the remarks recorded at the legendary 1985 meeting when the barriers to admitting women finally came down. In the cast were a dozen or so women gathered at a genteel ladies' club to debate a motion to admit men. Throughout the discussion, the offending, chauvinistic remarks of 1985 were repeated verbatim, with only the gender changed. Among the cast, not surprisingly, was Anne Lazare-Mirvish, speaking in favour of the motion. And performing a few crossovers at stage rear was the indomitable Ed Mirvish, waving a placard that read "Unfair to Speaker's [sic] Husbands." Shades of 1975! The audience loved it.

Anthony Adamson, 1996. (*Jim Parr*)

Another major event took place the following month, one that enticed a large crowd to the Great Hall to pay tribute to Tony Adamson, one of the country's most admired architects. Members, friends, and heritage activists came out to wish him well and to offer thanks for a lifetime devoted to the preservation of our architectural history. When Tony spoke, his followers hung on every frequently humorous word.

A week after all this excitement, we were back at it again with "Shocked and Appalled: *The Globe and Mail* and Us." The guest speaker was Margaret Inwood-Hagarty, *The Globe*'s letters editor. On hand were a goodly number of members who had, over the years, written some of the "shocked and appalled" letters she was talking about. Warren Clements, also of *The Globe*, was referee for the spirited questions and comments that followed the talk. Ron Sorley assisted at the piano.

Herbert Whittaker, 2001, with his portrait by Barker Fairley. (*Alan Carrie*)

(*Above right*) Herbert Whittaker interviews R. H. Thomson, 1996, in the "Friends of Herbert" program.

In late October, a Bob Christie celebration was held to thank Bob's family for donating his library to the club. It was quite an evening. Bob, a fine actor and past president, was one of our most admired members. The cream of the country's theatrical community turned up to pay their respects to a man whose life had been, in Herb Whittaker's words, "the story of professional theatre in Canada." Seated at the head table with four of Bob's children—daughters Dinah and Fiona, and sons David and Matthew—were Don Harron, Tom Kneebone, Araby Lockhart, Mavor Moore, and Bill Needles, all warmly recalling their work with Bob. His most remarkable attribute, said Mavor, was his modesty. As an added treat, everyone present received a souvenir booklet, *Five Fond Tributes*, designed by Barbara Howard and Richard Outram. The brief essays by Robertson Davies, Don Harron, Tanya Moiseiwitsch, Mavor Moore, and Herb Whittaker paid tribute to their friend and colleague. Bob was, unfortunately, too ill to attend; he died the following year.

Years of retrospective Group of Seven worship made the club's next accomplishment seem almost *de rigueur*—the publication of *The Group of Seven: Why not Eight or Nine or Ten?: Revelations by Members of The Arts and Letters Club.* The slim yet stylish booklet was published in 1995 to celebrate the Group's seventy-fifth anniversary. Designed by Ray Cattell, it included more than sixty seldom-seen drawings by members of the Group and three short essays by Archie Arbuckle, Jack Carr, and Fergus Cronin, each telling previously unrecorded stories of the Group. The booklet was launched in November at a special dinner with descendants of some of the painters on hand to provide their own personal recollections. Also to celebrate the Group's anniversary, the club played host to the Canada Post Corporation to thank them for the release of ten stamps, each featuring a painting by one of the Group, including the three later members—A. J. Casson, L. L. FitzGerald, and Edwin Holgate. The stamps, beautifully packaged and accompanied by a small informative brochure, were a fitting tribute to those artists whose paintings captured "a feeling for the sublime mystery of the Canadian landscape, which is the physical and spiritual heritage of every Canadian." These were, by no means, the first stamps featuring club artists. Many from earlier years are on display at the club.

Events were unfolding at a rapid pace. A serious topic of discussion at the members' dinner in March 1996 was the cuts to the arts in Canada, with that particular year described as "the worst...since the Second World War." In April, Herb Whittaker was on centre stage for a couple of club nights. At the first he interviewed author and social activist June Callwood, and then two weeks later, actor Douglas Campbell. There were also three splendid musical evenings that month and a three-night stage revue, *Spring to Life*. Before each performance, club artists offered a pre-show midway, similar to the 1991 fun fair.

In May, on a more serious note, the club signed an agreement with U of T whereby the university would "house, conserve, and restore the club archives on an ongoing basis, with the club continuing to hold title to the archives." This wise decision was taken because the club did not have, and never could have, the resources—human, financial, and physical—to maintain its archives adequately. Since then, the club's early scrapbooks and other valuable memorabilia have been safely housed in the Fisher Rare Book Library. Also that month, Ezra Schabas became the club's fiftieth president—and the fifth professional musician to serve in that position. He brought with him a host of talents, both musical and administrative: he was a professor of music at U of T, a talented clarinetist, the author of several books, and a pioneer for a number of programs to help launch young musicians.

By September, a bright new idea had surfaced—the establishment of an annual Arts and Letters Award that would honour each year a Torontonian who had made a significant contribution to the arts in the city. The recipient would be given a $1,000

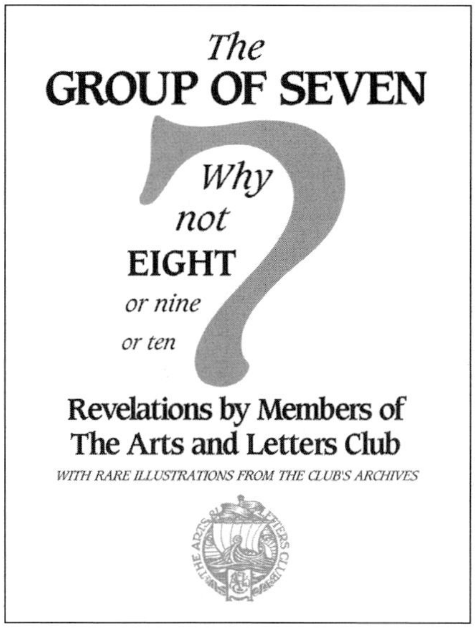

The Group of Seven: Why not Eight or Nine or Ten? 1995.

Ezra Schabas, President, 1996–1998. (*Neville Clarke*)

Arts and Letters Award medal, designed by Anne Lazare-Mirvish.

cheque and a one-year membership in the club, along with a handsome medallion designed by sculptor Anne Lazare-Mirvish. John McKellar chaired the committee and kindly contributed the initial funding. In the following years, the award was funded by a generous donation from Julian Mulock.

On the walls of the Great Hall that month were photographic portraits of sixty-some club members, a labour of love by Jim Parr. Then, in October, came a hilarious members' dinner, during which soprano Mary Lou Fallis brought us a program based on Sara Binks, the "sweet songstress of Saskatchewan." Fallis sang a number of Binks songs, from "Hi, Sooky, Ho, Sooky" to "Reflections While Translating Heine," all set to music by John Greer. Mark Morash was at the piano. What a show!

If 1996 had seemed busy, 1997 was even more so, beginning in January with magician David Ben and journalist Patrick Watson presenting "The Making of the Conjuror." One week later was the annual Burns Supper with, as usual, "its tribute to the bard's immortal memory, its naughty jokes, and its plenitude of scotch whiskey.... The highlander enjoys two things naked, one of them being his whiskey." This event was emceed by the irrepressible Reverend Malcolm Sinclair, with a toast to "the lassies" by Reg Wallace, and a clever reply from Zora Buchanan. Adding to the levity was Jim Parr, who once again turned his fertile mind to doggerel, this time drawing attention to the club's Mona Lisa, a treasured relic from some earlier spring revue. Mona Lisa and the doggerel both hang in the men's washroom:

By the A&L urinal
Mona Lisa's smile divine'll
Scare the pants off men of letters
As she sizes up their wetters.

Not from her the old "come hither,"
For her gauging glance will wither
Manliness, however brawny,
To the wispiest macaroni.

That is why each man afraid is
When he's asked to join the ladies.

Anne Lazare-Mirvish (centre) presents the 2002 Arts and Letters medal to Albert Schultz and Susan Coyne of Soulpepper Theatre. (*Ted Brock*)

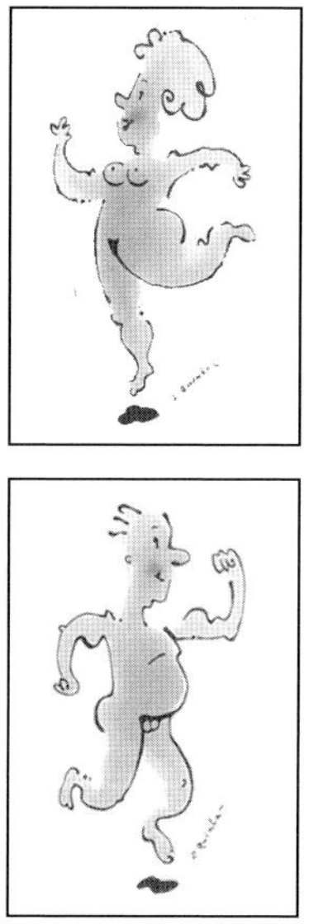

(Above left) Mona Lisa, a spring revue prop painted by Al Collier, oversees the "Gents."

(Above right) Creativity in washroom signage. (*Stephen Quinlan*)

September began on a controversial note with a special meeting to discuss leasing space in our building to the St. George's Society. Several weeks of heated discussion had preceded the meeting. As always, members had firmly held opinions, some pro and some con. After considerable debate, however, all was resolved. In due course, the Society moved into bright and newly renovated office space on the lower level. It still enjoys, as we do, this mutually advantageous arrangement. Later that month, Mary Lou Fallis became the first recipient of our Arts and Letters Award—a popular choice all around.

Plans had been underway since the spring for a tribute to sculptor Walter Allward, his Vimy Memorial, and the more than 3,000 Canadians who died in the battle of Vimy Ridge. It would be a major endeavour on the eightieth anniversary of "Canada's coming of age." Don Pounsett, John Twomey, Margaret McBurney, and their spouses drove to Ottawa to research the contributions made by club members during World War I. They were welcomed at the Canadian War Museum and at Vimy House, the museum's vast storage facility for the works of art and artifacts from that war, including more than three hundred paintings and sketches by members of the Group of Seven. On their return, work began on a twelve-page publication, *Remembering a Forgotten War: A Tribute to Walter Allward and Those Members of The Arts and Letters Club of Toronto Who Served in the Great War.* It includes brief biographies of the fifty-three members who served and the fifteen members who were official war artists, a short article by Fergus Cronin about the memorial, and poems by Richard Outram and J. P. McKerry expressing gratitude and respect for those who served their country with quiet dedication.

The twelve-day tribute began on November 10, with a theatrical production *For What?*, written and staged by club actors. The title was taken from Varley's masterful painting that hangs in the War Museum. We displayed paintings, posters, and war memorabilia throughout the building and opened our doors to the public for two afternoons so that a wider audience could view the exhibits. We welcomed guest speakers, held literary discussions, and showed films, all on World War I. It was a fitting tribute to Allward's magnificent memorial—the noblest monument in Europe—and to all who served.

As a fine example of blending two of our disciplines, Art Steven and Tom McNeeley gave a talk later that month to the literary table. They were addressing the role of artists—

Arthur Gelber. (*Andy Donato*)

both as designers and as illustrators—in book production. Art had been an art director and board member with the Ryerson Press and Tom's expertise was in illustration.

On New Year's Day 1998, one of Canada's leading philanthropists, Arthur Gelber, died. He had resigned from the club three years earlier, tired of what he saw as our only half-hearted support for the arts in the world outside the club. He had been an enthusiastic member of the committee concerned with the cultural implications of free trade in the late eighties, so it's not as though we were doing nothing. For Gelber, however, it was not enough.

The highlight of LAMPS week that year was a visit from the National Gallery's Charles Hill. He came to town specially for the occasion and spoke about visual arts at the club in its first decade and "how the creative energy permeating the former court house on Adelaide Street East fueled the movement that developed into the Group of Seven."

Another art initiative that spring was the Open Art Competition, the art committee's special project to celebrate our ninetieth birthday, open to any artist in Ontario. Doug Purdon, the committee's chair, reported a great response—close to four hundred works, from which forty-five were chosen for a club exhibition and final judging. Ontario Minister of Citizenship, Culture, and Recreation Isabel Bassett opened the gala show. The winner of the $1,000 first prize was Tom La Pierre, RCA, a former instructor at the Ontario College of Art. The club was open to the public for the two weeks of the show.

Sandy (left) and Pat Stewart.

That spring, too, members learned, with sorrow, of the imminent death of one of our most colourful and cherished members, Sandy Stewart. A CBC producer, Sandy had reached young viewers with shows like *Razzle Dazzle* and *Reach for the Top*. He had also written two books about the CBC. Although he knew his life was drawing to an end, he had no intention of going gently "into that good night." He faced his last few months with acceptance and great courage. The club lent a helping hand one evening in March by staging a "Salute to Sandy." There was standing room only as family, friends, and club members gathered to tell Sandy with great flair and humour just how much he meant to them. When it came his turn, Sandy treated his audience to some rollicking off-the-cuff descriptions of many of the people he had known at the CBC, and then he summed up for everyone how grateful he was for having such a wonderful family and such loyal friends, and he spoke of how much the club meant to him. The audience was on its feet and still dry-eyed until, as the crowd filed from the Great Hall, someone at the piano began quietly to play "We'll Meet Again." And so ended a truly memorable evening. Sandy died the following August.

A month or so after the "Salute to Sandy," another loyal member, Michael Spence, was honoured with a dinner to thank him for his "inde-SPENCE-able" contributions to the club, as "president, electrical engineer, building manager, carpenter, and general dogsbody." It was a fitting tribute to someone who has worked tirelessly—and with unfailing good humour—during his many years with the club.

When the annual meeting rolled around, the art committee reported with justifiable pride that, thanks to an auction held two years previously, it had raised enough money to install the state-of-the-art halogen lighting and Velcro-covered wall panels in the Great Hall that have greatly improved our exhibits ever since. Ezra Schabas, in his farewell column for *LAMPSletter*, wrote that he had enjoyed being president and was already wondering what he could do for the club after his final annual meeting. "Serving the club is not only fun," he said, "it's what membership is all about." When Margaret McBurney was elected the next president, she donned an elegant new red velvet robe, a gift to the club from Betty Oliphant. After one look at the tired stained garment that had served dozens of earlier presidents, Betty had said to McBurney, "Well, we're not going to let you wear *that* old thing!" and promptly arranged to have a new one made by the head costume designer at the National Ballet School. It has been worn by five presidents since then.

Margaret McBurney, President, 1998–2000. (*Barbara Howard*)

In July we opened our doors to inner city kids from Dixon Hall, to give them a venue to stage their musical, *Cinderella*. We provided the space free of charge and mounted their artwork on the walls of the Great Hall. The kids and their parents were delighted. And Gelber, no doubt, would have approved. That year, as well, we decided to keep the club open during August for the first time in decades. It was a boon to both members and staff, and we even broke even.

We presented our second annual Arts and Letters Award in September to Tom Kneebone, an actor who had achieved acclaim on the international stage and was at the time serving as director-producer for the Smile Theatre Company, a unique troupe that brings topnotch theatre to senior citizens in hospitals and retirement homes across the province.

Everything seemed to be going smoothly until, in true arts and letters fashion, a kerfuffle arose because of an anonymous letter in the September issue of *LAMPSletter* (by one J. F. C.) that complained about a poem on display in a showcase in our lower level. The title of the poem was "St. Penis," and its author was one Barry Dempster of Montreal. The letter writer accused the club of "accepting the philosophy of the gutter." In the next issue, at the request of a naughty Richard Outram, the entire poem was published, so that those who had not had a chance to view it in the showcase, "would be able

Ruth Morawetz performs in *'S Wonderful, 'S Gershwin*, 1998.

to decide for themselves on the issue." Donald Gillies, in a splendid letter to the editor, protested the club's publishing *any* anonymous letter. "Consider the impression that such a letter would have on a potential new member." Ann Robson, editor of *LAMPSletter*, survived "the hornet's nest buzzing about her" and before long all was forgotten.

For three nights in October, our theatre crew presented an entertaining light comedy, D. L. Coburn's *The Gin Game,* directed by Julian Mulock and starring Beth Firstbrook and Gordon Fulton. Two weeks later it was the musicians' turn with *'S Wonderful, 'S Gershwin*, a black-and-white attire extravaganza written by John Wimbs, Jr. and featuring club musicians Tanya D'Anger, Ruth Morawetz, Patrick Rose, Ezra Schabas, and John Wimbs.

Six weeks after that memorable evening came the final event of the club's ninetieth anniversary celebrations—a performance of *South of North,* a work for baritone and piano, commissioned by the club's music committee under John Lawson's leadership. The poetry was by Richard Outram with music by Srul Irving Glick. James Westman was the baritone, Albert Krywolt was at the piano, and announcing it all was a stunning poster by Tom McNeely. An audience of club members and distinguished guests packed the great hall.

In January 1999, the club staged a reading of Tom Stoppard's *The Invention of Love*—its North American debut. It was directed by *The Globe and Mail*'s "critic emeritus"—and Stoppard's friend—Herb Whittaker, and starred John Neville as A. E. Housman. The cast also included Tom Kneebone, Jamie Mainprize, Julian Mulock, John Rammell, and four students from Ryerson University. Morna Wales served as stage manager for this truly memorable evening. At a literary table the next day, to complement the event, Sandy Leggatt discussed the work of the play's protagonist, A. E. Housman. March saw Tom Kneebone back again, this time with his longtime associate and fellow actor, Dinah Christie, daughter of Bob Christie. In their inimitable fashion they staged their *I've Been to a Marvelous Party*, a celebration of the one-hundredth anniversary of Noel Coward's birth. It was another great evening for the club and for Tom's Smile Theatre Company.

The Invention of Love, by Sir Tom Stoppard, 1999, with director Herbert Whittaker (second row, third from right) and the cast, including John Neville (second row, second from right).

More renovations got underway during the summer, with the quietly competent architect Ian McGillivray in charge. On the second floor the archives/library office was enlarged and a new washroom installed. On the lower level the grungy, dank, dressing rooms were refurbished and a larger cloakroom added. Motion detectors were also put in place—a "closing the barn door" decision after a break-in a few months earlier during which five paintings were stolen. (As of this writing, they have not been recovered.)

In September, impresario Giuseppe Macina became our third Arts and Letters Award recipient, in recognition of his work with young opera singers. At a members' dinner that month, architects Jack Diamond and Donald Schmitt presented a virtual (computer-generated) tour through their proposed new opera house. Concerns were also surfacing about the possible demolition of Vincent Massey's boyhood home on Jarvis Street. Club members had a strong connection to this house—Henry Sproatt and Ernest Rolph had designed a major addition to it earlier in the century and adorned it with a number of fine murals by Emanuel Hahn.

Later that year, David Ben invited members and friends to see a rehearsal of his Christmas production, *The Conjurer's Suite*, at the Royal Ontario Museum. He donated the receipts to the club, earmarking them for junior members' projects, with a pool table (that never materialized) topping his wish list. By this time we were enjoying a newly refurbished building, and all was in readiness for the coming festive season: our annual Boar's Head, two Christmas luncheons, a "new millennium" New Year's Eve bash, and—a first for the club—a New Year's levee, with the president and members of the executive on hand to welcome members and their families for "music, magic, and refreshments." All came off without a hitch. Whew!

We were on a roll. In February 2000, for the final night of LAMPS week, we staged a *son et lumière* event at St. Anne's Anglican Church—a sold-out, star-studded, standing-room-only evening. Ruth Morawetz was the producer, and she had the help of an enthusiastic committee chaired by architect John Sullivan. Artist Andrew Sookrah climbed aboard with a stunning portrait of the church's interior. The performers included actors Dinah Christie, Tom Kneebone, and Gordon Pinsent, storyteller Stuart McLean, artist Charles Pachter, musicians John Avey, Michael Colvin, Mary Lou Fallis, Maureen Forrester, Mark Pedrotti, Brett Polegato, Catherine Robbin, and Sylvia Tyson, and musical groups—the Canadian Children's Opera Chorus, the Elmer Iseler Singers, the Quartetto Gelato, and the Ginger Group. All welcomed the opportunity to help save one of this country's iconic treasures. An astonishing $45,000 was raised that night for the restoration of the church's murals—the very ones that had been painted by club artists in 1923. Governor General Adrienne Clarkson had visited the church ten days prior to the big event with an entourage of journalists and photographers, and the publicity surrounding her visit had been a big boost to advance promotion. Ray Conlogue wrote in his column for *The Globe and Mail* the next day, "Like St. Anne's, the club is

(*Right*) Governor General Adrienne Clarkson and Reverend Peter Orme at St. Anne's (*Sgt. Julien Dupuis*)

(*Below*) Ezra Schabas with Maureen Forrester at St. Anne's.

a relic of old Toronto which many people will be surprised to learn still exists." St. Anne's is now officially designated a national historic site and is visited by countless tourists every year.

Another "first" that year was a CD-ROM about the club created by two bright young students at Sheridan College and their professor Bobbi Wagner. The work—donated to the club by its creators—presents a fresh look at the club, its history, its building, and its members. The same students also designed a web site using much of the same material.

In May, the affable Don Pounsett, a retired lawyer with a musical bent, became our next president. On a bright Sunday that month, dozens of enthusiastic members joined Jim Hubbard to greet the more than 1,200 visitors who streamed into the club for Toronto's first Doors Open. One of the city's most successful ventures, it had begun with a gleam in the eye of architect Cathy Nasmith when she saw what her distant relative Sir James Dunbar-Nasmith had achieved with a similar venture in Edinburgh in 1991. Thanks to her, Toronto was the first city in North America to follow suit.

The 2000 Arts and Letters Award was presented in September to visual artist Ernestine Tahedl. Later that fall, Duggan Melhuish, following in the footsteps of Fergus

(*Below left*) Gord Fulton conducts a tour of the club at Doors Open Toronto, 2002.

(*Below*) Donald Pounsett, President, 2000–2002. (*Mary Tuck Corelli*)

Open Mike on McMichael, 2001.
(*Warren Clements*)

Cronin, continued the series of biographical sketches in *LAMPSletter* under the new title "Introducing…."

In May 2001, we again welcomed visitors for the second Doors Open. Later in October, the Gelber Group (several members who had come together with a common interest in outreach) presented its first event, "Open Mike on McMichael," and played host to several notables from the art world who came to discuss the McMichael Gallery's controversial plan to de-acquisition more than 2,000 works of art from its contemporary collection. On the panel were the National Gallery's Charles Hill, McMichael's chief executive officer Vincent Varga, former chair of the McMichael collection Joan Goldfarb, Royal Canadian Academy of Arts president Ron Bolt, and the *Toronto Star*'s urban issues reporter Christopher Hume. Kate Graham, a club artist whose works are in the McMichael Gallery's collection, directed several pointed questions to the assembled guests. The general mood of the evening was a protest against the proposed de-acquisitioning. It was all quite an eye-opener.

In September, Rollo Myers, an architectural heritage enthusiast who now serves as manager of the Architectural Conservancy of Ontario, was presented with that year's Arts and Letters Award—something that would have pleased the late Eric Arthur, one of our leading architect members who had been a founder of the Conservancy many years before. Club actors were back on stage in November with George Bernard Shaw's *Dark Lady of the Sonnets* directed by Herb Whittaker, produced by Mike Spence, and designed by Rudi Stussi. The cast included Iris Bannerman, Juliana Gianelli, Julian Mulock, John Neville, and Jim Webster.

Early in 2002, it was time for another special dinner to recognize John McKellar, who has contributed greatly to the club ever since joining our ranks in 1980. He served as president, produced several spring revues and has brought distinction to the club in numerous ways through his untiring efforts on our behalf. In February, the Gelber Group presented "What's Happening to Heritage?" Attending the event were architects, archaeologists, museologists, journalists, authors, historians, academics, municipal heritage committee representatives, and politicians. At the annual meeting in May, we welcomed Julian Mulock, an accomplished visual artist and amateur actor, as our next president.

Julian Mulock, President, 2002–2004. (*Gerald Sevier*)

We continued to attract an impressive array of guest speakers. In 2003 alone we heard Richard Gwyn of the *Toronto Star* on "Canada and the World"; Roy McMurtry, Chief Justice of Ontario, on "The Role of the Judiciary in the Age of Terrorism"; Matthew Teitelbaum, Director of the AGO, on its vision for the future; novelist Nino Ricci on his most recent book, *Testament*; Dr. David Leighton, chairman of the National Arts Centre, on its renaissance; and Robert Storr, senior curator at the Museum of Modern Art in New York, on "Contemporary Painting and the Problems Facing Artists."

That year's Arts and Letters Award went to art historian Robert Stacey. He was being recognized for his splendid biography, *J. E. H. MacDonald: Designer*. It seemed a particularly fitting award, since the medallion presented to Stacey bore the club's beloved logo, MacDonald's "Viking ship with sails full spread before the rising sun to remind us of the open sea and the great adventure."

Stage

In the beginning was the word LAMPS. However, the final S stood for sculpture, not stage. Presumably drama was hidden under literature's umbrella, a fact that in 1920 caused then club president Vincent Massey to pen the following lines:

Five arts there are within this panorama,
But there is one omission still—the drama.
The club persists in keeping out this art:
In L-A-M-P-S, D plays no part.

In truth, within two years of the club's move to its first permanent location at the courthouse in 1910, drama had become an integral and thrilling part of its activities.

In a city lacking theatrical excitement, a nucleus of creative talent was at work in those drafty upper chambers of the old court building that would have a profound effect on Toronto's theatrical scene over the next fifty years and beyond. At the time, there were no rules to inhibit the enthusiasm of club members, no censors, and no need to make a profit. In fact, the stated intention was to put on plays otherwise inaccessible to Torontonians. Here the experimentalism could be nurtured.

The first full-length production took place in April 1911 when Maeterlinck's *Interior* was staged—probably its first performance in Canada. It was produced and directed by Roy Mitchell, who was crucial to the success of the club's early theatrical activities. Working conditions were primitive. The stage was made up of 150 movable boxes that had to be set up for each performance. Lighting consisted of spotlights with tin reflectors. There was no proscenium arch, no wings, no scenery—restrictions that resulted in the introduction of a stylized expressionistic school of stage setting. Here the players performed within the audience's space, thus bringing an immediacy and excitement to productions that allowed the audience to be intimate participants in the action rather than simply spectators. Necessity had produced a thrust stage in Canada, fifty years ahead of its time.

Over the next decade, in a series of triumphs of improvisation, plays both well known and obscure were staged—many for the first time in Canada, even North America. Club audiences had an eclectic choice: commedia del arte, Japanese Noh plays, Tagore's *The Post Office* and *Chitra*, J. M. Synge's *Riders to the Sea*, and Lady Gregory's *Rising of the Moon* were just a few of the highlights staged by this talented and dedicated band of thespians.

By now it had become obvious that a proper theatre, not the inadequate clubroom facilities, was needed. Plans were drawn up for a most ingenious little theatre and art gallery combined, but World War I forced their abandonment.

In 1920, the club moved to 14 Elm Street, and the following year—1921—the first play to be presented there was J. M. Synge's *The Shadow of the Glen*. There was still no proscenium, just a low platform fronted by a flimsy curtain running on a wire. It would be several years before a proper stage and dressing rooms would be built.

Still breaking new ground at a time when the expression "Canadian plays" was an oxymoron, the club encouraged homegrown playwrights such as Fred Jacob, Merrill Denison, Britton Cooke, and Welwyn Griffin by staging their plays. Much later, the club would stage plays by Herman Voaden and the internationally known John Coulter.

The move to new premises coincided with the establishment of Hart House Theatre and its better facilities soon attracted our members away from the club. Vincent Massey appointed Roy Mitchell its first director, and Mitchell's group of visionaries at the club shifted their theatrical experimentation from Elm Street to the university. In fact, nearly all the male actors appearing at Hart House in those early days were club members. Drama still flourished at Elm Street, of course, but the flame that had burnt so brilliantly during those pioneering days lost some of its intensity.

As a sidebar to this history, an event took place in 1933 that in its way reflects one of the finer qualities of our club. An all-black choir, leaving behind the humiliating reality of its segregated homeland, came to Toronto to perform *The Green Pastures*. Augustus Bridle recalled how "it was decided that, as this democracy had never recognized the colour line, we might have a midnight jamboree with the entire company of sixty-five as guests." Chartered buses brought the troop to the club where members and wives greeted them. Supper was provided. After midnight, the entire company spontaneously broke into "Joshua fit de battle ob Jericho," even though their contract prohibited them from singing any part of the show off their own stage. When President Napier Moore inquired, "What will de Lawd's people do next?" the reply was "Everything." What a night that must have been! What an occasion to remember!

During the years between the two world wars, the club was fortunate in counting among its members several gifted directors: Earle Grey, Edgar Stone, Frank Hemingway, and Sterndale Bennett. Their creative leadership kept drama in the forefront of the club's activities. During the twenties, three full-length plays were presented each year. In the thirties, the club won repeated acclaim for its entries in the Dominion Drama Festival, an annual event that was of great importance to the theatrical life of the country. It nurtured many writers and actors who later became well known to Canadian audiences. In 1936, for instance, festival adjudicator Harley Granville-Barker, an actor and playwright of international renown, judged our *Napoleon Crossing the Rockies* by Percy Mackaye. He found it almost perfect in its presentation and "could hardly pick a flaw" in Ivor Lewis's performance as the old fiddler.

Today Toronto has become a major theatrical centre. If the club's involvement in dramatic activity is not as intense as in earlier years it is because there is such a wide choice of fine professional theatre elsewhere in the city. However, the tradition continues. The lights dim, the audience is hushed, and the curtains part to reveal another theatrical event. Perhaps it is Robertson Davies' *Fortune My Foe*, or a Parr-McGrath musical, or an evening of Noel Coward's inimitable words and songs. And it was theatre critic-director Herbert Whittaker's friendship with Sir Tom Stoppard that secured for us the first North American performance of his *The Invention of Love*. The dramatic reading starred John Neville, with a large cast of members and, for the first time, students from Ryerson University's Theatre School.

Still experimenting, still aiming for excellence, still bringing first-class entertainment to audiences in the Great Hall, drama remains an integral part of the club's activities.

John Rammell

CHAPTER 6

Approaching One Hundred

2004–2007

Four years of accomplishment
Celebrating our centenary

The four years leading up to our centenary are too immediate to be handled in the same detail as the earlier chapters. If there are more stories to tell, they will have to wait for the next history to be written. So this one will focus only on the highlights—a once-over-lightly of recent events, with a glimpse of what lies ahead. Rest assured, the upcoming centennial celebrations will be creative, exciting, and, in true Arts and Letters fashion, memorable. Some will be more successful than others but, as we say, "that's club!"

As Julian Mulock's presidency came to an end at the annual meeting in May 2004, it was announced that our membership had reached more than six hundred—the highest in our history. Peter Hart became our next president. A retired engineer with a love of theatre, Peter had appeared on the club's stage on many occasions. After Peter, it was Lorna Kelly's turn—the second woman to don presidential robes. She had previously served the club as vice president (house) and had, before her retirement, been a professor at Ryerson University, where she chaired the School of Interior Design for ten years.

As for our staff, the club has been very, very lucky. In spite of inevitable glitches, misunderstandings, and the occasional curmudgeonly member, the young men and women on our staff have been unfailingly patient and pleasant. Those who have been with us for some years share a sense of involvement with the members. They even seem to enjoy working for us. Jason Clark, who served for several years as the club's general manager, wrote a year or so after returning to his home province of Nova Scotia that he hadn't realized until he left that "not all private clubs were as wonderful as the Arts and Letters!"

(*Above left*) Peter Hart, President, 2004–2006. (*Dennis Rose*)

Current president Lorna Kelly, 2006–2008. (*Brian Summers*)

From left:
Fiona McKeown, General Manager, 2007. (*George Lobb*)

Naomi Priddle Hunter, Membership Services, 2001

Ken Peace, Chef de Cuisine, 2007. (*George Lobb*)

Bill Buchanan, fundraiser, 1993. (*Alan Carrie*)

And so, with membership at an all-time high, it would seem that we must be doing something—many things—right. We continue to use every creative approach we can to encourage junior members since our future success lies in their hands. Bright ideas such as Michael Symonds' fun-filled Friday night Ad Lib events continue to be popular with young and old alike. Club access for the handicapped was installed in 2004, in large part thanks to Bill Buchanan's fundraising skills. Those in wheelchairs have welcomed both the ramp and the lift, which allow the club to remain available to them. And just recently, the Historic Sites and Monuments Board of Canada designated our building a national historic site, a fitting recognition of our first century. But challenges remain. We're keeping a wary eye on gender balance, since women now slightly outnumber men. And maintaining our constitutionally mandated sixty-forty professional-nonprofessional membership ratio continues to require constant vigilance.

There has been much to celebrate during the past few years, with members from all the LAMPS disciplines offering a continuing array of fine programming. The weekly literature and music lunches are thriving. The artists enjoy working on the third floor on a regular basis. Their thematic art shows continue to grace the walls of the Great Hall and the lounge, and their outdoor sketching weekends, to which non-artists are also invited, are convivial indeed. As in the past, our goodly number of architects and interior designers keep a low professional visibility, choosing to limit their formal contribution to hosting a guest speaker for LAMPS week and to mounting an occasional special event. In true interdisciplinary fashion, however, many of them maintain visibility as painters or writers or actors. Our thespian members continue to mount special productions throughout the year—a play, a reading, or a skit. And along with writers, directors, stagehands, technicians, set designers, choreographers, and costume designers, they continue to make spring revues a major focus.

At the Literary Table, Brenda Davies and daughter Jennifer read from Robertson Davies' posthumously published work, 1998. (*Alan Carrie*)

Monday club nights continue to be informal—featuring musicians, art openings, films, and speakers on a regular basis. Friday's TGIF lunches are just that—a regular and frequent opportunity for everyone to unwind and meet friends. For more formal monthly members' dinners there is usually a high-profile guest speaker—in 2004, for example, we welcomed Jackie Maxwell, the Shaw Festival's new artistic director; Pauline Michel, Canada's poet laureate; and Laura Brandon, the Canadian War Museum's curator of war art. Special events throughout the year continue to include a Boar's Head, Christmas lunches, a New Year's Eve party, a Burns Supper, LAMPS week, a week-long spring revue, and, in May, our annual meeting. There's rarely a dull moment.

The annual Arts and Letters Award continues to be presented every fall to a person (or persons) who has made a significant contribution to the arts in Toronto. In 2004, the winners were Bruce Ubukata and Stephen Ralls, recognized for their many contributions to music. The following year, the recipient was George Brough, a pianist "who holds a unique place in the history of music in this country and in the hearts of the musical community."

Hamilton & Scourge Project, subject of panel discussion, 2005.

March 2005 saw the sixth—and last—Gelber Group event when, as reported in a *Globe and Mail* editorial, "a remarkable thing happened under the auspices of the Arts and Letters Club of Toronto." The evening meeting was devoted to saving the *Hamilton* and the *Scourge,* two American schooners that sank in Hamilton Harbour during the War of 1812. On hand for the panel discussion was a leading naval historian and a top archaeologist, both from Washington, DC, two archaeologists from Parks Canada in Ottawa, and an historian from Hamilton. All had come "to talk about collaborating to safeguard these bi-national treasures and figure out what to do with them." Since that memorable evening, the spot where these vessels rest has been designated an underwater archeological site. As such, it receives special protection, with a marine archeologist on site to monitor any activity. Parks Canada is now playing a significant role in the project, and the City of Hamilton has also contributed funding. Everyone involved agrees that "this remarkable thing" would not in all probability have happened without the club's initial impetus. Charles Currelly and Robert Flaherty would be delighted, for it was they who, in the club's earliest days, introduced archaeology to fascinated members.

Videography workshop led by Peter Fleming, 2003.

(Above left) Artists in the third-floor studio. (*George Lobb*)

In April, members and visitors from England, France, and the United States, and from across Canada arrived at the club for a memorial evening to honour two of our most admired and beloved members—artist Barbara Howard, RCA, and her husband, poet Richard Outram, a man described by Alberto Manguel as "one of the finest poets in the English language." Barbara had died unexpectedly in December 2002. Richard, having coped with grief for the following two years, took his own life in January 2005.

That year also brought the welcome announcement that John Lawson had agreed to take charge of wide-ranging plans for the celebration of our centennial, three years down the road. A retired lawyer, John brought to the position his devotion to the arts and an intimate knowledge of the club and its members. Before long, he had lined up Mary Jane Large as vice chair, and representatives of each LAMPS discipline were appointed to help with the planning.

Richard Outram and Barbara Howard, 1994. (*Jim Parr*)

A defining moment in the club's history occurred in January 2006 when pianist William Aide sat down at the club's new Steinway concert grand for its inaugural concert. The piano, which replaced the larger of our two pianos, was built in New York in 1971–1972. It had been completely restored with original Steinway parts and refinished with a high

Centenary Committee, 2007. From the left: George Hume, Roland de Corneille, Peter Hart, John Lawson (chair), George Edmonds, Peter Moon, Pat Wardrop, Vernon Mould, Ellen Edmonds, Mary Jane Large, John Rammell, John Caldwell, John Hore, Peter Large, and Scott James. (*George Lobb*)

Executive Committee, 2007. Standing, from the left: Malcolm McGrath, Peter Large, Frances Webster, Peter Alberti, Peter Moon, Michael Symonds; (seated, clockwise from the left) Lorna Kelly, Michelle Bouchard, Zora Buchanan, Roger (Rod) Carruthers, Carol McGirr, Peter Fleming, Kay Montgomery, Penelope Cookson, Helen Mitchell, Robert White; (absent) Chester Gryski, Jonathan Krehm. (*George Lobb*)

William Aide at the new Steinway, 2007. (*Frances Webster*)

ebony polish finish. Our two Steinways will continue to bring great pleasure to countless members and guests in the coming years, as they did recently for two young artists who came to the club to perform a duo piano recital for us: "Wow! I've got a Steinway!" said one. "Wow! So have I!" said the other.

On a club night in mid-February, we celebrated the twentieth anniversary of "Women at the Heart of the Club" with a valentine dinner and a thoughtful keynote address given by John McKellar. Paintings by charter women artists were on the walls, and a short play written by Bill Whiteacre and directed by Nancy Kee was performed on the stage. Soprano Jean Edwards also sang that evening. Alan Stein presented his list of the forty charter women—those who joined the club between May 1985 and July 1987—that now hangs in the LAMPS Room. Fittingly, Ed and Anne Mirvish were on hand as well, Anne carrying with her the hat she had worn while picketing the club in 1975.

During the summer, the Fisher Rare Book Library mounted "Pungent Personalities," an exhibition of Arthur Lismer sketches—whimsical caricatures of club members—all from our archives. Our archivist, Scott James, prepared a fine catalogue to accompany the show, and the library hosted a gala opening.

In the fall, our Honorary Member for stage, R. H. Thomson, was commissioned by the federal government to write a staged reading, *Words from Vimy*, for the unveiling of Walter Allward's newly restored Vimy Memorial in April 2007, the ninetieth anniversary of the Battle of Vimy Ridge. Our archives were a major source for his project, since they hold considerable information about that battle and the memories of some of our early members—Agar Adamson, Jack McLaren, and others—who served in it.

On a cold and rainy weekend in October, more than thirty members travelled to Rochester, New York to celebrate an art exhibition held jointly by the Arts and Letters Club and the Rochester Art Club. It was, to our knowledge, the first time that a Canadian and an American private club have collaborated in this way. Twenty-nine of our artists had works in the show and it was a great success. Plans are already underway for a repeat exhibition—to be held in Toronto this time as part of our centennial celebrations. In late November, designer, illustrator, and painter Roger Hill was named the 2006 Arts and Letters Award winner. His work included sixteen commemorative stamps for Canada Post and a one-dollar coin for the Royal Canadian Mint.

Opening of the first joint exhibition with the Rochester Art Club, 2006. (*Gordon Fulton*)

Guests at the club today might be forgiven for assuming that most of our members have been around ever since the doors first opened. Well, hardly. While it's true that many are no longer young, we are also fortunate to have a growing coterie of talented and keen junior members. Whatever their age, our members arrive full of enthusiasm, looking forward to whatever that particular day has to offer, entertaining friends, or just settling in for a chat with anyone who happens to be there. Boredom is rarely an option. In one of his more insightful moments, Hector Charlesworth wrote that the club's vitality "derives from the urge toward companionship and the genial exchange of opinion which brought it into being." The *New Yorker*'s Adam Gopnik puts it another way—a club is for "convivial people who are in need of other people as a mirror in which to see their better selves."

The question of how private we are as a private club has been an issue ever since day one, with privacy usually holding sway. But with our centenary approaching, this issue was recently revisited by our executive. With the backing of John Lawson's committee and spearheaded by Peter Moon, it was decided that the club would, on specified occasions, welcome the media in order to "garner significant public recognition of our contributions to Canada." We have, of course, been mentioned countless times by the

Les Tibbles (left) and John Joy on an outdoor sketching trip, 1991.

Peter Large, President-Elect, 2008–2010. (*Brian Little*)

media in the past, but now the welcome will be official. Perhaps some of the old guard are turning in their graves.

The club is still a vital place. Our members simply enjoy being with like-minded people. They love the club for all that it offers within its walls, for its intimate and informal atmosphere, for its connection to the community, and for the lasting friendships formed therein. For many, it has become a surrogate family. They feel proprietary about the club—which is at the same time both its greatest strength and its greatest weakness.

For the better part of a century, despite occasional rows and resignations and disagreements, there has been a general consensus about the kind of club we want. And it all goes back to the beginning—to Gus Bridle, who urged us to "help civic art" and remain a "shirtsleeve democracy," to charter member Joseph Clark's description of his fellow members as men "whose main object in life is not to make money," and to George Locke's insistence that we never become an "upholstered" club. We have succeeded on all counts and welcome new challenges as our second century stretches invitingly ahead.

Spring Revues

Did you know that the club once hired an ecdysiast to perform in a spring revue? Or that a prominent federal cabinet minister and his wife, both in full evening attire, were covered in flour during a performance? These are just two of many fascinating stories about past spring revues. Napier Moore initiated the events in 1930 to present original skits for the entertainment of members and guests. A sampling of titles gives an idea of their scope: "Saps Running" (1933), "Speakeasia" (1957), "Let's All Hate Toronto" (1966), "Oh Hell" (1972), "Out of Your Mind" (1980), "You've Got to Be Dreaming" (1990), "Nuts in May" (2000), and "Out of Control" (2002). Many of the skits have been satirical, poking fun at politicians and bureaucrats at international, national, and local levels. Others have been based on everyday situations.

Before 1930, comedy sketches were common fare at monthly dinners, and sometimes repeated for ladies' days. As Napier Moore wrote, "It was a pity that the results of so much work and talent should be seen only by a limited audience." He proposed that every spring there be a club revue for which tickets could be sold. Programs would be made up of the best acts staged during the previous year. The idea was approved, and Moore was appointed producer. On April 2, 1930, the old blue curtains that ran on a wire strung across the low platform parted. Pianist Percy Schutte and a small chorus burst out with "We're Members of Rather an Odd Sort of Club." The first revue, "April Foolies," was launched. It played for two nights and was repeated a month later as "May Gambols."

By 1932 the show was running for a full week. The performances were for members and guests only. The absence of the press allowed freedom to satirize public figures. Those who were the butt of the wit revelled in it. Word spread. People travelled from far away to see the show. Soon sufficient money had accumulated for a permanent proscenium, a proper switchboard and lighting equipment, and adequate dressing rooms. These improvements gave added zest to other club productions.

In "Round the Corner" (1934), Jack McLaren had the audience rolling in the aisles with his cooking school, in which he prepared for a cocktail party by mixing various "alcoholic" concoctions and tasting each in turn. The pipe organ act in "Spring Is Cub" (1935) started with the swelling strains of an organ. The curtains opened to reveal Harvey Robb seated at an enormous console studded with keys and stops. Above him towered a mighty array of pipes, painted on a scrim. As the music reached its climax, the lighting changed to make the scrim transparent and to reveal forty men blowing on real organ pipes. Robb had "borrowed" the pipes surreptitiously from Bloor Street United Church. Ernest MacMillan had rehearsed the organ blowers. Only John Robins had the lung capacity to produce a sound from the eight-foot bass pipe.

McLaren achieved immortality in "Old Skit Bag" (1939). So realistic was his furnace in "How to Light a Furnace" that, when the curtain rose, the applause lasted a full minute. Then Jack, in evening clothes, proceeded to build the fire. He smashed up furniture for kindling. He played mashie shots with pieces of coal—with unerring aim. It was a property man's nightmare. The audience was in stitches. When McLaren lit the fire there was an explosion. Clouds of smoke—flour—were blown out of the furnace to settle all over the front row, transforming the beautifully gowned ladies and black-coated gents—including the afore-mentioned cabinet minister and his wife—into ghosts! Members of his party howled with glee. "We've never had such fun," said their host.

One memorable show included a nude female posing as a garden statue. She was covered from head to toe with gold body cream. Walter Packman decided that as lighting man he should assist with the application of the cream. All proprieties were, however, decently observed since the model was always accompanied by her mother.

Over the years, hundreds of members have contributed to spring revues. Musical numbers boast of contributions by Scott Malcolm, Reg Godden, David Ouchterlony, Ernest MacMillan, and the two-piano team of Jack Yocom and Wilf White. More recently, pianist Ruth Morawetz has contributed her considerable talents. Directors have included luminaries Napier Moore, Reg Godden, Bob Christie, Pat Hume, John Snell, Gary Hall, Jim Morris, Jim Webster, Peter Hart, John Rammell, Julian Mulock, and Betty Trott. Acting talent, both professional and non-professional, has often been outstanding. Before women were included, the *corps de ballet* was composed entirely of men in dance attire. In the mid-sixties, Morna Wales Daniel, Norma Crawford, Anne Marie Hurley, and Jean Edwards joined the stalwart group of male dancers—Bill Shelden, Elmer Phillips, Eric Ford, Norm McMurrich, Gary Hall, Cal Wilson, and Brent Rowe. Pat Hume's many humorous numbers in the seventies, eighties, and nineties are just examples of the contributions of our many talented club writers.

Our artists have contributed to the design, construction, and painting of elaborate stage sets, including some ingenious mechanisms such as the above-mentioned furnace, a piano torn apart nightly, and a computerized bank machine. Designers have included Oxford MacNeill, York Wilson, Al Collier, John Snell, Chris Adeney, Geoff Armstrong, Steve Quinlan, Jim Webster, Loi Hathaway, and Murray Oliver—each adding his or her own spark of creativity to the show. Costume makers have also contributed to the total visual experience. Di Hore, Margaret Spence, and Virginia Cooper have followed in the footsteps of Michael Schilder, who had the resources of Malabar Costumes at his disposal.

Let's not forget the backstage workers. Stage manager emeritus Roly Pincoe can count over forty consecutive revues. Other crew members include John Morrow, Ran MacDonald, Hugh Westren, Wentworth Walker, Jim Dooley, Jim Hubbard, Bill McCoy, Steve Walker, Irena Corbelo, Michael Spence, David Skene-Melvin, Ken Judd, Chris Nanos, and David Briant.

Throughout the years, spring revues have been the place where many artistic talents come together. Each year some fifty or more dedicated members make sure that the ideas contributed by the script writers are brought to fruition. It is always a team effort, culminating in some truly memorable and enjoyable performances.

Michael Spence

Honours

Nobel Laureates

Frederick Grant Banting
John James Richard Macleod

Knighthoods

Frederick Grant Banting
Beverley Baxter
Wyly Grier
Ernest MacMillan
William Mulock
Edmund Walker

Historic Sites and Monuments Board of Canada: Historic Persons

Walter Seymour Allward
Sir Frederick G. Banting
Charles-Marius Barbeau
John Murray Gibbon
Lawren Stewart Harris
Alexander Young Jackson
Charles William Jefferys
Arthur Lismer
George Herbert Locke
James E. H. MacDonald
Sir Ernest MacMillan
Charles Vincent Massey
Peter McArthur
E. J. Pratt
George Agnew Reid
Bernard Keble Sandwell
Duncan Campbell Scott
Frederick Varley
Sir Byron Edmund Walker
Horatio Walker
Homer Ransford Watson
Healey Willan

Order of Canada: Companions

Lincoln Alexander
Louis Applebaum
Eric R. Arthur
Charles S. Band
Marius Barbeau
Mario Bernardi
Claude T. Bissell
Floyd S. Chalmers
Donald G. Creighton
Robertson Davies
Maureen Forrester
Northrop Frye
Lawren S. Harris
A. Y. Jackson
Arthur Lismer
Hugh MacLennan
Ernest MacMillan
Vincent Massey
Marshall McLuhan
J. Mavor Moore
Betty Oliphant
Christopher Plummer
Healey Willan
J. Tuzo Wilson

Order of Canada: Officers

Anthony Adamson
Harry Adaskin
Murray Adaskin
Edmund Charles Bovey
Harry J. Boyle
Jack Bush
Alfred J. Casson
Charles F. Comfort
Thomas Cullen Daly
Richard E. G. Davis
Dora de Pedery-Hunt
H. Lovat Dickson
Arnold Edinborough
Barker Fairley
Clarence B. Farrar
Victor Feldbrill
James Douglas Fleck
Kenneth K. Forbes
Harry Freedman
Herman Geiger-Torel

Arthur E. Gelber
William Glassco
Jack Lawrence Granatstein
Donald Harron
Robert Hall Haynes
Thomas Best Hendry
Walter B. Herbert
John W. Holmes
Hugh Hood
Cleeve Horne
Robert Hamilton Hubbard
W. Arthur Irwin
Elmer Iseler
Marsh Jeanneret
John Francis Leddy
David S. R. Leighton
John B. Macdonald
J. Keiller Mackay
Alexander Gordon McKay
Kenneth William McNaught
Edwin Mirvish
William O. Mitchell
Mary Morrison
Louis Boyd Neel
Walter George Pitman
Arthur Porter
Gerald Pratley
Laure E. Rièse
Roderick George Robbie
Richard H. Rohmer
Malcolm M. Ross
Murray G. Ross
Peter Russell
Lister S. Sinclair
Arnold Cantwell Smith
Gordon Hamilton Southam
Edward E. Stewart
Vincent Tovell
Peter Trueman
Tommy Tweed
Arnold M. Walter
Herbert W. Whittaker
Joyce Wieland

Order of Canada: Members

Lanfranco Amato
Paul Rodney Arthur
Gerald Bales
Clare Bice
John Burgon Bickersteth
David Lloyd Blackwood
Michael Bliss
John F. Brook
G. Allan Burton
Douglas Campbell
Humphrey Stephen Mumford Carver
Christopher Martin Chapman
H. Spencer Clark
Austin Chesterfield Clarke
Kenneth H. J. Clarke
John Robert Colombo
J. Douglas Crashley
Brian Doherty
Jack M. Dow
J. Alexander Edmison
Sorel Etrog
Robert Farnon
Charles Henry Foss
John Anderson Fraser
Gregory Francis Gatenby
Sheldon Jay Godfrey
Helen Frances Gregor
Lyman G. Henderson
George William Bligh Hostetter
James Nairn Patterson Hume
Richard Johnston
Franc R. Joubin
Tom Kneebone
G. Blair Laing
Heath R. Lamberts
Bruce Jarvis Legge
Reginald William Lewis
Marion Bell MacRae
Leon Major
Charles A. G. Matthews
Graeme Donald McDonald
Frank F. McEachren
John Duncan McKellar
Alasdair J. McKichan
Robert McMichael
Ruby Mercer
Robert N. Munsch
John Neville
Will Ogilvie
Charles Pachter
Charles Peaker
Kati Rekai
Roseann Runte
Ezra Schabas
Paul Siren
Taylor Statten
Clair Cuthbert Stewart
Grant Strate
Mary Alice Stuart
Dennis Sweeting
Alan Miller Thomas
Tony van Bridge
J. Bryan Vaughan
Herman Voaden
William J. Withrow
Elwy Yost

Bibliography

Adams, John Coldwell. *Sir Charles God Damn: The Life of Sir Charles G.D. Roberts.* Toronto: University of Toronto Press, 1986.

Adamson, Agar. *Letters of Agar Adamson, 1914 to 1919: Lieutenant Colonel, Princess Patricia's Canadian Light Infantry 1914 to 1919.* Edited by N. M. Christie. Toronto: CEF Books, 1997.

Adamson, Jeremy. *Lawren S. Harris: Urban Scenes and Wilderness Landscapes 1906–1930.* Toronto: Art Gallery of Ontario, 1978.

Anthony, Geraldine. *John Coulter*. Boston: Twayne Publishers, 1976.

Armstrong, Frederick H. *Toronto: The Place of Meeting.* Burlington: Windsor Publications, 1983.

Arthur, Eric. *Toronto: No Mean City*. Toronto: University of Toronto Press, 1986.

Arts and Letters Club of Toronto. *Year Book of Canadian Art 1913*. Toronto: J. M. Dent, 1913.

Bissell, Claude. *The Young Vincent Massey.* Toronto: University of Toronto Press, 1981.

Bliss, Michael. *Banting: A Biography*. Toronto: McClelland and Stewart, 1984.

Bliss, Michael. *The Discovery of Insulin*. Toronto: McClelland and Stewart, 1982.

Bridle, Augustus. *Sons of Canada*. Toronto: J. M. Dent, 1916.

Bridle, Augustus. *The Story of the Club.* Toronto: The Arts and Letters Club of Toronto, 1945.

Brooke, Rupert and James Strachey. *Friends and Apostles: Correspondence*. New Haven: Yale University Press, 1998.

Brooker, Bertram, ed. *Yearbook of the Arts in Canada.* Toronto: Macmillan of Canada, 1929.

Canadian Press Association. *Who's Who and Why: A Biographical Dictionary of Men and Women of Canada and Newfoundland*. Vancouver: International Press, 1914.

Chalmers, Floyd S. *Both Sides of the Street: One Man's Life in Business and the Arts in Canada.* Toronto: Macmillan of Canada, 1983.

Chalmers, Floyd S. *A Gentleman of the Press: The Story of Colonel John Bayne Maclean and the Publishing Empire He Founded.* Toronto: Doubleday, 1969.

Coulter, John. *In My Day: Memoirs.* Toronto: Hounslow Press, 1980.

Dendy, William and William Kilbourn. *Toronto Observed: Its Architecture, Patrons, and History.* Toronto: Oxford University Press Canada, 1986.

Denvir, Bernard. *A Most Agreeable Society: A Hundred and Twenty-five Years of the Arts Club.* London: Arts Club/Studio Editions, 1989.

Douglas, Francis, R., Richard Jones, and Donald B. Smith. *Destinies: Canadian History Since Confederation.* Toronto: Nelson, 2004.

Fairley, Barker. *Barker Fairley Portraits.* Toronto: Methuen, 1981.

Firth, Edith. *Toronto in Art: 150 Years through Artists' Eyes.* Toronto: Fitzhenry & Whiteside/City of Toronto, 1983.

Frye, Northrop. *The Diaries of Northrop Frye, 1942–1955.* Edited by Robert D. Denham. Toronto: University of Toronto Press, 2001.

Fulford, Robert. *Accidental City: The Transformation of Toronto.* Toronto: Macfarlane Walter & Ross, 1995.

Gatenby, Greg. *Toronto: A Literary Guide.* Toronto: McArthur & Company, 1999.

Gatenby, Greg, ed. *The Very Richness of That Past: Canada Through the Eyes of Foreign Writers.* Toronto: Alfred A. Knopf Canada, 1995.

Granatstein, J. L. *Who Killed Canadian History?* Toronto: HarperCollins, 1998.

Grigor, Angela Nairne. *Arthur Lismer, Visionary Art Educator.* Montreal: McGill-Queen's University Press, 2002.

Guillet, Edwin C. *Pioneer Inns and Taverns.* Toronto: University of Toronto Press, 1954.

Gwyn, Sandra. *The Private Capital: Ambition and Love in the Age of Macdonald and Laurier.* Toronto: McClelland and Stewart, 1984.

Gwyn, Sandra. *Tapestry of War: A Private View of Canadians in the Great War.* Toronto: HarperCollins, 1992.

Harper, J. Russell. *Painting in Canada: A History.* Toronto: University of Toronto Press, 1966.

Harriott, Ted. *Sunday Morning with Cass: Conversations with A. J. Casson.* Mississauga: Purpleville Publishing, 1993.

Henderson, Maxwell. *Plain Talk! Memoirs of an Auditor General.* Toronto: McClelland and Stewart, 1984.

Hill, Charles C. *The Group of Seven: Art for a Nation.* Ottawa: National Gallery of Canada, 1995.

Housser, F. B. *A Canadian Art Movement: The Story of the Group of Seven.* Toronto: Macmillan of Canada, 1926.

Hunter, Martin. *Romancing the Bard: Stratford at Fifty.* Toronto: Dundurn Press, 2001.

Jones, Donald. *Fifty Tales of Toronto.* Toronto: University of Toronto Press, 1992.

Kapica, Jack, ed. *Shocked and Appalled: A Century of Letters to the Globe and Mail.* Toronto: Lester & Orpen Dennys, 1985.

Kilbourn, William. *Intimate Grandeur: One Hundred Years at Massey Hall.* Toronto: Stoddart, 1993.

Kilbourn, William. *Toronto Remembered: A Celebration of the City.* Toronto: Stoddart, 1984.

Kilgour, David, ed. *A Strange Elation: Hart House, The First Eighty Years.* Toronto: Hart House, 1999.

Kluckner, Michael. *Toronto: The Way It Was.* Toronto: Whitecap Books, 1988.

Koch, Eric. *The Brothers Hambourg*. Toronto: Robin Brass, 1997.

Lamb, Robert J. ed. *The Canadian Art Club 1907–1915.* Edmonton: Edmonton Art Gallery, 1988.

Larisey, Peter. *Light for a Cold Land: Lawren Harris's Work and Life.* Toronto: Dundurn Press, 1993.

MacKenzie, David. *Arthur Irwin: A Biography*. Toronto: University of Toronto Press, 1993.

MacNeil, Robert. *Wordstruck: A Memoir*. Markham: Viking, 1989.

MacTavish, Newton. *Ars Longa*. Toronto: Ontario Publishing Co., 1938.

MacTavish, Newton. *The Fine Arts in Canada*. Toronto, 1925

Martin, Sandra and Roger Hall. *Rupert Brooke in Canada*. Toronto: PMA Books, 1978.

Massey, Raymond. *A Hundred Different Lives.* Toronto: McClelland and Stewart, 1979.

Massey, Raymond. *When I Was Young.* Toronto: Little Brown and Co., 1976.

Massey, Vincent. *What's Past is Prologue: The Memoirs of the Right Honourable Vincent Massey, C.H.* Toronto: Macmillan of Canada, 1963.

McCarthy, Doris. *A Fool in Paradise: An Artist's Early Life.* Toronto: Macfarlane Walter & Ross, 1990.

McCarthy, Pearl. *Leo Smith.* Toronto: University of Toronto Press, 1957.

McConnell, Newton. *McConnell's Vanity Fair: A Portfolio of Caricatures.* Toronto: Printed by W. S. Johnston, 1912.

McHugh, Patricia. *Toronto Architecture: A City Guide*. Toronto: Mercury Books, 1985.

McInnis, Graham. *Finding a Father.* London: H. Hamilton, 1967.

McKillop, A. B. *The Spinster and the Prophet: Florence Deeks, H. G. Wells, and the Mystery of the Purloined Past*. Toronto: Macfarlane Walter & Ross, 2000.

McLaren, John. *J. W.: The Life Story of J. W. McLaren*. Toronto, 2006.

McLeish, John A. B. *September Gale: A Study of Arthur Lismer of the Group of Seven.* Toronto: Dent, 1973.

Mellen, Peter. *The Group of Seven*. Toronto: McClelland and Stewart, 1970.

Middleton, Jesse Edgar. *The Municipality of Toronto, A History*. Toronto: Dominion Publishing Co., 1923.

Miller, Muriel. *Bliss Carmen: Quest and*

Revolt. St. John's: Jesperson Press, 1985.
Mirvish, Ed. *Honest Ed Mirvish: How to Build an Empire on an Orange Crate, or 121 Lessons I Never Learned in School.* Toronto: Key Porter Books, 1993.
Mitchell, Roy. *Creative Theatre.* New York: John Day, 1929.
Moore, Mavor. *Reinventing Myself.* Toronto: Stoddart, 1994.
Morgan, Henry J. *The Canadian Men and Women of the Time: A Hand-book of Canadian Biography.* Toronto: W. Briggs, 1898.
Murray, Joan. *Canadian Art in the Twentieth Century.* Toronto: Dundurn Group, 1999.
Reid, Dennis. *A Concise History of Canadian Painting.* Toronto: Oxford University Press, 1973.
Saddlemyer, Ann, ed. *Early Stages: Theatre in Ontario 1800–1914.* Toronto: University of Toronto Press, 1990.
Saddlemyer, Ann and Richard Plant, eds. *Later Stages: Essays in Ontario Theatre from the First World War to the 1970s.* Toronto: University of Toronto Press, 1997.
Schabas, Ezra. *Sir Ernest MacMillan: The Importance of Being Canadian.* Toronto: University of Toronto Press, 1994.
Schabas, Ezra. *There's Music in These Walls: A History of the Royal Conservatory of Music.* Toronto: Dundurn Group, 2005.
Sewell, John. *Doors Open Toronto: Illuminating the City's Great Spaces.* Toronto: Alfred A. Knopf Canada, 2002.
Smith, Donald B. *From the Land of Shadows: The Making of Grey Owl.* Saskatoon: Western Producer Prairie Books, 1990.
Snell, Gordon. *Yes! Even More Canadians!: Hysterically Historical Rhymes.* Toronto: Doubleday Canada, 2000.
Stacey, Robert. *The Canadian Poster Book: 100 Years of the Poster in Canada.* Toronto: Methuen, 1980.
Stacey, Robert and Hunter Bishop. *J. E. H. MacDonald, Designer: An Anthology of Graphic Design, Illustration and Lettering.* Ottawa: Archives of Canadian Art, 1996.
Staples, Rod. *Owen Staples: Painter of Canada's Past.* Toronto: Hogarth Productions, 1994.
Stewart, Sandy. *From Coast to Coast: A Personal History of Radio in Canada.* Toronto: CBC Enterprises, 1985.
Thom, Ian M. *The Cartoons of Arthur Lismer: A New Angle on Canadian Art.* Toronto: Irwin, 1985.
Tippett, Maria. *Art in the Service of War: Canada, Art, and the Great War.* Toronto: University of Toronto Press, 1984.
Tippett, Maria. *By a Lady: Celebrating Three Centuries of Art by Canadian Women.* Toronto: Viking, 1992.
Tippett, Maria. *Making Culture: English-Canadian Institutions and the Arts Before the Massey Commission.* Toronto: University of Toronto Press, 1990.

Tippett, Maria. *Stormy Weather: F. H. Varley—A Biography*. Toronto: McClelland and Stewart, 1998.
West, Bruce. *Toronto.* Toronto: Doubleday Canada, 1967.
White, Randall. *Too Good to Be True: Toronto in the 1920s*. Toronto: Dundurn Press, 1993.

Photo Credits and Sources

Almost all the images in this book are from the Arts and Letters Club collection. In addition to the already credited images in the book, the photographs of the Curtiss Jenny propeller (page 31); the bust of Hector Charlesworth (page 113); the Birds of a Feather clay pipes (page 121); the Life Member medallion (page 130); both St. George's Hall plaques (page 148); the Fun Fair poster (page 149); the Arts and Letters Award medal (page 156); the Mona Lisa in the Gents and the washrooms signs (page 157); and Dennis Rose's portrait of Peter Hart (page 168); and the colour section photographs of Wyly Grier's portrait of Gus Bridle were taken by George Lobb.

The photographs of A. J. Casson's *Christmas Scene*; Bertram Brooker's *Autumn Arches*; Frederick Challener's *Artist's Studio*; J. W. Beatty's *Falling Leaves Meadow Vale*; Franklin Carmichael's *Winter Scene*; Leonard Hutchinson's *Desjardins Canal*; Fred Banting's *Medicine Lake*; Franklin Arbuckle's *The Bridge*; Fred Haines' *Trees Eastern Ontario*; Joachim Gauthier's *Old Beech Trees in Carnarvon*; Nicholas Hornyansky's *Boreas (North Wind)*; the Executive lists; Barker Fairley's portrait of Herbert Whittaker; Eric Aldwinckle's portrait of Alfred Chapman; John Joy's *Toronto Houses*; Phillipa Faulkner's *Baicelong*; William Sherman's *Phillipa Faulkener's Art Class*; Leonard Brooks' *Vase of Morning Glories*; Donald M. Houston's *A Time to Sow*; Raymond Victor Cattell's *Narrows at Penetang*; and Arthur Steven's *Log Boom, Savona, BC* were also taken by George Lobb. The photograph of J. E. Sampson's *The Old Club* was taken by Brian Summers.

The photographs of the St. Charles Hotel (page 2); Sir William Mulock and Sir Wilfrid Laurier (page 21); G. G. Nasmith (page 37); and the Royal Ontario Museum (page 83) are from the City of Toronto Archives.

The photograph of Herman Voaden (page 88) is from the Collection of Jane Ricketts.

The photograph of Owen Staples (page 94) is from the Archives of Ontario.

Index